LINUX DESK REFERENCE

SCOTT HAWKINS

Prentice Hall PTR
Upper Saddle River, NJ 07458
www.phptr.com

Editorial/production supervision: *Kathleen M. Caren*
Cover design director: *Jerry Votta*
Cover designer: *Talar Agasyan*
Series interior design: *Gail Cocker-Bogusz*
Manufacturing manager: *Alexis R. Heydt*
Acquisitions editor: *Miles Williams*
Editorial assistant: *Noreen Regina*
Marketing manager: *Kate Hargett*

Prentice-Hall, Inc.
Upper Saddle River, New Jersey 07458

Prentice Hall books are widely used by corporations and government agencies for training, marketing, and resale.

The publisher offers discounts on this book when ordered in bulk quantities. For more information, contact Corporate Sales Department, Phone: 800-382-3419; FAX: 201- 236-7141;
E-mail: corpsales@prenhall.com
Or write: Prentice Hall PTR, Corporate Sales Dept., One Lake Street, Upper Saddle River, NJ 07458.

Printed in the United States of America
10 9 8 7 6 5 4 3 2 1

ISBN 0-13-016391-0

Prentice-Hall International (UK) Limited, *London*
Prentice-Hall of Australia Pty. Limited, *Sydney*
Prentice-Hall Canada Inc., *Toronto*
Prentice-Hall Hispanoamericana, S.A., *Mexico*
Prentice-Hall of India Private Limited, *New Delhi*
Prentice-Hall of Japan, Inc., *Tokyo*
Prentice-Hall (Singapore) Pte. Ltd., *Singapore*
Editora Prentice-Hall do Brasil, Ltda., *Rio de Janeiro*

DEDICATION

I would like to dedicate this book to my grandmothers, Emma Louise Hawkins and Viola Knoll.

TABLE OF CONTENTS

PART 2 MANIPULATING DATA & TEXT FILES

PART 3 COMMON TASKS

PART 4 NETWORKING

FOREWORD

Books are very important to me, particularly books about Linux. Not just because we sell books on LinuxMall.com, either. Rather the reason is that books about Linux help people learn more about Linux, empowering themselves and helping the Linux OS grow in the process.

As acceptance of the Linux OS grows, more and more people are liberated and empowered by the ability to have a powerful computing infrastructure that they can control, rather than just be controlled by megalithic software companies that think they know what is good for everyone. Freedom has always required responsibility, with self education being part of that responsibility.

Not long ago, in 1994 to be exact, I wrote an essay entitled "Why Linux is Significant." Basically, I outlined the reasons that I thought that Linux was going to thrive and take a significant place in the world of computing. I gave Linux about five years to become a common standard, and sure enough Linux has done, and is continuing to do just that.

It's gratifying to see my predictions becoming reality. This book, and every book about Linux, is a testament to the popularity of Linux. That's what LinuxMall.com is all about, and I'm happy to see so many other companies getting behind Linux as well.

Just a few years ago, books on Linux were few and far between. Today becoming Linux-literate is increasingly important, and Scott's book will provide newbies, UNIX gurus and everyone in-between with a valuable reference for their journey with Linux. The Linux Desk Reference is a well-organized and complete Linux companion that will assist you in learning and using all the power Linux has to offer. I hope this book, and Linux serve you well!

Mark Bolzern

CEO LinuxMall.com

PS: For those who care, "Why Linux is Significant" can be found at:

http://www.LinuxMall.com/announce/lxsig

"State of the State"

The Linux kernel is eight years old as I write this. In September of 1991, a 21-year-old student at the University of Helsinki uploaded version 0.01 of the Linux kernel. Linus Torvalds could not have predicted that the code that he had written would be the core of an industry less than a decade later.

What we know as the Linux operating system now, however, is much more than Linus' kernel. The kernel only handles the core functions of an operating system; it does not provide a user interface or tools for everyday use. Happily, the Free Software Foundation's GNU project had already developed most of the tools for a UNIX-style system. Most of the work toward a free OS had already been done; what was lacking was the vital piece that Linus provided.

Slowly at first, and with a little more momentum each month, people began downloading and using Linux. Because the code was available as well, they began refining it and adding to it, and returning the changes to Linus to be incorporated to new versions of the kernel. Thanks to the General Public License, anyone could look at and improve the code, and many of them did.

To make Linux more easily accessible, people started putting together "distributions," that is, creating installation programs and generally simplifying the process of using Linux. If you think installing Linux off of a CD-ROM is hard, imagine having to gather the source code for all the parts of the OS, compiling them and putting them in the right place, writing all the configuration files by hand and doing everything manually.

To make Linux even more readily available, a few companies started selling Linux distributions. At the time, many people thought that this was a little crazy, because everyone knew that you couldn't make money off free software. When it turned out you could make a successful business case for Linux, big companies started to get interested in Linux. Taking a cue from Eric S. Raymond's "The Cathedral and the Bizarre," Netscape decided to try to go the Open Source route as well.

While the Mozilla project has not been as successful as hoped, Netscape's foray into Open Source brought a lot of attention to Open Source software—especially Linux. The more people and businesses heard about Linux, the more they liked.

It's been only a little over a year since Netscape went Open Source, and Linux has grown tremendously. Companies are stumbling over one another to make announcements with "Open Source" or "Linux" in them. Hardly a day passes without a major company issuing a press release declaring their commitment to Linux. Almost every major software and hardware company has made some kind of commitment to Linux, with one notable exception.

Wall Street apparently likes Linux as well. Red Hat's IPO went through the roof. Starting at $14 a share in August, Red Hat's stock has consistently been valued over $100 a share. Several other Linux companies are poised to go public soon as well.

Linux has long been regarded as a technical success, and now it has become a commercial success as well. Linux has come a long way from its humble beginnings. While it is not clear how far Linux will go, it is clear that Linux is here to stay. The growth of Linux, and the impact Linux has had on the computer industry, is nothing short of amazing. That doesn't mean that Linux has "won" yet—there's quite bit of ground to cover yet. I'm sure that the next eight years are going to be even more exciting for Linux than the last eight have been.

The Chinese curse "may you live in exciting times" rings true as well. Now that "there's gold in them thar hills," everyone wants to get into the Linux act. Companies are consolidating at an alarming rate and existing players who have built the Linux Community are in danger of losing their shirts to newcomers desiring a piece of the Linux pie. The house that Linus built doesn't rest on code alone. We can only hope that the newcomers to the party don't trash this house by treating it like any other industry.

Microsoft is unlikely to take Linux lying down, either. Their recent "Linux Myths" page is evidence that the giant is beginning to awaken to the threat that Linux represents to Microsoft. Unlike companies that have threatened Microsoft's hegemony, Linux represents more than a threat to a singular revenue stream for the software monolith. Linux and Open Source are nothing less than a revolution against Microsoft's business model. It will be interesting to see how the beast from Redmond takes on Linux. Old tactics of FUD (fear, uncertainty, doubt) are unlikely to work, and Microsoft can't just buy the competition either. The proverbial 800 pound gorilla may be going on a diet soon.

The biggest threat to Linux—if there is one—is from within, not without. The Community has shown the ability to take the technical hurdles in stride. The question is how we'll handle money.

However, I think that the roots of Open Source are too strong to be rotted by creeping commercialism. Yes, Linux will be a money-maker for companies willing to invest in it. However, I see Linux changing the way in which computer companies make money in the long run. Service, support and source will all be required for successful software and hardware companies, in the not so distant future.

Many companies and individuals have already seen the advantages that Open Source and Linux offer. If you're new to Linux you'll find that it offers a much richer computing environment than the proprietary offerings of Microsoft, Apple and others. Not only is Linux comparable to other server and desktop OSes now, you can expect that at its present rate of development, Linux will surpass these systems in features and stability in short order.

Whether you are a seasoned UNIX or Linux hacker, or if you're new to Linux and just want to see what all the fuss is about, Scott's ***Linux Desk Reference*** should serve you well. This book can serve as a cornerstone to your Linux education if you are new to Linux, or as an essential reference if you are already familiar with Linux. Almost everything you need to know about Linux is between these covers.

Enjoy!

Joe "Zonker" Brockmeier
Editor of the *Linux Newsletter*

ACKNOWLEDGMENTS

First and foremost, let me thank my editor, Miles Williams of Prentice-Hall PTR, a good editor and a hell of a human being. My illustrator, Shannea Maggio, turned my more or less illegible ball-point napkin sketches into human readable drawings. My reviewer, Zonker Brockmeier, provided excellent feedback and notes. Also, in no particular order, Robert Oakman, Manton Matthews, Jerahd Hollis and Joe Morris have been invaluable references. Last but not least, let me mention my idiot dogs: Puppy Dog, the Mighty Bebos, Igor, Renfield, and (most recently) the nine nuggets, who served as footrests during the creation of this manuscript and (for the most part) refrained from doing terrible things to my reference books and network infrastructure.

INTRODUCTION

I hope you get a lot of use out of this book. Since I first got started in Unix in 1986, I've spent a ton of cash buying reference books. I've always been a bibliophile, and computer books have the advantage of being tax deductible, so I've amassed quite a collection. It always annoys me when I get home and the glitzy, well-packaged 400 page document-o-rama I just shelled out $50 for turns out to contain only 5 pages of actual information or, worse, to be full of information but so poorly organized that it's more trouble than it's worth to find what I need. I've got a shelf full of them, which I will sell cheap.

What I've tried to do here is incorporate the best features from my collection. I know what I like—a good index, thorough technical coverage, relevant examples, and concise explanations (in English). Also, in the process of writing this book I've become almost supernaturally attuned to the subject of computer reference books—you can whisper "Linux in a Nutshell" from thirty feet away across a crowded room and my ears will perk up like a retriever on point. The number one complaint I hear about reference books is "not enough examples." I'm not unsympathetic; thinking up, configuring, and testing all the examples for this book slowed the writing process down to a crawl. But, as my editor pointed out, I'm not doing this for my health. So you will find that for every command in this book there is an accompanying example.

To some extent, Linux commands tend to come in clusters. For example, there are a dozen or so that handle filesystems, another half dozen for fiddling with disks, a whole slew that do things with files. Sometimes the command clusters follow a naming convention, as in the case of the "remote" commands (**rlogin**, **rsh**, ...); other times they do not. It occurred to me it wouldn't be entirely wrong to group the Linux commands into clusters (one for users, another for disks, etc.) and then treat the clusters as data structures. Technically, a data structure consists of two things:

- a specification for how data will be stored
- a specification of methods by which the data will be accessed

That's not a perfect description of how the chapters are arranged, but it isn't bad either. At the beginning of each chapter there is a high-level discussion of what purpose each "data structure" serves, how that service is accomplished, and the jargon that has sprung up around it. That provides background for the detailed description of commands which follows. Hopefully, this will provide enough information for newcomers to get started and perhaps be of some value for experienced users as well.

Of course, as you can tell from a quick glance through the contents, the main thrust of this book is information on actual user commands. I have collected what I believe to be a fairly thorough subset of the most useful Linux commands, together with their options and some suggestions for use. Information on configuration and use of the various subsystems (e.g. NIS, Samba, Networking) is also included, either explicitly or as part of the examples.

How to Use This Book

When You Know Exactly What You Need

For the advanced users who know exactly what command they are after and are looking only for **example**s or **command line options**, the book has two command indexes:

- all commands are indexed in the back of the book, as are term definitions, procedures, and the rest of the content.
- there is a second index in the front for executable programs only.

When You Know What You Need But Not What It's Called

Did you ever find yourself digging around looking for a command that you know must exist, only you don't have any idea what it might be called? Back when I was in school I clearly remember fumbling around for an hour trying to figure out what command I'd use to lower the priority of a running process. There was nothing in the man pages under "priority" or "process", but I knew it had to be out there somewhere.

This book is arranged by concept. If you want to find out how to do something with filesystems, flip to the chapter on filesystems. In each chapter, there's a brief discussion of relevant **terms and concepts**, followed by a one-line summary of all the relevant commands, a list of **related files**, and finally a complete listing of the **commands** with **options** and **examples**.

When You're Just Getting Started

This book explains all of the **basic concepts** you need to understand in order to use your Linux system. If you're not familiar with particular **terms**, they are defined in the text and indexed in the back. There's also a **glossary**. For every command, there is at least one **example**. For the more popular or confusing commands, there are frequently two or more. Where I thought it would be helpful, I included **diagrams** and **sample output**.

Conventions of This Book

Introductions

There's a certain amount of overhead involved in learning the Linux system. Some of the concepts can be counterintuitive at first glance, particularly if you're still in the process of switching over from one of the lesser operating systems. Each chapter in this book starts off with a few of pages of notes about the concepts, terms, and theory underlying the commands. Hopefully, this will help you get a feel for how the commands make up subsystems and how the subsystems make up Linux.

Related Files

Most Unix commands take configuration or startup information from one or more files. The entries in this section are a listing of the files associated with the commands in each chapter.

Commands

Each chapter contains a detailed listing of commands, together with options and examples. The typographical conversions used in the command section are explained below:

Commands are in large bold italic print.

Options are listed line by line in bold italics.

Tips are set off with the following icon:

TIP

File names and ***paths*** are listed in bold italics.

Examples are centered and in bold print:

example

Commands which must be run as the superuser are indicated with the following icon:

ROOT

Occasionally I will put comments within an example command. In that case, the command will appear as usual, but the comment will be off to the side, not in bold type, and indicated with the pound sign (#).

command# comment

Sample output of system commands is listed in plain text:

```
This is typed exactly as it appeared on screen.
```

A Final Word

Any single book that purports to cover the entire Linux operating system is probably lying. There's so much going on that what you can fit between two covers is, of necessity, a reflection of the experiences and prejudices of its author. To the extent that I neglected <your favorite command/suite/utility> I really do apologize. If it's any consolation, it wasn't from lack of effort. If you have comments, corrections, or suggestions for improvement, feel free to contact me at:

s_hawkins@mindspring.com

As a post script, some of you may be wondering about the significance of the Minotaur on the cover of this book. Tradition has it that Daedalus, a mythological inventor and the spiritual ancestor of hackers everywhere, built a large and complex maze in Crete (the Labyrinth, capital L) at the behest of king Minos. The Minotaur was a bastard child of the Queen Pasiphae (Minos' wife) and some unusually attractive livestock. He had a man's body and the head of a bull which (understandably) made him a bit shy and grumpy. Territorial and ferocious, he lived in the center of the Labyrinth, which he ran with an iron fist. He guarded its secrets jealously, and was famous throughout the kingdom for biting the heads off ignorant newbies. When I was asked to suggest a creature for the cover of this guide to deciphering the intricacies of the Linux OS, there was really only one choice.

COMMAND LIST

CHAPTER

1

DOCUMENTATION

Introduction

There are a wide variety of sources for documentation on Linux. The quality of the information provided ranges from nearly poetic in its eloquence and usefulness all the way down to misleading or even blatantly wrong. *Caveat emptor.*

Most commercial packages provide a variety of FAQ's and HOWTO's in addition to the standard online documentation (**man**, **info**, ...). These are generally centered around some non-trivial task (e.g., running X-Windows, communicating with the lesser operating systems).

Usenet has dozens, if not hundreds, of newsgroups devoted to the various facets of Linux. Be advised that they are usually segregated according to level of expertise and the locals can be grumpy about inappropriate newbie questions—you should (as always) read the FAQ (frequently asked questions) before posting.

Similarly diverse information can be found on the Web. Probably the best site is *http://metalab.unc.edu/LDP*, the official Linux Documentation Project Web site.

Because Linux is a variation of the Unix operating system, the published Unix references will, for the most part, apply to Linux as well. Also, as Linux gains popularity, more Linux-specific periodicals are available at bookstores.

Of course, your first source of information should be your own machine. Most questions can be answered by a careful reading of the online documentation.

The commands covered in this section tell you how to use the resources on your machine to answer questions. They include:

apropos	Search the whatis database.
info	Provide hypertext documentation.
locate	Search for a file in the locate database.
man	Access on-line manual pages.
makewhatis	Create the whatis database.
manpath	Specify the search path for the man command.
updatedb	Update the locate database.
whatis	Search the whatis database for information.
whereis	Locate source files and documentation.

Related Files

/etc/man.config	Default man.conf file.
/usr/sbin/makewhatis	Create the whatis database.

Commands

apropos *keyword*

Search the whatis database for *keyword*. Provides terse but thorough documentation. Good place to start looking if you're clueless. You must run **makewhatis** before using.

Example: To retrieve information on the various files and executables dealing with passwords:

apropos passwd

info options *keyword*

Info is a hypertext reader which searches and displays online documentation about the specified keyword.

Example: To look up information on the cd command:

info cd

Example: To look up information on the grep command and store it in output file grep.doc:

info -o grep.doc grep

--directory DIRECTORY-PATH, -d DIRECTORY-PATH	Look for info files in the specified directories.
--file FILENAME, -f FILENAME	Search the specified filename for information about keyword.
--node NODENAME, -n NODENAME	Force display of the specified info node.
--output FILENAME, -o FILENAME	Direct all output to FILENAME rather than standard output.
--subnodes	Recursively output the nodes appearing in the menu of each node being output.
--help, -h	Output a description of the available options for info.
--version	Display the version information.

locate [-d path] [--database=path][--version][--help] *pattern*

Search the *locate* database for pattern. This command serves some of the same purposes as **find**, but it is quicker and not as thorough.

Note that in order for this command to work, the **updatedb** command must first be run. If you get in the habit of using **locate**, you probably ought to put a line in your **crontab** to run **updatedb** every night; otherwise, your information will get out of date quickly.

Example: To get **locate** to search its database for HOWTO files pertaining to XFree86:

locate HOWTO | grep XFree86

➠

TIP If the file you're after was created since the last time **updatedb** was run, **locate** won't find it. Use the **find** command instead.

-d path, --database=path	Search the specified path instead of the default path.
--version	Display the version number.
--help	Display help info.

makewhatis options

Create the **whatis** database, an on-line database of commands used by the **whatis** command. Generally, **makewhatis** needs to be run only once.

Example: To update the whatis database after you've installed a new batch of man pages:

ROOT

makewhatis -w

-u	Update database with new man pages.
-v	Operate verbosely.
-w	Use manpath obtained from man --path.

man [-acdfhkKtwW] [-m system] [-p string] [-C config_file] [-M path] [-P pager] [-S section_list] [section] *name* ...

Format and display on-line manual pages. Manual pages are prepared documents associated with a particular command. They describe the command syntax, the usage, the associated files, and occasionally provide usage examples. The following environment variables apply:

MANPATH	Specify the path to be searched for man pages.
MANROFFSEQ	Determine the set of preprocessors run before **nroff** or **troff**.
MANSECT	Specify which sections of the manual to search (if set at all).
MANWIDTH	Specify the width at which man pages are displayed.

MANPAGER	Specify the paging program used to output man pages.
LANG	Specify the subdirectory where man first looks for entries.

Example: To search for the manual page for the ls command:

man ls

Example: To search for all manual pages (not just the first one) on the **mke2fs** command and display using the **less** pager:

man -a -P less mke2fs

***-C** config_file*	Specify the configuration file used by man. Default is /etc/man.conf.
***-M** path*	Specify the list of directories to search for man pages.
***-P** pager*	Specify which program is used to present the output to the user. Default is /usr/bin/less-is.
***-S** section_list*	Specify a list of man sections to search (list delimited by colons).
-a	Force man to display all man pages matching the name argument, not just the first.
-c	Force man to reformat the source page, regardless of whether an up-to-date cat page exists.
-d	Print debugging information instead of actual man pages.
-D	Display and print debugging information.
-f	Force man to behave as if it were the whatis program.
-h	Print a succinct help message.
-k	Force man to behave as if it were the apropos program.
-K	Force man to search for the specified string in all man pages. Painfully slow.
***-m** system*	Specify an alternate set of man pages to search based on the system name given.

***-p** string*	String is a sequence of preprocessors to be run before nroff or troff.
-t	Use /usr/bin/groff -Tps-mandoc to format the man page.
-w or --path	Instead of the man page, print the path of the man page that would be displayed.
-W	Like -w (above) but only prints file names one per line.

updatedb [options]

Update the file database used by **locate**.

Example: To update the database used by **locate**:

updatedb

TIP If you use **locate**, you should run this command nightly via **cron**.

***--localpaths=**'path1 path2...'*	Non-network directories to put in the database.
***--netpaths=**'path1 path2...'*	Network (NFS, AFS, RFS, etc.) directories to put in the database. Default is none.
***--prunepaths=**'path1 path2...'*	Directories to not put in the database, which would otherwise be. Default is ***/tmp /usr/tmp /var/tmp /afs***.
***--output=**dbfile*	The database file to build. Default is system-dependent, but typically ***/usr/local/var/locatedb***.
***--netuser=**user*	The user to search network directories as, using su(1). Default is daemon.
--old-format	Create the database in the old format instead of the new one.
--version	Print the version number of ***updatedb*** and exit.
--help	Print a summary of the options to ***updatedb*** and exit.

whatis *keyword ...*

Search the **whatis** database for keyword. The **whatis** database contains short descriptions of system commands. Note that in order to be usable, you must first run the **/usr/sbin/makewhatis** command.

Example: To get a brief description of the **cron** command:

whatis cron

whereis [-bmsu] [-BMS directory... -f] *filename ...*

Locate source files and applicable manual sections for the specified files.

Example: To search for source files and manual selections for the **/etc/hosts** file:

whereis /etc/hosts

-b	Search for binary files only.
-m	Search the manual pages only.
-s	Search for source files only.
-u	Search for unusual entries. An unusual entry is a file in the current directory which has neither a binary, a man page, nor a source file associated with it.
-B	Specify where to look for binaries.
-M	Specify where to look for man pages.
-S	Specify where to look for source files.
-f	Used as a delimiter on the command line. Indicates that the directory list has ended and the file list is about to begin.

PART

1

SYSTEM STRUCTURES

CHAPTER

2

FILES

Introduction

In the Linux environment, a file is defined by its **inode**. Though most users never have occasion to directly access the inode, it is one of the fundamental components of the operating system, and thus it is very useful to have at least a cursory understanding of it.

The inode is a data structure which contains all the information the system needs to know about a particular file. This includes a unique identifying number (the **inode number**), the **name** of the file, its **size**, the file's location on the device, the most recent **access** and **update times**, the file's (numeric) **owner** and **group ids**, **access permissions**, and a pointer to the first block of data which the file contains.

In Unix, everything that isn't a running process is a file. Actually, there are also files corresponding to processes (see the ***/proc*** filesystem), though the classic definition of file is distinct from an executing process. The various file types are listed below. The first column of Table 2-1 corresponds to the letter displayed when an **ls -l** command is run:

ls -l

Code	Type	Description
-	regular file	Traditional file containing data.
b	block special file	Block input/output access device.
c	character special file	Raw (character based access) device.
d	directory	A file whose purpose is to group other files.
l	symbolic link	A pointer to another file.
p	named pipe	first-in/first-out interprocess communication mechanism.
s	socket	Interprocess communication mechanism associated with a port.

Also, note that the inode does not itself contain the file's data. Instead, it contains the addresses of the disk blocks which store the data. These blocks are probably not even next to each other; the data for a single file is usually scattered all around the file system. Of course, all of this scattering is invisible to the user who sees only a single file.

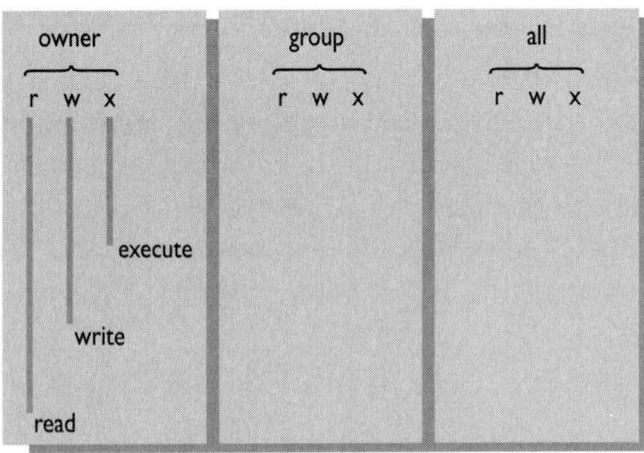

Figure 2-1 **File Implementation**

Note that all of the following commands may potentially be used on your own files, but to use them on someone else's you will need to have superuser privileges.

You will see the above properties appear in various ways throughout the commands listed below:

chgrp	Change the group ownership of the file.
chmod	Change the mode (access permissions) of the file.
chown	Change the owner of the file.
cksum	Calculate the checksum of a the file.
cp	Copy the file.
dd	Copy file and possibly fiddle with the format.
file	Determine file type.
install	Copy file(s), preserving permissions.
ln	Create a link to a file.
lockfile	Create a semaphore.
ls	List the contents of a directory.
lsattr	List the attributes of a file.
mv	Rename a file.
pathchk	Check filename for portability.
rm	Remove (delete) a file.
stat	Display the contents of the file's inode.
sum	Calculate a checksum.
symlinks	Scan a directory for symbolic links.
touch	Update access times or, potentially, create a file.

Related Files

/etc/passwd	Contains the user names and ids referenced by the inode.
/etc/group	Contains the group names and ids referenced by the inode.

Commands

chgrp [OPTION]... *GROUP FILE...*

Change the group membership of the file(s) to GROUP. Group must be a valid option as defined in ***/etc/groups***. Depending on your current access permissions for the target file, this command may or may not work for you. In general, if you already have access to FILE, you can grant access permission to someone else. If you do not currently have permission to access the file, you cannot grant access to yourself.

Example: To change the group ownership of the file testfile to group2:

chgrp group2 testfile

-c, --changes	Print out a confirmation for each file whose permission is successfully changed.
-f, --silent, --quiet	Suppress any error messages generated by the chgrp command.
-h, --no-dereference	In the case where the target file is a symbolic link, make any changes to the link itself rather than the file to which it points.
-v, --verbose	Verbose output.
-R, --recursive	In the case where the file is a directory, also change the contents of the directory (including any subdirectories).

chmod [OPTION]... NEW_PERMISSIONS *FILE...*

Change the permissions (mode) of the target FILE(s) to NEW_PERMISSIONS. NEW_PERMISSIONS may be one of two forms:

[+ | -] [r | w | x]

for [adding | subtracting] one of the three permission types [**r**ead | **w**rite | e**x**ecute].

Unless otherwise specified, using the +|- syntax in chmod will cause changes to apply to everyone. If you want to be more specific, you can specify whether to apply to the **u**ser (u), the **g**roup (g), **e**veryone (e) or **a**ll of the above (a).

This generates commands like the following:

Example: Grant read access to the file to *user, group* and *everyone*:

chmod a+r file1

Example: Revoke execute access on the file from the *group*:

chmod g-x file2

Alternatively, you may specify the new permissions in octal notation. Each file has three sets of permissions associated with it: those for the file's **owner**, those for the owner's **group**, and those for the rest of the **world**. Within each set there are three possible permissions: **read**, **write**, and **execute**.

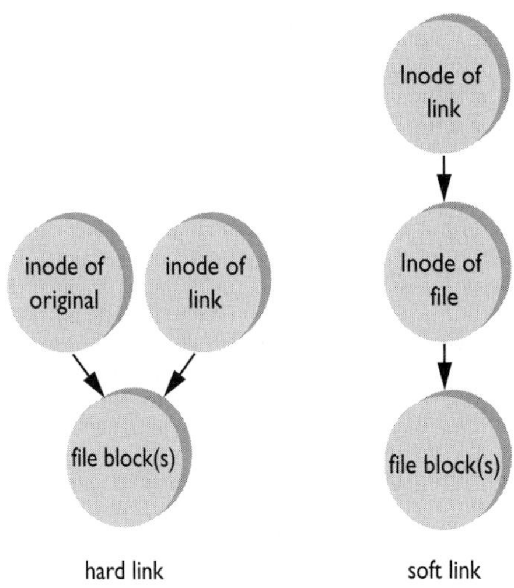

Figure 2-2 **Permissions**

To understand the use of octal notation, think of each of the three sets as being a separate number between 0 and 7. Notice how a 1 in the *binary* column means there will be a corresponding permission in the *permissions* column.

Octal	Binary	Permission	English Translation
0	000	---	No permissions.
1	001	--x	Execute only.
2	010	-w-	Write only.
3	011	-wx	Write and execute.
4	100	r--	Read only.
5	101	r-x	Read and execute.
6	110	rw-	Read and write.
7	111	rwx	Read, write, execute.

Use of the octal permission set generates commands like the following:
Example: Grant the file's *owner* read, write, and execute permission (octal = 7). Grant the owner's *group* read permission (octal = 4). Deny any access to the rest of the *world* (octal = 0).

chmod 740 file

Example: Grant read and execute access to the user (octal = 5). Grant execute access to the owner's group (octal = 1). Grant no access to the outside world (octal = 0).

chmod 510

-c, --changes	Print out a confirmation for each file whose permission is successfully changed.
-f, --silent, --quiet	Suppress any error messages generated by the **chgrp** command.
-h, --no-dereference	In the case where the target file is a symbolic link, make any changes to the link itself rather than the file to which it points.

-v, --verbose	Verbose output.
-R, --recursive	In the case where the file is a directory, also change the contents of the directory (including any subdirectories).

chown [OPTION]... NEW-OWNER[[:|.]GROUP] *FILE...*

Change the owner of FILE to be NEW-OWNER. Optionally, also change the group associated with the file. NEW-OWNER is either a user-id number or a user name as found in the ***/etc/passwd*** file.

Note: For non-trivial use of this command (i.e., changing ownership to anyone other than yourself) you need superuser privileges.

The OWNER value may be either the login name of a valid user or the numeric value associated with that user (see the ***/etc/passwd*** file for user id's). The GROUP may be either a group (from the ***/etc/group*** file) or a numeric group id.

If you omit the NEW-OWNER argument, but do supply an argument for NEW_GROUP, this command will behave like the **chgrp** command.

Example: Change the owner of the file bigfile to be "rcowan", the group of the file to be "compsci."

chown rcowan:compsci bigfile

Example: Change the owner of the file otherfile to be "bob." Because there is a colon after bob's user name but no group id provided, the group id will be changed to bob's login group.

chown bob: otherfile

-c, --changes	Print out a confirmation for each file whose permission is successfully changed.
-f, --silent, --quiet	Suppress any error messages generated by the chgrp command.
-h, --no-dereference	In the case where the target file is a symbolic link, make any changes to the link itself rather than the file to which it points.

Files

-v, --verbose	Verbose output.
-R, --recursive	In the case where the file is a directory, also change the contents of the directory (including any subdirectories).

cksum [OPTION]... *[FILE]...*

Compute and print the Cyclic Redundancy Check for each file specified. The primary use for this command is to verify that a file you have just transferred via some potentially unreliable means has arrived in one piece. That is, if you calculate the checksum from the original file and compare it to the transferred copy, the sums will be identical if and only if it was transferred correctly.

Example: To verify that rcp copied testfile from host1 to host2 correctly:

```
host1>  cksum testfile
        4294967295 329 testfile
host1>  rlogin host2
host2>  rcp hostfile:/tmp/testfile
host2>  cksum testfile
        4294967295 329 testfile
```

cp [OPTION]... *SOURCE TARGET*

Create an copy of the file SOURCE at TARGET. TARGET may be a file or a directory. If TARGET is a directory, **cp** will create a copy of SOURCE in that directory with the same name as the source file. Note that this command is distinct from **mv** in that an entirely new file is created with a different inode number and a different location in the filesystem.

By default, **cp** doesn't copy directories. However, you can force it to do so by specifying the -r option.

Example: To copy the file ch08.txt to ch09.txt without prompting before overwriting (-f option) the existing copy of ch09.txt:

cp -f ch08.txt ch09.txt

Example: To recursively copy all files in the subdirectory Linux.book to the subdirectory Reference:

cp -r Linux.book Reference

-a, --archive	Preserve as many of the attributes of the original as possible.
-b, --backup	Make backups of the files that are about to be overwritten.
-d, --no-dereference	In the case where the file is a symbolic link, copy the link itself rather than the file to which it points.
-f, --force	Force the removal of target files.
-i, --interactive	In the case where TARGET is an existing file, prompt the user before removing it.
-l, --link	Rather than copying a file, instead create a hard link.
-p, --preserve	Preserve the owner, group, permissions, and timestamp of the original file.
-P, --parents	When copying a SOURCE which is specified by a directory path as well as a file name, retain the directory path (by creating subdirectories, if necessary) at the TARGET.

Example: Create a subdirectory "etc" under myhomedir and place the file "passwd" within it.

cp /etc/passwd myhomedir

-r, -R, --recursive	In the case where SOURCE is a directory, recursively copy any subdirectories under it.
--sparse=[auto / always / never]	In the case where a file is sparse (that is, contains a sequence of zero bytes which occupy no disk blocks, a common space saving technique in modern filesystems) treat the sparse sequence as specified.

auto	If the SOURCE is sparse, the TARGET is sparse. This option is the default.

Files

always	The TARGET is always sparse.
never	The TARGET is never sparse.

-s, --symbolic-link	Create symbolic links instead of actual copies.
-S SUFFIX, --suffix=SUFFIX	In the case where use of the -b option is about to generate backup files, append the specified SUFFIX to the backup.
-u, --update	In the case where the target file already exists and has a more recent update time than the source, do not make the copy.
-v, --verbose	Verbose output. (Print the file name before copying.)
-V METHOD, --version-control=METHOD	Used in conjunction with the "-b" option. The METHOD argument is one of the following: [numbered | t] [existing | nil] [never | simple]
-x, --one-file-system	In the case where copying recursively, skip any subdirectories not on the current file system.

dd [OPTION]...

Copy a file with a changeable I/O blocksize. By default, copying is done from standard input to standard output. **dd** is usually used to perform conversions from one file format to another.

Example: To copy and convert an EBCDIC formatted source file (file.mainframe) into ASCII format (file.linux):

dd if=file.mainframe of=file.linux conv=ascii

if=*FILE*	Read from FILE instead of standard input.
of=*FILE*	Write to FILE instead of standard output.
ibs=*BYTES*	Input the specified number of bytes at a time.

***obs=**BYTES*	Output the specified number of bytes at a time.
***bs=**BYTES*	Input and output the specified number of bytes at a time.
***cbs=**BYTES*	Convert the specified number of bytes at a time.
***skip=**BLOCKS*	Skip the specified number of blocks in the input file before beginning to copy.
***seek=**BLOCKS*	Skip the specified number of blocks in the output file before beginning to copy.
***count=**BLOCKS*	Copy only the specified number of bytes from the input file and then stop.
***conv=**CONVERSION[,CONVERSION]...*	Convert the file from one format to another. CONVERSION is one of the following:

ascii	EBCDIC to ASCII.
ebcdic	ASCII to EBCDIC.
ibm	ASCII to alternate EBCDIC.
block	For each line in the input, output exactly the number of bytes specified by the “cbs” argument, padding with spaces as necessary.
unblock	Replace the trailing spaces in each “cbs”-sized input block with newline.
lcase	Change uppercase letters to lowercase.
ucase	Change lowercase letters to uppercase.

swap	Swap every pair of input bytes.
noerror	Continue after read errors.
notrunc	Do not truncate the output file.
sync	Pad every input block to size of "ibs" with trailing zero bytes.

file [-vbczl] [-f namefile] [-m magicfiles] file ...

The **file** program tests all the files listed on the command line in an attempt to determine their type.

Example: To determine the types of the files named in the file filelist:

file -f filelist

-v	Display version information and exit.
-m	Specify a different source for the "magic numbers" used to determine file type.
-z	Attempt to look at the contents of compressed files.
-b	Brief mode.
-c	Print out the parsed magic file.
-f namefile	Read the list of file names to be tested from namefile.
-L	Follow symbolic links.

install [OPTION]... *SOURCE DEST*

install works much like the **cp** command. It copies files but also attempts to set their permissions, owner, and group. DEST may be either a file or a directory. It is most commonly used in Makefiles to copy compiled programs into their destination directories.

Example: To copy the executable interest into the directory */usr/bin* with read and execute permissions while at the same time backing up any existing copy of interest:

install -b -m 555 interest /usr/bin

-b, --backup	Create backups of files about to be overwritten.
-c	No action. Included for backward compatibility.
-d, --directory	Create the directory specified by DEST.
-g *GROUP,* ***--group=****GROUP*	Set the group attribute of installed files as specified by GROUP.
-m *MODE,* ***--mode=****MODE*	Set the permissions attribute of installed files as specified by MODE.
-o *OWNER,* ***--owner=****OWNER*	Set the ownership attribute of installed files to a value of OWNER.
-s, --strip	Strip the symbol tables from installed binary executables.
-S *SUFFIX,* ***--suffix=****SUFFIX*	In the case where a backup file is being generated as a result of the use of the -b option, append SUFFIX to the backup file.
-V *METHOD,* ***--version-control=****METHOD*	Used in conjunction with the "-b" option. The METHOD argument is one of the following: [numbered | t] [existing | nil] [never | simple]

Files

ln [OPTION]... SOURCE [DEST]

Create a link between files or directories. This link may be either "hard" or "soft" (see Figure 2-2). A hard link is effectively a new file name for the existing file. A soft link is a special type of file that is a pointer to the original file. For most purposes, the links behave as if they were the file itself.

Example: To create a symbolic link called junk to the ***/tmp*** directory:

ln -s -d /tmp junk

-b, --backup	Create backups of files about to be overwritten.
-d, -F, --directory	Allow hard links to directories (superuser only).
-f, --force	Force the removal of previously existing destination files.
-i, --interactive	Prompt the user before removing existing destination files.
-n, --no-dereference	In the case where the DEST value is itself a symbolic link, treat the DEST as if it were an actual file. That is, create a link to DEST, rather than a direct link to the (third) file which DEST is already a link to.
-s, --symbolic	Create symbolic rather than hard links.
-v, --verbose	Print the name of each file before linking.
-S *SUFFIX*, ***--suffix=****SUFFIX*	In the case where use of the **-b** option generates a backup file, append SUFFIX to each backup file created.
-V *METHOD*, ***--version-control=****METHOD*	Used in conjunction with the "**-b**" option. The METHOD argument is one of the following: [numbered | t] [existing | nil] [never | simple]

lockfile -sleeptime | -r retries | -l locktimeout | -suspend | -! | -ml | -mu | *filename* ...

lockfile is used to create a semaphore file. A semaphore file is used to determine whether another file (e.g., a system mailbox) is currently in use. If it is unable to create the specified lockfile, it will wait (by default) 8 seconds to try again. By default, this retrying will go on indefinitely. Arguments can be specified anywhere on the command line and apply only to files listed after the argument.

Example: To unlock your system mailbox:

lockfile -mu

-!	Invert return value of lockfile.
-h, -?	Help.
-SLEEPTIME	Sleeptime specifies the number of seconds to wait between retries.
-s	Sleep n seconds after the forced removal occurs.
-r *retries*	Stop after specified number of retries.
-ml	Lock your system mailbox.
-mu	Unlock your system mailbox.

ls whole_lot_of_options

The ls program displays information about files or directories. The output is presented in alphabetical order by default.

ls is inarguably the single most used command in the Unix world. I have taken my cue from the man page authors and organized the options by functional area.

Example: Frequently, the files output by the **ls** command will occupy much more than a single screen. If so, pipe the output of the **ls** command to the **less** paginator for easy viewing:

ls | less

Example: To suppress listing of subdirectory contents (that is, list the directory name only):

ls -d

Example: To list the contents of the /etc directory in reverse alphabetical order:

ls -r /etc

Example: To list the contents of the current directory, including files beginning with a period (".") and including access times and inode information:

ls -ali

TIP

Take the time to familiarize yourself with the options to ls. Once you've got them in your mental toolchest, you'll be amazed at how often they come in handy.

Create a couple of entries in the .alias file in your home directory for your favorite options to ls.

alias ll='ls -al'

If you're running Linux on a color terminal, include the --color option in your alias. Using that, you can distinguish file types at a glance.

Options which specify which files to list

-a, --all	List all files in directories, including files that start with a period (".").
-A, --almost-all	List all files in directories, including files which start with ".", but do not list "." and "..".
-B, --ignore-backups	Do not list files ending in "~".
-d, --directory	List the names of directories rather than their contents.
-I, --ignore PATTERN	Ignore files whose names match the shell pattern PATTERN.
-L, --dereference	Show file information for the reference of symbolic links rather than the links themselves.
-R, --recursive	Recursively list contents of directories.

Options which specify the information to be listed

-D, --dired	Print an additional line specifying the unsigned integers which record the byte position of the beginning and end of each file name in the output.
-G, --no-group	Do not display group information.
-i,--inode	Include the inode number in the listing.
-l, --format=*long,* ***--format=****verbose*	Include file type, permissions, hard link count, owner name, group name, size, and modification time. The third character of each set (owner, group, all) of permissions may be one of the following codes:

s	Indicates the setuid or setgid bit and the corresponding executable bit are both set.
S	Indicates the setuid or setgid bit is set but the corresponding executable bit is not set.
t	Indicates the sticky bit and the other-executable bit are both set.
T	Indicates the sticky bit is set but the other-executable bit is not set.
x	Indicates the executable bit is set and none of the above applies.
-	Otherwise.

-o	Long listing without group information.
-s, --size	Include the size (in 1024-byte) blocks in the listing.

Ordering the output

***-c, --time=**ctime, **--time=**status*	Sort output by status chante time ("ctime" of the inode).
-f	List files in the order they are stored within the directory.
-r, --reverse	Reverse whatever ordering might otherwise apply.
***-S, --sort=**size*	Order files by size from largest to smallest.
***-t, --sort=**time*	Order files by modification time, most recent first.
***-u, --time=**atime, **--time=**access,**--time=**use*	Order files by access time.

***-U, --sort=**none*	Do not sort.
***-X, --sort=**extension*	Order by file extension.

Output Appearance

***-1, --format=**single-column*	List one file per line.
***-C, --format=**vertical*	List in columns.
***--color [=**WHEN]*	Specify whether to use color for distinguishing between file types.
-F, --classify	Append a character to each file name indicating the file type.
--full-time	Print out any time values in full, rather than abbreviating.
-k, --kilobytes	Display any sizes in kilobytes.
-m, --format=commas	List files horizontally, separated by commas.
-n, --numeric-uid-gid	List the numeric user id and group id as opposed to the actual names.
-p	Append a character to each file name indicating the file type.
***-x FORMAT, --format=**across, **--format=**horizontal*	List the files in columns, ordered horizontally.
***-T COLS, --tabsize=**COLS*	Set tabstop to be COLS columns wide.
***-w, --width=**COLS*	Set screen width to be COLS columns wide.

Specify filename printing style

-b, --escape	Display nongraphic characters in file names using alphabetic and octal backslash sequences like those in C.
-N, --literal	Do not quote file names.
-q, --hide-control-chars	Do not attempt to print nongraphic control characters. (Use "?" instead.)
-Q, --quote-name	Enclose file names in double quotes, also quote nongraphic characters.

mv [options] source target

mv moves (effectively renames) a file. If the target argument is a directory, **mv** moves the source files into that directory without changing the file name. Only regular files can be moved across filesystems.

Example: To rename the file program.c to be program.old, regardless of whether or not there is already a file called program.old (-f):

mv -f program.c program.old

TIP

The main difference between **mv** and **cp** is in what happens with (update time, inode number, etc). **mv** retains the inode number and the inode. **cp** creates an entirely new file with new inode information, changing only the filename and access time.

-b, --backup	Create backups of files that are about to be overwritten.
-f, --force	Overwrite existing target files without prompting the user.
-i, --interactive	Prompt the user before overwriting a target file.
-u, --update	In the case where a target file has the same name as the source, and the target file's most recent modification time is more recent than that of the source, do not move.

-v, --verbose	Display the name of each file before moving.
***-S** SUFFIX, **--suffix=**SUFFIX*	In the case where use of the -b option generates a backup file, append SUFFIX to the filename of each backup file created.
***-V** METHOD, **--version-control=**METHOD*	Used in conjunction with the "-b" option. The METHOD argument is one of the following: [numbered | t] [existing | nil] [never | simple]

pathchk [OPTION]... NAME...

Determine whether NAME is a valid and portable Unix filename. Returns a message if:

1. a directory in NAME does not have execute permission.
2. the length of NAME is outside the filesystem's limits.
3. the length of any component of NAME is outside the filesystem's limits.

Example: If you've got a program directory that you're planning to send out into the world, you ought to check it as follows:

pathchk my_baby

-p, --portability	Performs tests using the POSIX minimum limits for portability.

rm [OPTION]... [FILE]...

Remove (delete) a file. By default, **rm** does not remove directories. By default, **rm** will prompt you before getting rid of anything.

Example: To recursively remove all the files in the directory tree useless_crap without prompting the user at each file:

rm -rf useless_crap

TIP

The **-rf** options are handy, but before you hit <Enter>, take a second and think about what you're doing, especially if it's after midnight.

-d, --directory	Remove directories via "unlink" (as opposed to rmdir). Does not require that a directory be empty before removal. Use with caution.
-f, --force	Force removal without prompting the user.
-i, --interactive	Prompt the user before removing a file.
-r, -R, --recursive	Recursively remove the contents of any subdirectories.
-v, --verbose	Print the name of any file before removal.

stat filename...

Print the contents of the inode associated with filename. This includes:

File	Filename
Size	Size in bytes
Filetype	Regular, block device, link...
Mode	Access permissions
Uid	User id of file owner
Gid	Group id of file owner
Device	Device number of device containing file
Inode	Inode number of file
links	Number of links to file
Access	Time file last accessed (e.g., catted out)
Modify	Time file last modified (e.g., edited)
Change	Time file last changed (e.g., touched, copied)

Example: To print out the inode information on the file /etc/passwd.

stat /etc/passwd

sum [OPTION]... *[FILE]...*

Print the checksum for each FILE followed by the number of blocks in the file. Generally used before and after transmission of a file to verify that everything arrived OK.

Example: To print the BSD checksum for the file traveller:

sum -r traveller

-r	Compute checksums via BSD algorithms.
-s, --sysv	Compute checksums via System V algorithms.

symlinks [-cdrv] *dirlist*

This command scans directories for symbolic links, listing them to standard output. Each link is classified as one of the following:

relative	A link expressed as a path relative to the directory in which the link resides.
absolute	A link given as an absolute path from the root directory.
dangling	A link whose target does not currently exist.
messy	A link containing unnecessary slashes or dots in the path.
lengthy	A length using "../" more than necessary in the path.
other_fs	A link whose target resides on a different filesystem.

Example: To search all the subdirectories under your home directory (-r option) for symbolic links, removing any dangling links found (-d option):

symlinks -r -d ~

-c	Convert absolute links to relative links.
-d	Remove dangling links.
-r	Recursive operation (within a single filesystem).
-s	Detach lengthy links.
-t	Test what would happen if -c was specified but don't change anything.
-v	Include relative links in the output (by default, they are excluded).

Files

touch [OPTION]... *FILE...*

Change the access and modification times of FILE to the current time. If FILE does not exist, it is created as an empty file.

Example: To create an empty file named blah:

touch blah

TIP

Use the **touch** command in shell scripts. If you're writing a script that does something (removes, moves) a file and the file isn't there, the script will bomb. If you **touch** the file first, it is guaranteed to be there. **touch** won't alter the contents of the file or the access and modification times.

***-a, --time=**atime, **--time=**access, **--time=**use,*	Change the access time only.
-c, --no-create	Do not create any files which do not exist.
***-d --date=**time*	Use the specified time instead of the current time.
-f	No effect. Included for backward compatibility.
***-m, --time=**mtime, **--time=**modify*	Change the modification time only.

-r FILE, --reference=*FILE*	Use the times of the reference file rather than the current time.
-t MMDDhhmm[[CC]YY][.ss]'	Use the time as specified rather than the current time.

CHAPTER

3

PROCESS

Introduction

A **process** is a program which is currently running. It consists of the executable instructions for the program, the program data, and stack data. Processes are uniquely identified by their number, called **PID** or process id.

Processes are always created by other processes via the fork() system call. For example, when you type **ls** and hit <enter>, the process which is your shell forks, creating a nearly exact (everything is the same except the **pid**) duplicate of itself. The copy then immediately cedes control of its system resources to the **ls** program by running an exec() system call. In this way, all processes are descended from **init**.

The process created via a fork() is referred to as the **child**, the process which forked is called the **parent**. In some process information listings you will see a **PPID** field; this contains the Process ID of the processes' Parent.

Processes may communicate with each other via **signals**, standardized numeric messages corresponding to a variety of system events. (See ***/usr/include/linux/signal.h*** for details).

Processes have a **priority**, a numeric value between -19 (highest priority) and 20 (lowest priority) used by the kernel to calculate who gets next crack at the CPU. By default, processes are created with a priority of 0.

Processes may be run in the **foreground** (visibly executing on your display) or in the **background** (running but not in control of your terminal). It is possible to explicitly move running processes between the foreground and background; see the entries for **&, ^Z, bg, fg**, and **jobs**.

A **zombie process** is a process which has been killed and had its system resources freed but has not yet been removed from the list of running processes.

The following are some of the commands which deal directly with processes:

&	Run the specified process in the background.
^Z	Suspend the current foreground process.
bg	Put the specified process in the background.
fg	Bring a specified process to the foreground.
fuser	Display the pid of any process using a specified file.
jobs	Display a list of background processes.
kill	Stop the execution of a process.
killall	Kill all processes executing a specified command.
nice	Change priority of a process.
nohup	Run a process that will ignore signaling.
pidof	Locate and print the process id of the specified program.
ps	Get process status information.
pstree	Display family tree of running processes.
renice	Change the id of a running process.
top	Display CPU usage information.

Related Files

/proc	Location of the process filesystem.
/usr/include/linux/signal.h	List of valid signals.

Commands

&

The **&** command, used on the command line, forces the specified process to run in the background.

Example: To start a lengthy program running in the background:

sort_everything &

TIP

As soon as they are successfully invoked, background processes release control of your terminal to the shell which invoked them. This means that you can continue to work without waiting for a lengthy process to finish.

^Z

The **^Z** command stops the current foreground process.

Example: This command works on any process. For example, say you're running a lengthy sort and you want to check what time it is:

$ biglongsort	# Start lengthy process
^Z	# Suspend with ^Z
[3]+ Stopped (signal)	
$ date	# Check time
Sun Jul 11 12:22:41 EDT 1999	
$ fg 3	# Restart process

bg *job_num*

The **bg** command takes a stopped job and starts it in the background.

Example: Say you started running a **find** command and it was taking forever. You've got only one window available, so you want to move it to the background without restarting it:

```
$ find / -type f -print | grep sammich
^Z                          # Stop current job
$ jobs                      # Display job list
[2]+ Stopped      find / -type f -print | grep sammich
$ bg 2                      # Run job in background
```

TIP To use this command, you will need to know the job number. Obtain the job number with the **jobs** command.

fg *job_num*

The **fg** command moves a running background job to the foreground.

Example: To get the job numbers of your background and stopped jobs, start **bigsort** running in the foreground:

```
$ jobs                      # Tell system to display job list
[2] Running      bigsort
[3] Stopped      find / -type f -print | grep sammich
$ fg 2                      # Move bigsort to foreground
```

TIP To use this command, you must know the job number. Obtain the job number with the jobs command.

fuser [-a|-s] [-n space] [-signal] [-kmuv] name ... [-][-n space] [-signal] [-kmuv] *name ...*

fuser -l

fuser -V

The **fuser** command is used to display the PID of any process(es) using a specified file. The various types of access are indicated as follows:

c File is process' current directory.

e	Process is running file as executable.
f	File is open for modification.
r	File is process' root directory.
m	Mmap'ed file or shared library.

Example: To find and kill all processes running the file ***/bin/program***:

ROOT

fuser -k /bin/program

-a	Show all files listed on the command line, whether accessed or not.
-k	Attempt to kill any process accessing the file.
-l	List signal names.
-m	If the file listed is s mounted filesystem, list all processes accessing members of that filesystem.
-n	Space select a different name space.
-s	Silent operation.
-signal	Use the specified signal instead of SIGKILL when killing processes.
-u	Include the user name of the process' owner in output.
-v	Verbose output. Include PID, USER, COMMAND.
-V	Output version number.
-	Return all options to their default values.

jobs

The **jobs** command displays a list of the current background processes.

Example: Say you had two jobs, bigsort and a find, running in the background. If so, **jobs** might display the following output.

```
$ jobs
[2] Running      bigsort
[3] Stopped      find / -type f -print | grep sammich
```

kill [-s *signal* | -p] [-a] *pid* ...

kill -l [*signal*]

Kill a process. More specifically, the **kill** command sends one of a variety of possible signals to the specified process. The default signal is TERM. The *pid* parameter is a process id, which may be obtained using the **ps** command. You need to be superuser to use this command on anyone other than yourself.

Example: To kill process 1234 immediately without giving it a chance to finish what it is doing:

kill -9 1234

TIP One way to kill processes by process id number. To get the process id number, run **ps aux** and **grep** for the name of the command you're targeting. Another is to kill by job number:

kill %1

TIP To kill someone else's process, you must be superuser.

-s signal

Use the specified signal, rather than the default.

-p	Print the pid of the named process, but do not signal it.
-l	Output a list of possible signals.

killall [-eiqvw] [-signal] *command_name* ...

killall -l

killall -V

killall attempts to kill all processes executing the command specified by command_name. By default, this is accomplished by use of the SIGTERM signal. However, other signals may be specified either by name (see /usr/include/linux/signal.h) or by number.

Example: To kill all processes (not just those owned by you) currently running the **mail** command:

killall mail ROOT

-e	Requires long filenames (> 15 char) to be matched exactly.
-i	Prompt the user for confirmation before killing.
-l	List possible signals.
-q	Run quietly. Suppress error messages.
-v	Run verbosely. Display a message for each successful termination.
-V	Output version information.
-w	Wait for signaled processes to die.

Process

nice [OPTION]... [COMMAND [ARG]...]

Start a command with the specified priority rather than the default. By default, commands are run with a priority of zero. To give your command a lower priority (and thereby make it run slower), you may specify a value between 1 and 19. To make it run faster, you may specify a value between -1 and -20. You must be the superuser to specify a negative value.

Example: To start up big_program but force it to yield some of its processor time to other programs:

nice 19 big_program

Example: To start up big_program, but enable it to snatch some processor time from other, less deserving programs:

nice -20 big_program

Use **renice** to modify the priority of a command which is already running. 

To start a process with a higher priority (e.g., a lower priority number) you must be superuser. TIP

-n *ADJUSTMENT*	
-ADJUSTMENT --adjustment=*ADJUSTMENT*	Use the specified ADJUSTMENT instead of the default.

nohup COMMAND [ARG]...

Execute the specified command, ignoring the hangup signals (particularly those sent when you logout). The idea is that the command will continue to run after you logout. Also, **nohup** increases the scheduling priority to 5, which means it will run a bit slower. Output is sent to nohup.out.

Example: To start up big_program telling it continue to run even after you're at home asleep:

nohup big_program

pidof [-s] [-x] [-o omitpid] [-o omitpid..] *program* [*program..*]

Locate and print the process id of the specified program.

Example: To learn the process id of the sendmail program:

pidof sendmail

-s	Limit output to a single pid.
-x	If "program" is a script, also output the pid's of shells running the script.
***-o** omitpid*	Ignore processes with the specified pid.

ps [-] [lujsvmaxScewhrnu] [txx] [O[+|-]k1[[+|-]k2...]] [pids]--sortX[+|-]key[,[+|-]key[,...]], --help, --version

ps (Process Status) retrieves and displays information about currently running processes. Depending on the command line options, the output of this command will include various permutations of the following:

Column	Description
%CPU	Rough percentage of CPU time consumed.
%MEM	Rough percentage of system memory consumed.
COMMAND	Command which started process.
NI	Nice value of process.

PID	Process ID.
PPID	Process Parent ID.
RSS	Real memory used.
SIZE	Virtual memory consumed by process.
STA	Current process state. One of

R	Running
S	Sleeping
D	Uninterruptible sleep
T	Stopped or Traced
Z	Zombie

START	Time process started.
TIME	Total CPU time used.
TTY	Terminal associated with process.
UID	User id of process originator.
USER	User name of process originator.
WCHAN	Event process is waiting for.

Example: To display a long list of information about my current processes:

ps l

```
FLAGS      UID   PID    PPID PRI   NI   SIZE    RSS WCHAN       STA  TTY  TIME COMMAND
   100      0   390     1   0    0   1232    808 wait4       S     1  0:00 -bash
100100      0   391     1   0    0    724    296 read_chan   S     2  0:00 /sbin/min
100100      0   392     1   0    0    724    296 read_chan   S     3  0:00 /sbin/min
100100      0   393     1   0    0    724    296 read_chan   S     4  0:00 /sbin/min
100100      0   394     1   0    0    724    296 read_chan   S     5  0:00 /sbin/min
100100      0   395     1   0    0    724    296 read_chan   S     6  0:00 /sbin/min
100000      0   420   390   0    0   1200    648 wait4       S     1  0:00 sh /usr/X
   100      0   421   420   0    0   1828    656 wait4       S     1  0:00 xinit /us
100100      0   424   421   0    0   2968   1944 do_select   S     1  0:01 /usr/X11R
100100      0   433   424   0    0   1496    724 nanosleep   S     1  0:00 wmclock -
100100      0   878   424   0    0   2488   1656 do_select   S     1  0:00 xterm -sb
100100      0   970   424   0    0   2448   1620 do_select   S     1  0:00 xterm -sb
```

```
   100     0   879   878   0   0   1240   808 wait4       S   p1   0:00 bash
100100     0   884   879   0   0   1244   768 do_signal   T   p1   0:00 vi
100100     0   911   879   0   0   1268   720 do_signal   T   p1   0:00 top
100100     0  1016   879   0   0   1388   752 do_select   S   p1   0:00 vi t
   100     0   971   970  10   0   1236   796 wait4       S   p2   0:00 bash
100000     0  1020   971  11   0    956   492             R   p2   0:00 ps l
```

Example: To display full (**f** option) process information about all (**e** option) processes to standard output:

ps ef

Example: To display full (**f** option) process information about all processes associated with user jones (**u** option) to standard output:

ps fu jones

l	Long format.
u	User format—include user name and start time.
j	Jobs format—pgid sid.
s	Signal format.
v	Vm format.
m	Displays memory information (combine with p flag to get number of pages).
f	"Forest" family tree format for command line.
a	Show processes of other users, too.
x	Show processes without controlling terminal.
S	Add child cpu time and page faults.
c	Command name from task_struct.
e	Show environment after command line and "+".
w	Wide output: Don't truncate command lines to fit on one line.
h	No header
r	Running processes only.

n	Numeric output for USER and WCHAN.
txx	Look only at processes with controlling tty xx.
O[+/-]k1[,[+/-]k2[,...]]	Order the output by the sequence of sort keys k1, k2,... - reverses default order of sort. There are a lot of possible sort keys:

SHORT	LONG	DESCRIPTION
c	cmd	Simple name of executable.
C	cmdline	Full command line.
f	flags	Flags as in long format F field.
g	pgrp	Process group ID.
G	tpgid	Controlling tty process group ID.
j	cutime	Cumulative user time.
J	cstime	Cumulative system time.
k	utime	User time.
K	stime	System time.
m	min_flt	Number of minor page faults.
M	maj_flt	Number of major page faults.
n	cmin_flt	Cumulative minor page faults.
N	cmaj_flt	Cumulative major page faults.
o	session	Session ID.
p	pid	Process ID.
P	ppid	Parent process ID.

r	rss	Resident set size.
R	resident	Resident pages.
s	size	Memory size in kilobytes.
S	share	Amount of shared pages.
t	tty	The minor device number of tty.
T	start_time	Time process was started.
U	uid	User ID number.
u	user	User name.
v	vsize	Total VM size in bytes.

Sort order

-Ou , --sort:user	-Oc , --sort:cmd
-OU , --sort:uid	-Op , --sort:pid
-OP , --sort:ppid	-Og , --sort:pgrp
-Oo , --sort:session	-Ot , --sort:tty
-OG , --sort:tpgid	-Ok , --sort:utime
-OK , --sort:stime	-Oj , --sort:cutime
-OJ , --sort:cstime	-Oy , --sort:priority
-OT , --sort:start_time	-Of , --sort:flags
-Om , --sort:min_flt	-On , --sort:cmin_flt
-OM , --sort:maj_flt	-ON , --sort:cmaj_flt
-Ov , --sort:vsize	-Or , --sort:rss

-OC , --sort:pcpu	-Os , --sort:size
-OR , --sort:resident	-OS , --sort:share

xpids	Restrict output to only the listed processes.
--help	Output a help message.
--version	Display version information.

pstree [-a] [-c] [-h] [-l] [-n] [-p] [-u] [-G|-U] [pid|user]

pstree -V

Output the family tree of running processes. If no process id or user name is specified, the tree is rooted at init. Identical branches are merged in the display by prefixing the process name with a count.

Example: Say your xinit process has a PID of 430. To display it and all its descendants in tree form with their PIDs (see output, below):

pstree 430 -p

```
xinit(431)-+-X(432)
           `-wmaker(434)-+-wmclock(443)
                         |-xterm(637)---bash(638)
                         |-xterm(715)---bash(716)---pstree(2118)
                         |-xterm(718)---bash(719)---top(720)
                         |-xterm(721)---bash(722)---vi(2051)
                         `-xterm(724)---bash(725)
```

-a	Include command line arguments in the display.
-c	Do not compact the identical subtrees.
-G	Graphical display. (Use vt100 line drawing characters). Very cool.
-h	Highlight family tree of current process.
-l	Do not truncate long lines.
-n	Numeric sort by PID.

Process

-p	Include PIDs in display.
-u	Include uid transitions in display.
-U	Graphical display. Uses UTF-8 (Unicode) graphical characters in display.
-V	Display version information.

renice priority [[-p] pid ...] [[-g] pgrp ...] [[-u] user ...]

renice enables you to alter the scheduling priority of running process(es). The default priority is 0. To make a process run faster, specify a negative priority value (you must be root to do this). To give a process a lower priority (and thereby make it run slower), specify a positive priority. The priority value must be in the range -20 <= priority <= 19.

Example: To play a funny joke on your buddy, "Tim," and make all his stuff run really slowly:

renice 20 -u tim

You must be superuser to be this funny.

TIP To give a running process a higher priority (by decreasing its priority number) you must be superuser.

-g	Include processes belonging to the specified group in any modifications.
-u	Include processes belonging to the specified user in any modifications.
-p	Include the specified process in any modifications.

top [-] [d *delay*] [q] [c] [S] [s] [i]

Top displays a listing of the processes utilizing the CPU. Output may be ordered by CPU usage, memory usage or runtime. Note that **top** is itself a CPU-intensive task, so use it sparingly. To change options while **top** is running, use the **s** command at the prompt and specify the new options.

Example: In my experience, **top** is generally run without arguments.

top

It produces output like the following:

```
8:59am  up 3 days, 16:42,  3 users,  load average: 0.00, 0.00, 0.00
39 processes: 38 sleeping, 1 running, 0 zombie, 0 stopped
CPU states:  0.9% user,  0.0% system,  0.0% nice, 99.1% idle
Mem:   95460K av,  87380K used,   8080K free,  17648K shrd,  33748K buff
Swap: 104384K av,      0K used, 104384K free                37184K cached

  PID USER     PRI  NI  SIZE  RSS SHARE STAT  LIB %CPU %MEM   TIME COMMAND
 6543 root      19   0   716  716   556 R       0  0.9  0.7   0:00 top
    1 root       0   0   388  388   328 S       0  0.0  0.4   0:03 init
    2 root       0   0     0    0     0 SW      0  0.0  0.0   0:00 kflushd
    3 root     -12 -12     0    0     0 SW<     0  0.0  0.0   0:00 kswapd
    4 root       0   0     0    0     0 SW      0  0.0  0.0   0:00 md_thread
    5 root       0   0     0    0     0 SW      0  0.0  0.0   0:00 md_thread
  402 news      19   0   708  708   576 S       0  0.0  0.7   0:00 innwatch
 1287 root       0   0   796  796   656 S       0  0.0  0.8   0:00 bash
  395 root       0   0   296  296   248 S       0  0.0  0.3   0:00 mingetty
   36 root       0   0   364  364   312 S       0  0.0  0.3   0:00 kerneld
  210 bin        0   0   332  332   264 S       0  0.0  0.3   0:00 portmap
  224 root       0   0   472  472   396 S       0  0.0  0.4   0:00 syslogd
  233 root       0   0   536  536   324 S       0  0.0  0.5   0:00 klogd
  244 daemon     0   0   404  404   328 S       0  0.0  0.4   0:00 atd
  255 root       0   0   472  472   392 S       0  0.0  0.4   0:00 crond
  267 root       0   0   396  396   328 S       0  0.0  0.4   0:00 inetd
  278 root       0   0  1168 1168   580 S       0  0.0  1.2   0:00 named
```

-d	Use the specified delay (in seconds) between updates.
-q	Refresh constantly with no delay.
-S	Include in usage calculations the usage of the process' children.
-s	Run in secure mode.
-i	Tells top to ignore idle or zombie processes.
-c	Include the process' entire command line in the output

Summary of display values

Uptime	How long the system has been running, plus the average number of processes ready to run in the last 1, 5, and 15 minutes.
Processes	count of the number of processes running at the last update.
CPU states	Percentage of CPU time in user mode, system mode, niced tasks and idle.
Mem	Memory statistics (total K, free K, used K, shared K, buffer K).
Swap	Swap statistics (total K, available K, used K, cached)

PID	PID of the process.
PPID	PID of the process' parent.
UID	UID of the process' owner.
USER	User name of the process' owner.
PRI	Priority of the task..
NI	Nice value of the task.
SIZE	Size of code + data + stack space, in kilobytes.
TSIZE	Code size of the task.
DSIZE	Size of data + stack space.
TRS	Text Resident Size.
SWAP	Size of part of task currently swapped out.
D	Size of dirty memory pages.
LIB	Size of library pages.
RSS	Total amount of physical memory used by the task.
SHARE	Amount of shared memory used by the task.
STAT	State of the task (Z=zombie, S=sleeping, T=stopped).
WCHAN	Show the address or name of the kernel function task is sleeping in.
TIME	Total CPU time used by task since invoked.
%CPU	Percentage of CPU time used by task since last update.
%MEM	Percentage of physical memory used by task.
COMMAND	Name of command which started task.

Once invoked, top may be used interactively. The following are supported:

<space>	Update display information immediately.
^L	Repaint the screen.
h, ?	Display help information.
k	Kill a process—top will prompt for pid.
i	Ignore zombie processes and idle processes.
n, #	Show the specified number of processes.
q	Quit.
r	Renice a process.
S	Toggle cumulative mode on/off.
s	Specify new delay (in seconds) between updates.
f, F	Add specified fields to display.
o, O	Change order of displayed fields.
l	Toggle display of load average and uptime information.
m	Toggle display of memory information.
t	Toggle display of CPU state and process information.
c	Toggle display between command name/full command line.
M	Order display by memory usage.
P	Order display by CPU usage.
T	Order display by time/cumulative time.
W	Write current setup to ~/.toprc.

CHAPTER

4

STANDARD INPUT, OUTPUT, AND ERROR

Introduction

The concept of a **standard input** and a **standard output** is one of the most useful features of Unix-like operating systems. The idea is that every program, no matter how diverse, should be reading input and generating output in a uniform, clearly understood way. Once you have that, it makes it much easier for programs to talk to one another directly. It is also possible to write generic programs which bridge the in-and-out of any two programs, which is an amazingly handy ability to have.

To put it another way, for the most part, standard input and standard output are nothing more than the keyboard and the monitor, respectively. But if you want to, you can redirect the output that would have gone to your monitor to somewhere more useful—like a file, or even the input of another program. Similarly, you can set up files that contain sheaves of data and use that as input to some command, or read the input for command A directly from the output of command B.

In addition, a third mechanism known as **standard error** has been provided to programs for displaying error messages.

>	Send standard output to a file.
<	Read standard input from a file.

2>	Redirect standard error as specified.
>>	Append standard output to the specified file.
|	Couple the standard output of one program to the standard input of another program.
tee	Copy standard input to a file and also to standard output.
script	Save the activity on your screen in a file
xargs	Read multiple arguments from standard input and use them as arguments to some specified command.

Commands

>

Send **standard output** to somewhere other than the monitor.

Example: To save the output of a directory listing to the file "myhome.base":

ls -l > myhome.base

<

Read **standard input** from somewhere other than the keyboard.

Example: To get a list of expressions to evaluate from the file "myexpr.ksh":

test < myexpr.ksh

2>

Redirect **standard error** as specified. The 2 in this command comes from the Unix tradition that standard input has a file number 0, standard output is numbered 1 and standard error is numbered 2.

Example: To send standard error messages to the file error:

cc -o interest interest.c 2> error

>>

Append standard output to the specified file without overwriting the existing contents.

Example: To append Mail directory information to the file "myhome.base":

dirname $MAIL |xargs ls -l >> myhome.base

|

The pipe character is used to link the standard output of one program to the standard input of another program.

Example: To look through all the subdirectories of your current directory for a file named "important.c":

find . -type f -print | grep "important.c"

In this example, the standard output from the **find** command (a list of file names) is piped to the standard input of the **grep** command, which searches for a text string.

tee [OPTION]... [FILE]...

Copy standard input to standard output and to any file(s) given as arguments. Useful for saving a copy of stuff being written to the screen. So named because it's like the T joint in plumbing.

Example: To **grep** through the output of a lengthy **find** and also save a copy of the **find** results for possible later perusal:

find / -type f -print | tee find.results | grep "important.file"

-a, --append	Append any output to the specified files rather than overwriting.
-i,--ignore-interrupt	Ignore any interrupts sent.

script [-a] [file]

Record what is happening on the terminal and save it into a file. By default, the file is "typescript" in your current working directory, but you can specify any one you like. Exit with CTRL-D.

Example: To record the output of multiple commands in the file "homework.220":

script homework.220

<Type a bunch of commands>

<Press Ctrl-C>

-a	Append any subsequent information to the existing script file—do not overwrite.

xargs [-0prtx] [-e[eof-str]] [-i[replace-str]] [-l[maxlines]] [-n max-args] [-s max-chars][-P max-procs] [--null] [--eof[=eof-str]] [--replace[=replace-str]] [--max-lines[=max-lines]] [--interactive] [--maxchars=max-chars] [--verbose] [--exit] [--max-procs=maxprocs] [--max-args=max-args] [--no-run-if-empty] [-version] [--help] [command [initial-arguments]]

Read arguments from standard input, construct a command line using those arguments and arguments provided on its own command line, and execute the constructed commands.

Example: Say you have some time on your hands and you want to **grep** through every file in the **/usr/local** filesystem for the string "datum". First, generate a list of the files using the **find** command, then pipe the results of that find to **grep** via the **xargs** command (if you don't use **xargs**, **grep** will look only at the names of the files for the string "datum", not look in the files themselves).

find /usr/local -type f -print | xargs grep "datum"

--null, -0	Input files are terminated by Null rather than the end of file character.
--eof[=eof-str], -e[eof-str]	Treat the specified string as the end-of -file marker.
--help	Display a listing of the possible arguments to xargs.

--replace[=*replace-str****], -i[****replace-str****]***	Replace occurrences of replace-str in the initial arguments with names read from standard input.
--max-lines[=*max-lines****], -l[****max-lines****]***	Limit commands to at most max-lines nonblank lines per command (default 1).
--max-args=*max-args,* ***-n*** *max-args*	Limit commands to at most max-args.
--interactive, -p	Prompt the user before executing a generated command line.
--no-run-if-empty, -r	If the generated command line is empty, don't run it.
--max-chars=*max-chars,* ***-s*** *max-chars*	Specify a maximum length for a command line.
--verbose, -t	Before executing the command, display it to standard output.
--version	Output the version number and exit.
--exit, -x	Exit if the size specified by -s is exceeded.
--max-procs=*max-procs,* ***-P*** *max-procs*	Specify an upper limit of processes to be simultaneously executed.

CHAPTER

5

DIRECTORIES

Introduction

A **directory** is a special kind of file which is used to arrange other files into groups. For example, in writing this book I have created a directory ***Linux*** into which I'm placing the files associated with each chapter:

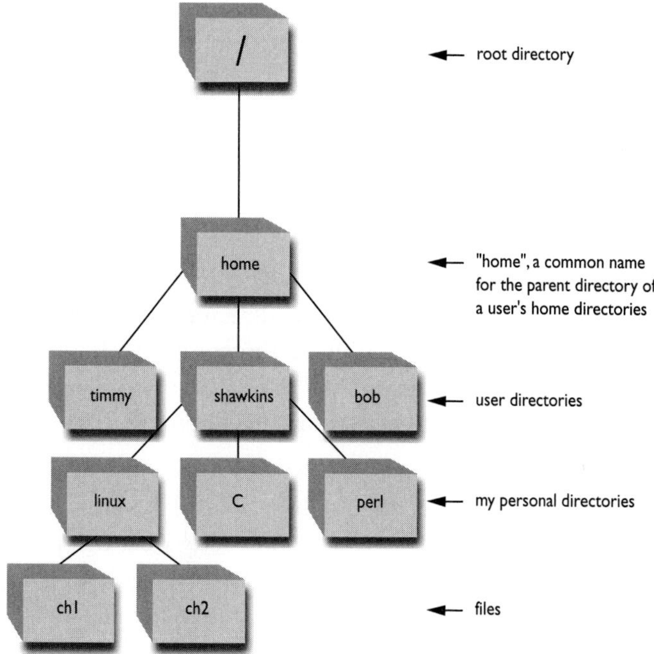

Figure 5-1 Sample Directory Tree

Directories are arranged under the root directory, "/", in a structure called the **directory hierarchy** or **directory tree**.

The internal construction of directories is similar to that of files in most ways. Directories have owners and groups associated with them. They have permissions associated with their owner, group, and the rest of the world. (See the **chmod** command in the chapter on files for a bit more information about permissions). They have access times, modification times, and change times, all stored within the inode. The biggest difference between files and directories is that where the inode of a file contains pointers to data blocks, the inode of a directory contains pointers to other files.

Directories are pervasive, so there is a substantial collection of specialized jargon associated with them. Here are some of the highlights:

home directory—A user's home directory is the directory where he or she is placed at login. Home directories for a given user are defined in that user's entry in the ***/etc/passwd*** file. Because it is so common to need to specify files relative to your home directory, a specialized symbol has been defined for each user's home directory: The tilde, "~", can be used in shell commands to indicate your home directory. In the examples below, assume that we're still talking about my home directory, ***/home/shawkins***.

Abbreviation	**Equivalent to**	**Example**
~	/home/shawkins	cd ~
~/linux	/home/shawkins/linux	cd ~/linux

current directory—Whenever you're logged in, you have a current working directory, your current location in the directory tree. This is the output of the **pwd** command. When you enter the command **ls -a**, the current directory shows up with a filename of "**.**". The shell variable for your current directory is **$PWD.** To change your current directory, use the **cd** command.

TIP I get sick of typing **pwd** all the time, so I set up my bash shell prompt to display my current working directory. It works pretty well, except when I get more than 4 or 5 levels deep in the directory tree. At that point the shell prompt starts cutting seriously into my typing space. If you're interested in trying this out for yourself, add the following line to your ~/.bashrc file:

```
export PS1='$PWD> '
```

You'll have to re-source your .bashrc file, either by logging out and then back in, or by typing:

. ./.bashrc

before the new command prompt will take effect. (Note: "PS1" is the shell variable for your command line prompt.)

parent directory—For any given directory, the directory above it in the directory tree. The parent directory also has a shorthand symbol, "..", which can be used in commands. For example, say your current working directory is ***/home/shawkins/linux***. If you type the command:

cd ..

your new current working directory will be ***/home/shawkins***.

subdirectory—Any directory below another in the directory tree. ***/home/shawkins*** is a subdirectory of ***/home***, and ***/home/shawkins/linux*** is a subdirectory of ***/home/shawkins***.

The commands covered in this section include:

cd	Change directories.
mkdir	Create a new directory.
pwd	Print the current working directory.
rmdir	Remove the specified directory.
symlinks	Find symbolic links.

Related Files

~	Your home directory.
/	The root directory of the Linux system.

Commands

cd *target_directory*

Change directory. This command makes target_directory your current working directory. It is a strong contender for the single most commonly used command in Linux. *target_directory* may be either a relative path, an absolute path, a shell symbol, or a shell variable.

Example: In the examples below, assume that the shell variable **$BOB** stands for ***/home/bob***. The directory tree is the same as the sample directory tree printed in the front of this chapter.

Starting Directory	target_directory Type	Example Command	Ending Directory
/home/shawkins	relative	cd linux	/home/shawkins/linux
/home/shawkins	absolute	cd /home	/home
/home/shawkins	shell symbol	cd ..	/home
/home/shawkins	shell variable	cd $BOB	/home/bob

mkdir [OPTION]... *NAME...*

Create a directory.

Example: To create a new directory called ***tcl_stuff*** under your current working directory:

mkdir tcl_stuff

***-m** MODE, **--mode=**MODE*	Set the file permissions as specified.
-p, --parents	Make any missing parent directories for each argument.
--verbose	Verbose output. Display a message for each directory created.

pwd

Display the fully resolved name (that is, the full pathname starting at the root directory) of the current directory.

Example: To display the current directory:

pwd

rmdir [OPTION]... *DIRECTORY...*

Remove the specified directory(ies). All directories specified must a) exist and b) be empty.

Example: To remove the directory ***tcl_stuff***:

rmdir tcl_stuff

-p, --parents	Tell rmdir to remove any parent directories that may become empty after one of the subdirectories is removed.

symlinks [-cdrv] *dirlist*

This command scans directories for symbolic links, listing them to standard output. Each link is classified as one of the following:

relative	A link expressed as a path relative to the directory in which the link resides.
absolute	A link given as an absolute path from the root directory.
dangling	A link whose target does not currently exist.
messy	A link containing unnecessary slashes or dots in the path.

lengthy	A length using "../" more than necessary in the path.
other_fs	A link whose target resides on a different filesystem.

Example: To search all the subdirectories under your home directory (**-r** option) for symbolic links, removing any dangling links found (**-d** option):

symlinks -r -d ~

-c	Convert absolute links to relative links.
-d	Remove dangling links.
-r	Recursive operation (within a single filesystem).
-s	Detach lengthy links.
-t	Test what would happen if -c was specified but don't change anything.
-v	Include relative links in the output (by default they are excluded).

CHAPTER

6

USERS

Introduction

The concept of a user on a Linux system is fairly rigidly defined and more numeric than you might think. At the login prompt, you type in some string of characters (e.g., shawkins, root) called your **user name**. The system takes this string, compares it to the entries in the ***/etc/passwd*** file, and finds the encrypted password associated with that user. It then prompts you for a password. Whatever string you type in is encrypted and the result of the encryption is compared to the password string stored in ***/etc/passwd***. If they match, the system acknowledges your right to exist and begins the login process.

The **login** program sets your user id and group id (see below) forks (creates a copy of itself) and the copy turns into whatever shell is specified as your preference in ***/etc/passwd***. That shell is told that its current working directory is whatever file specified as your home directory in the (can you guess?) ***/etc/passwd*** file.

From login on, your existence on the system is largely defined by two numbers: your **user id** (**uid**) and **group id** (**gid**). These two numbers are how the system thinks of you—they are found in the inodes of your files, in the innermost recesses of the kernel's CPU allocation algorithms, and in the processes you run. The **user** and **group** names that one typically sees when running commands (ls, ps, ...) are looked up in ***/etc/passwd*** file, as necessary. The system doesn't care about names.

Entries in the ***/etc/passwd*** file are of the following format:

```
name:encrypted_password:UID:GID:user name:home_directory:shell
```

Your primary group is specified in ***/etc/passwd***. However, you can belong to more than one group. Groups and their membership are defined in the file ***/etc/group***.

Various program exist to display your current set of user attributes and allow you to modify them.

chfn	Change information displayed by finger.
chpasswd	Change user passwords in bulk.
finger	Display information about a user.
groupmod	Modify information in the system group files.
grpck	Check system group files for validity.
id	Display information about a user.
passwd	Change a user's password.
pwck	Check system password files for validity.
su	Change to a new user id.
useradd	Add a new user to the system.
userdel	Delete a user from the system.
usermod	Modify user information on the system.
users	Display a list of current users.
who	Display a list of current users.

Related Files

/etc/group	Group information.
/etc/gshadow	Secure group information.
/etc/passwd	Definitive source of user information.
/home	Filesystem which usually contains the home directories of users.

Commands

chfn [-f *full-name*][-o *office*][-p *office-phone*] [-h *home-phone*] [-u] [-v] [*username*]

This command is used to change the information displayed when someone **finger**s you. If no information is entered on the command line, **chfn** will prompt you interactively for each field.

Example: To change your home phone as stored on the system:

chfn -h 1234567890

-f, --full-name	Enter your real name.
-o, --office	Enter office or room number.
-p, --office-phone	Enter office phone number.
-h, --home-phone	Enter home phone number.
-u, --help	Display help information and exit.
-v, --version	Display version information and exit.

chpasswd [-e]

This command accepts a list of user name + password pairs from standard input and uses the information to update the passwords of existing users. The input lines are formatted:

user:password

Example: After you've set up the file "newpasswords" containing the user name/password pairs, use **chpasswd** to update the password information on the system:

chpasswd < newpasswords

TIP Use this command on a security-conscious system to do periodic bulk updating of passwords.

TIP It is a terrible idea to store unencrypted passwords anywhere on the system.

-e	Specify that the input password will already be encrypted.

finger [-lmsp] [user ...] [user@host ...]

This command displays information about system users.

Example: To find out if user dsatter is logged on and doing stuff:

finger dsatter

might produce output like the following:

```
Login: dsatter                    Name:
Directory: /home/dsatter          Shell: /bin/bash
On since Sat Jul 24 10:42 (EDT) on tty1
No mail.
Plan:
Go away and leave me alone.
```

TIP If you keep a file called ".plan" in your home directory, the contents of that file will be displayed when someone **finger**s you. The original intent was to provide a mechanism for letting people know you were at lunch, what you were working on, etc., but in practice it's become a window into the personality of the user, not unlike the .signature file in e-mail.

-s	Display login name, real name, terminal name, write status, idle time, login time, office location and office phone number.
-l	Display a multi-line output, including all the information included with the -s option and also user's home directory, home phone number, login shell, mail status, and (finally), the contents of their .plan, .project, and .forward files.
-p	Suppress printing of the .plan and .project files.
-m	Suppress matching of the user argument to user's real names.

groupmod [-g *gid* [-o]] [-n *group_name*] *group*

Modify the system account files pertaining to group information.

Example: To change the name of the group "chem" to "chemistry" (**-n** option) and at the same time make their new group id be 127 (**-g** option):

ROOT **chgrp -g 127 -n chemistry**

***-g** gid*	Specify a new numeric group ID. By default, this value must be unique. Values less than 100 are reserved for system groups (by convention). Values may not be negative.
-o	Permit use of non-unique group IDs.
***-n** group_name*	Specify a new name for the group.

groups [USERNAME]...

Display group information for the specified user.

Example: To display information about all groups user shae belongs to:

groups shae

-help	Display help information and exit.
--version	Display version information and exit.

grpck [-r] [group shadow]

Check the entries in ***/etc/group*** and **/etc/gshadow** for validity (proper format and valid data).

Example: To test your group file for validity without modifying anything:

grpck

-r	Read-only mode.

id [OPTION]... [USERNAME]

Display user and group id information for the specified user or, if no user is specified, the running process.

Example: To display user and group information for the user Michael:

id michael

-g, --group	Restrict output to group id only.
-G, --groups	Display supplementary groups only.
-n, --name	Display user or group name rather than ID number. Must be used with one of -u, -g, or -G.
-r, --real	Display real, rather than effective user or group id.
-u, --user	Display the user id only.

passwd [-u] [*username*]

Change the specified user's password. You must be root to run this command on any user other than yourself.

Example: If you're root, you can reset Timmy's password by typing:

passwd timmy

and entering the password two times as prompted.

-u	Only update expired passwords.

pwck [-r] [*passwd shadow*]

Check the entries in ***/etc/passwd*** and ***/etc/shadow*** for validity.

Example: To run a sanity check on your password file:

pwck

-r	Read-only mode.

su [OPTION]... [USER [ARG]...]

Change identity to the specified user or, with no options, become superuser.

Example: To become superuser, type:

su

and enter the proper password at the prompt.

Example: To assume the user id of shawkins without changing your current environment variables, type:

su shawkins

and enter the proper password at the prompt

Example: To assume the user id of shawkins, replacing all your current environment variables with those of shawkins:

su - shawkins

***-c** COMMAND, **--command=**COMMAND'*	Run the specified command as the specified user without starting an interactive shell.
-, -l, --login	Make the shell a login shell. That is, the new shell will behave as if you had just logged in from a blank terminal as the specified user.
-m, -p, --preserve-environment	Do not change HOME, USER, LOGNAME, or SHELL environment variables.
***-s** SHELL, **--shell=**SHELL*	Run the specified shell rather than the shell from the user's password entry.

useradd [-c comment] [-d home_dir] [-e expire_date] [-f inactive_time] [-g initial_group] [-G group[,...]] [-m [-k skeleton_dir] | -M] [-s shell] [-u uid [-o]] [-n] [-r] login

useradd -D [-g default_group] [-b default_home] [-f default_inactive] [-e default_expire_date] [-s default_shell]

This command is used to create a new user account on the system. The user must supply a login name, but all other values are optional.

Example: To create a user "mary", with home directory (**-d** option) of ***/home/mary***, shell (**-s** option) ***/bin/bash***, and group (**-g** option) "chemistry":

ROOT

useradd -g chemistry -s /bin/bash -d /home/mary mary

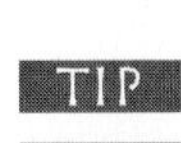

You're not done yet. Use the **passwd** command to give her a new password.

If you're the system administrator on a busy multiuser system, it will effectively add years to your life to write a script that will add new users with a minimum of work on your part (prompt with defaults for username, phone, home directory, etc). If you're not the system administrator on a multiuser system, you should do this anyway, for practice.

-c *comment*	Specify a value for the comment field of the password file.
-d *home_dir*	Specify the new user's home directory.
-e *expire_date*	Specify a date on which the new user account will cease to work. expire_date is of the format MM/DD/YY.
-f *inactive_days*	Specify how long to wait after a password expires before the account becomes disabled.
-g *initial_group*	This field contains the group name or number of the user's initial login group.
-G *group,[...]*	Define the user's supplementary groups.
-m	When this option is invoked, the user's home directory will be created if it does not already exist.
-M	Force useradd to NOT create the user's home directory.
-n	Tell useradd NOT to create a group corresponding to the new user's user name.
-r	Specify that the new user is a system account. (System accounts have UID values less than UID_MIN)
-s *shell*	Specify a login shell for the user.
-u *uid*	Specify a numerical UID value.

Changing Defaults

Useradd has certain defaults which may be either displayed or modified by invoking the command with the -D option. (Display only if no other options are provided; otherwise, the options are set as specified.)

***-b** default_home*	Specify an initial path for new home directories.
***-e** default_expire_date*	Specify a new account expiration date.
***-f** default_inactive*	Specify the number of days to wait after a password expired before cancelling an account.
***-g** default_group*	Specify a default group for new users.
***-s** default_shell*	Specify a new user's default login shell.

userdel [-r] *login*

Delete the specified login account. All entries pertaining to the specified user are deleted from system account files.

Example: To remove the user postalguy from the system:

ROOT **userdel postalguy**

-r	Scorched earth option. Remove all files in the user's home directory, as well as the directory itself.

usermod [-c *comment*] [-d *home_dir* [-m]] [-e *expire_date*] [-f *inactive_time*] [-g *initial_group*] [-G *group*[,...]] [-l *login_name*] [-s *shell*] [-u *uid* [-o]] login

This command enables the user to modify information contained in system account files.

Example: To change user Ajita's home directory to ***/home/chemdept***:

ROOT **usermod -d /home/chemdept ajita**

***-c** comment*	Change the comment field as specified.
***-d** home_dir*	Change the login directory to the specified value.

***-e** expire_date*	Change the account expiration date as specified.
***-f** inactive_days*	Specify the number of days to wait after the account password expires before permanently disabling the account.
***-g** initial_group*	Specify a new initial login group.
***-G** group,[...]*	Specify a list of additional groups of which the user is a member.
***-l** login_name*	Specify a new login name.
***-s** shell*	Specify a new login shell.
***-u** uid*	Specify a new numeric user ID.

users [*FILE*]

Display a list of users currently logged on.

Example: This command has no real options. To use, type:

users

FILE	Tell the command to look in a file other than *wtmp* for the necessary information.
--help	Display usage information and exit.
--version	Display version information and exit.

who [OPTION] [FILE] [am i]

Display information about the users currently logged in. With no options, the display includes: login name, terminal line, login time, remote hostname or X display.

Example: To find out who's logged in to the system:

who

FILE	If present, who will use this as the source for users logged on rather than /etc/wtmp.
-m	Same as "who am i".
-q, -count	Display only the count of users logged on and their login names.
-s	No effect; included for compatibility.
-i, -u, -idle	Include idle time in display. "." in the idle time field means the user has been active in the last minute; "old" means they have been idle for more than 24 hours.
-H, -heading	Print a line of column headings.
-w, -T, -mesg, -message, -writable	After each login name, print a character indicating the user's message status: + Allowing "write" messages - Disallowing "write" messages ? Cannot find terminal device

CHAPTER

7

PATHS

Introduction

The **path** to a file is an ordered specification of the subdirectories through which one must pass in order to find that file. Linux paths are delimited (separated) by the forward slash character, "/". A path which begins with a forward slash is assumed to start at the root directory and is called an **absolute path**. A path that does not begin with the forward slash character is called a **relative path** and is assumed to refer to files relative to the current working directory.

Occasionally when you're writing a script or program, it's handy to get access to the text string which is all or part of a path. The commands in this section help you do that. If you're looking for information on the environment variable PATH, check the chapter on terminal and environment.

basename	Take a full path and strip out all but the last element.
dirname	Take a full path and display all but the last element.
namei	Follow a path to the end, if it has one.
pathchk	Check paths for portability and validity.

Commands

basename NAME [SUFFIX]

This command takes a full UNIX path and strips away all but the last element. Generally used in scripting. If the optional suffix is supplied and it matches the last element, it is stripped away as well.

Example: Say your current working directory is ***/var/spool/mail***. In that case:

basename $PWD

would display

mail

Of course, **basename** can be used on text strings as well as environment variables:

basename /var/spool/mail

would also display

mail

--help	Display usage information.
--version	Display version information.

dirname NAME

This command takes a full UNIX path and displays all but the last element. Generally used in scripting.

Example: Say you were writing a script that needed to know the directory name of your mail folder:

dirname $MAIL

TIP This command is a good example of a general scripting principle: don't hard code. "Hard coding" means treating a value in your script (e.g., the mail directory, ***/var/spool/mail***) as a constant when it may not necessarily be constant.

For example, while ***/var/spool/mail*** is in fact a wise choice for a mail directory, I can flat-out promise you that the systems administrator of the company to whom you are pitching your million-dollar mail utility chose instead to specify ***/random/directory***. I can further promise that you won't notice this until the board of directors is assembled.

--help	Display usage information.
--version	Display version information.

namei [-mx] *pathname* [*pathname* ...]

When passed a standard UNIX path, **namei** will follow the path until a terminal point is found. If a symbolic link is in the path, **namei** follows that as well. Generally used for identifying excessive symbolic links (links to links to links to...). Output uses the following abbreviations:

f	The pathname we are currently trying to resolve
d	Directory
l	Symbolic link (both the link and it's contents are output)
s	Socket
b	Block device
c	Character device
-	Regular file
?	Error

Example: Say linkfile was a link to ***/usr/local***:

namei linkfile/hawksoft

would yield:

```
f: linkfile/hawksoft
l linkfile -> /usr/local
d /
d usr
d local
d hawksoft
```

-x	Display mount point directories as a "D".
-m	Include the mode of each file in the display.

pathchk [OPTION]... *NAME*...

Check the portability and validity of any specified path. Displays an error if any of the following conditions is met:

1. A directory in NAME does not have execute permission.
2. The length of NAME exceeds the filesystem's name length limits.
3. The length of any component of NAME exceeds the filesystem's component length limits.

Example: To check the portability of your baby before sending it out into the world:

pathchk /usr/local/hawksoft/eft-o-matic

-p,--portability	Test against the POSIX minimum limits for portability.

CHAPTER

8

THE BASH SHELL

Introduction

"Shell" is the name given to the program which handles user commands and starts other programs. The term "shell" is another one of those weak UNIX jokes; the "shell" is the program between you and the "kernel." After you log in, the shell prompt is the first thing you see. There are a lot of different shells available for Linux (e.g., Korn, Bourne, **csh**, **tcsh**); which particular one you use at login time is determined by your entry in the ***/etc/passwd*** file (it's the rightmost field on the line). One's choice of shell isn't quite the fountain of jihad that one's choice of operating system is, but it is still a semi-touchy issue.

Bash stands for Bourne Again SHell, a reference to the fact that **bash** is based on another shell (the Bourne shell, obviously). Bash contains features found in Bourne shell, csh (the C shell), Korn Shell, and some that are found in **bash** only. All of the Bourne shell built-in commands are available in **bash**.

Quick Overview of Shell Operation

When you log in or otherwise invoke the shell, it checks system variables and the ***/etc/passwd*** file to determine who you are and where your login session is supposed to begin. It then searches the system for default configuration files and looks for configuration files in your home directory. Typically, these system files set up a few aliases, do some security checks, configure your prompt, and perform half a dozen other user and site specific tasks limited only by your imagination. It then prints out a prompt and waits for you to type in a command.

When you do type in a command line, the shell first parses it. It identifies any redirection of standard input, output, and error, any background detachments, looks up any shell variables (e.g., $**DBDIR**) or aliases (**ll**) and replaces them with the values they represent. It expands any wildcard arguments (e.g., the "**c***" in "**ls -l c***") into lists of actual files and concatenates them into argument arrays suitable for passing to an actual command. The line you typed in is stored in whatever history mechanism the shell provides. The shell searches the directories specified in your $**PATH** system variable for the command you typed in. If it finds it, it constructs a list of arguments composed of that command and any expanded arguments, **forks()** a copy of itself, and **execs()** the specified command. When the command finishes executing, control passes back to the shell. It prints out another prompt and the whole process starts over.

TIP You can display your current environment variables and their values by typing:

env

Topics Covered

The topic of shell programming doesn't lend itself as neatly to a command-by-command reference as other subjects covered in this book. (There are a whole lot of little commands, most of which have few or no arguments.) Consequently, I'm going to break with the traditions of this book a little bit and arrange this chapter by subtopic.

Note: The notation used in this chapter may be a wee bit confusing. Here are some examples which hopefully might clear things up:

Notation	Means
<Tab>	Press the Tab key on the keyboard. Do not try to type the letter sequence T-a-b.
<Ctrl>-P	Press the Ctrl key and the P key at the same time.
<Meta>-r	Press the meta key (on my keyboard it's the <Esc> key; yours may be different) and the r key at the same time.

The subtopics covered in this chapter include:

Invoking bash	Command line options for bash.
Startup Files	Conditions under which startup/shutdown files are sourced.
Aliases	Set and unset command line aliases.
Command History	Access and manipulate command history.
Command Completion	How to exploit command completion features.
Command Line Editing	How to manipulate the current command line.
Word Designators	How to specify individual words on a command line.
Shell Variables	Listing of shell variables.
Shell Prompt	How to customize your shell prompt.
Shell Arithmetic	Shell arithmetic operators.
Looping Statements	Shell looping statements.
Conditional Statements	Syntax & examples.
Shell Functions	Syntax & examples.
Builtins	Built- in bash commands.

Related Files

~/.bashrc	Executed when starting a bash subshell.
~/.bash_profile	Executed at login time.
/etc/profile	Systemwide profile.
~/.bash_login	Synonym for *bash_profile.*
~/.bash_logout	Executed when a bash shell exits.

Commands

Invoking bash

Typically, the shells are invoked when you log in. The last thing the login program does is look in your ***/etc/passwd*** file to see what shell your system administrator has specified for you to use. If it isn't **bash**, you can either edit the ***/etc/passwd*** file or invoke **bash** from another shell by typing /bin/bash at the command line. The following options apply:

-norc	Don't read the "~/.bashrc" initialization file in an interactive shell.
-rcfile *FILENAME*	Execute commands from the specified file rather than ~/.bashrc in an interactive shell.
-noprofile	Don't load the system-wide startup file /etc/profile or any of the personal initialization files (~/.bash_profile, ~/.bash_login, ~/.profile).
-version	Display version information.
-login	Make this shell act as if it were directly invoked from login.
-nobraceexpansion	Do not perform curly brace expansion.

-nolineediting	Do not use the GNU Readline library to read interactive command lines.
-posix	Force bash to conform to the Posiz 1003.2 standard.
-c STRING	Read and execute commands from STRING after processing the options, then exit.
-i	Force the shell to run interactively.

Startup Files

When you log in or otherwise invoke **bash,** the shell looks at a variety of files and attempts to execute any shell commands contained in therein, a process known as **sourcing**. These files are where you set any configuration information (e.g., environment variables, aliases) or execute startup programs and scripts (**fortune**, **startx**).

Example: To set the environment variable **PATH** to include the directory ***/sbin***, include the following line in your ***~/.bash_profile*** file:

PATH=$PATH:/sbin

This sets the new value of **PATH** to be equal to the old value (**$PATH**) plus the directory **/sbin**.

Bash may be invoked interactively either at login time or from another shell, or non-interactively. Which files it attempts to source depend on how it was called.

Interactive Bash

At login: If the shell is being run as a normal, interactive shell, **bash** executes startup files at login time. Assuming the shell was invoked without the -noprofile option, files are sourced under the following circumstances:

1. If ***/etc/profile*** exists, then source it.
2. If ***~/.bash_profile*** exists, then source it,
   else if ***~/.bash_login*** exists, then source it,
   else if ***~/.profile*** exists, then source it.

At logout: If ***~/.bash_logout*** exists, source it.

Non-login Interactive bash

For non-login interactive shells (subject to the **-norc** and **-rcfile** options):

Startup Time: If ***~/.bashrc*** exists, then source it.

Non-interactive Shells

Startup Time: If the environment variable **ENV** is non-null, expand the variable and source the file named by the value. If **bash** is not started in Posix mode, it looks for **BASH_ENV** before **ENV**.

So, typically, your ***~/.bash_profile*** contains the line

```
if [ -f ~/.bashrc ]; then source ~/.bashrc; fi
```

TIP In non-interactive instances of **bash**, the **$PS1** variable is unset.

Aliases

Aliases are a shell mechanism which enable you to create shortened versions of common commands. You create an alias by typing the word "alias", the character sequence you want to be your new alias, an equal sign, and the value the alias expands to.

Example: These are two of my favorite aliases:

alias l='ls -a --color'

alias ll='ls -al --color'

TIP Create a file in your home directory called ***.alias*** and source it in one of your startup scripts. The .alias file is just a plain ASCII text file containing a list of your favorite aliases, exactly as you would type them on the command line. To source the alias file you might include the following line in the ***~/.bashrc*** file:

```
. ./.alias
```

This will give you back all your favorite aliases at login time and provide a central location for storing and referencing your aliases

alias [*NAME[=VALUE]* ...]

Without arguments, print the current list of aliases. Otherwise, define an alias. When the NAME is typed, **bash** will expand the name into VALUE and run VALUE as the command.

unalias [-a] [*NAME* ...]

Remove the specified NAME from the list of aliases. If **-a** is supplied, all aliases are removed.

Command History

As I mentioned in the introduction, **bash** stores commands in a history file (**$HISTFILE**) as you type them. Those commands are, of course, accessible at a later time. The following key combinations allow you to do various stuff with your command history:

<Enter>	Accept the line regardless of where the cursor is.
<Ctrl >-P	Move "up" through the history list.
<Ctrl>-n	Move "down" through the history list.
<Meta>-<	Move to the first line in the history.
<Meta>->	Move to the end of the input history.
<Ctrl>-r	Search backward starting at the current line and moving "up" through the history as necessary.
<Ctrl>-s	Search forward starting at the current line and moving "down" through the history as necessary.
<Meta>-p	Search backward starting at the current line and moving "up" through the history as necessary using a non-incremental search for a string supplied by the user.
<Meta>-n	Search forward starting at the current line and moving "down" through the history as necessary using a non-incremental search for a string supplied by the user.
<Meta>-<Ctrl>-y	Yank nth argument of previous command.
<Meta>-., M-_	Insert last argument to the previous command.

Alternatively, and (to my mind, at least) somewhat less conveniently, you have the ! (pronounced "bang"—honest) method of accessing your history:

!	Start a history substitution, except when followed by a space, tab, the end of the line, = or (.
!!	Refer to the previous command. This is a synonym for `!-1.

!n	Refer to command line N.
!-n	Refer to the command N lines back.
!string	Refer to the most recent command starting with STRING.
!?string[`?]	Refer to the most recent command containing STRING.
!#	The entire command line typed so far.
^string1^string2^	Quick Substitution. Repeat the last command, replacing STRING1 with STRING2. Equivalent to "!!:s/string1/string2/".

In addition, you also have the history command, which will display a listing of your command history.

history [N] [[-w -r -a -n] [*FILENAME*]]

Display the history list with line numbers.

-w	Write out the current history to the history file.
-r	Read the current history file and make its contents the history list.
-a	Append the new history lines.
-n	Read the history lines not already read from the history file into the current history list.

Command Completion

One of the niftiest things about **bash** is that it will do a lot of your typing for you.

<Tab>	Attempt to do completion on the text before the cursor.
<Meta>-?	List the possible completions of the text before the cursor.

<Ctrl>-x, <Ctrl>-r	Read in the contents of your init file, and incorporate any bindings or variable assignments found there.
<Ctrl>-g	Abort the current editing command and ring the terminal's bell (subject to the setting of "bell-style").
<Esc>	Make the next character that you type be metafied.
<Ctrl>-_, <Ctrl>-x, <Ctrl>-u	Incremental undo, separately remembered for each line.
<Meta>-r	Undo all changes made to this line.

Command Line Editing

Bash provides a slightly bewildering array of control characters for command line editing. These are most of them.

Handling Characters

<Ctrl>-b	Move back one character.
<Ctrl>-f	Move forward one character.
<Del>	Delete the character to the left of the cursor.
<Ctrl>-d	Delete the character underneath the cursor.
Printing characters	Insert the character into the line at the cursor.
<Ctrl>-u	Undo the last thing that you did. You can undo all the way back to an empty line.

Moving Around on the Line

<Ctrl>-a	Move to the start of the line.
<Ctrl>-e	Move to the end of the line.
<Meta>-f	Move forward a word.

<Meta>-b	Move backward a word.
<Ctrl>-l	Clear the screen, reprinting the current line at the top.
<Ctrl>-k	Kill the text from the current cursor position to the end of the line.
<Meta>-d	Kill from the cursor to the end of the current word, or, if between words, to the end of the next word.
<Meta>-DEL	Kill from the cursor the start of the previous word, or, if between words, to the start of the previous word.
<Ctrl>-w	Kill from the cursor to the previous whitespace. This is different from M-DEL because the word boundaries differ.
<Ctrl>-y	Yank the most recently killed text back into the buffer at the cursor.
<Meta>-y	Rotate the kill-ring, and yank the new top. You can do this only if the prior command is <Ctrl>-y or M-y.

Changing Text

<Ctrl>-d	Delete the character under the cursor.
<Ctrl>-q, C-v	Add the next character that you type to the line verbatim.
<Meta>-<Tab>	Insert a tab character.
<Ctrl>-t	Drag the character before the cursor forward over the character at the cursor, moving the cursor forward as well.
<Meta>-t	Drag the word behind the cursor past the word in front of the cursor moving the cursor over that word as well.
<Meta>-u	Uppercase the current (or following) word.
<Meta>-l	Lowercase the current (or following) word.
<Meta>-c	Capitalize the current (or following) word.

Killing & Yanking

<Ctrl>-k	Kill the text from the current cursor position to the end of the line.
<Ctrl>-x	Kill backward to the beginning of the line.
<Ctrl>-u	Kill backward from the cursor to the beginning of the current line.
<Meta>-d	Kill from the cursor to the end of the current word, or, if between words, to the end of the next word.
<Meta>-<Del>	Kill the word behind the cursor.
<Ctrl>-w	Kill the word behind the cursor, using white space as a word boundary.
<Ctrl>-y	Yank the top of the kill-ring into the buffer at the current cursor position.
<Meta>-y	Rotate the kill-ring, and yank the new top. You can do this only if the prior command is yank or yank-pop.

Key Bindings

<Ctrl>-a	Move to the start of the current line.
<Ctrl>-e	Move to the end of the line.
<Ctrl>-f	Move forward a character.
<Ctrl>-b	Move back a character.
<Meta>-f	Move forward to the end of the next word.
<Meta>-b	Move back to the start of this, or the previous, word.
<Ctrl>-l	Clear the screen and redraw the current line.

Word Designators

Bash allows you to specify words within a command line. These operators are primarily intended for use in shell programming.

Word Designation Operators

These operators allow you to specify one or more words within a command line.

:	Separate the event specification from the word designator.
0 (zero)	The "0"th word. Usually, the 0th word is the command word.
n	The Nth word.
^	The first argument; that is, word 1.
$	The last argument.
%	The word matched by the most recent "?string?" search.
x-y	A range of words; "-Y" abbreviates "0-Y".
*	All words except the 0th.
x*	Abbreviates "x-$".
x-	Abbreviates "x-$" like "x*", but omits the last word.

Modifiers

After the optional word designator, you can add a sequence of one or more of the following modifiers, each preceded by a colon (:).

h	Remove a trailing pathname component, leaving only the head.
r	Remove a trailing suffix of the form .SUFFIX, leaving the basename.
e	Remove all but the trailing suffix.
t	Remove all leading pathname components, leaving the tail.
p	Print the new command, but do not execute it.
q	Quote the substituted words, escaping further substitutions.
x	Quote the substituted words as with q.
s/old/new/	Substitute NEW for the first occurrence of OLD in the event line.

&	Repeat the previous substitution.
g	Apply change over entire event line.

Shell Variables

Technically, the variables including in this section include both shell variables and environments variables. Environment variables are a special subset of shell variables that are exported to all subprocesses of the shell (see the **export** command).

By convention, shell variables are usually composed of ALL CAPITAL LETTERS, but you do see lowercase shell variables in bash from time to time.

Shell variables are set with the equal sign (=). The syntax is **variable=***value*.

Example: To set the value of the HISTFILE variable (HISTFILE is the name of the file where your history commands are stored):

HISTFILE=/home/shawkins/.bash_history

You may also want to **export** the variable. Exporting makes the value of the variable available to any subprocesses invoked by the shell.

Example: To set and export the value of the HISTFILE variable:

export HISTFILE=/home/shawkins/.bash_history

The current values of shell variables can be displayed with **env** or **echo**:

Example: To display the current values of all your environment variables, type:

env

To display the current value of a particular environment variable, type **echo $**<variable>. The **$** tells the shell you're referring to the value of the variable.

Example: To display the current value of your CDPATH, type:

echo $CDPATH

Shell variables are built-in variables used by the shell for, uh, various stuff. For example, the PATH variable is a list of directories, separated by a colon, which the shell searches for the executable program corresponding to the command you typed in at the shell prompt.

TIP If you're getting "command not found" errors for programs you know are out there, you probably need to modify your PATH.

Bourne Shell Variables

BASH_VERSION	The version number of the current instance of bash.
CDPATH	Colon separated list of directories used as a search path for the cd command.
EUID	The numeric effective user id of the current user.
FIGNORE	A colon-separated list of suffixes to ignore when performing filename completion.
HISTCMD	The history number of the current command.
HISTCONTROL	Set to a value of "ignorespace", it means don't enter lines which begin with a space or tab into the history list. Set to a value of "ignoredups", it means don't enter lines which match the last entered line. A value of "ignoreboth" combines the two options. Unset, or set to any other value than those above, means to save all lines on the history list.
HISTFILE	The file containing the command history.
HISTFILESIZE	Number of commands to store in the history file.
HOME	Home directory of current user.
HOSTFILE	Contains the name of a file to be read when the shell needs to complete a hostname.
HOSTTYPE	A string describing the machine Bash is running on.
IFS	A list of characters that separate (delimit) fields; used when the shell splits words as part of expansion.
IGNOREEOF	Number of consecutive EOF's Bash will read before exiting.
INPUTRC	The name of the Readline startup file, overriding the default of *~/.inputrc*.

MAIL	Name of file to check for new mail.
MAILCHECK	The number of seconds to wait before checking for new mail.
MAILPATH	Colon separated list of files which the shell periodically checks for new mail.
nolinks	If present, do not follow symbolic links when doing commands that change the current working directory.
OLDPWD	Previous working directory.
OPTARG	Value of the last option argument processed by the getopts built in.
OPTIND	Index of the last option processed by the getopts built in.
OSTYPE	A string describing the operating system Bash is running on.
PATH	Colon separated list of directories in which the shell looks for commands.
PROMPT_COMMAND	If present, this contains a string which is a command to execute before the printing of each primary prompt ("$PS1").
PS1	The primary prompt string.
PS2	The secondary prompt string.
PS3	Used as the prompt for the select command.
PS4	Prompt printed before the command line is echoed when the -x option is set.
PWD	Current working directory.
RANDOM	Generate a random integer.
REPLY	Default variable for the read bulletin.
SECONDS	Number of seconds since the shell was started.

TMOUT	Interpret the value as the number of seconds to wait for input after issuing the primary prompt.
UID	The numeric real user id of the current user.

Shell Prompt

Shell prompts range from the trivial (">") to the thoroughly overboard (I once had a shell prompt so long I included a newline character in it so I'd have room to type commands). My current prompt is somewhere in between. I set it with the following command in my ***.bashrc*** file:

PS1='\h:$PWD> '

which produces prompts like the following:

odin:/home/root>

Note the use of an environment variable (**$PWD**) within the prompt. The following table describes the special characters which can appear in the **PS1** variable:

\t	The time, in HH:MM:SS format.
\T	The time in 12-hour HH:MM:SS format.
\@	The time in 12-hour am/pm format.
\d	The date, in "Weekday Month Date" format (e.g., "Tue May 26").
\e	ASCII escape character.
\n	Newline.
\s	The name of the shell.
\w	The current working directory.
\W	The basename of $PWD.
\u	Your username.
\h	The hostname.
\#	The command number of this command.

\!	The history number of this command.
\nnn	The character corresponding to the octal number nnn.
\$	If the effective uid is 0, #, otherwise $.
\\	A backslash.
\[	Begin a sequence of non-printing characters.
\]	End a sequence of non-printing characters.

Shell Arithmetic

As you might imagine, the shell has pretty much the full complement of arithmetic (including logic) operators. To specify an arithmetic expression, encase it in double parentheses.

Arithmetic Expansion

Arithmetic expansion allows the evaluation of an arithmetic expression and the substitution of the result. There are two formats for arithmetic expansion:

$[expression]

$((expression))

Example: The following expression adds the values of the variables A and B:

$((A + B))

Example: To print out the results of an arithmetic expression, use echo:

echo "A + B is $((A+B))"

Arithmetic Builtins

let EXPRESSION [EXPRESSION]

Perform arithmetic on shell variables.

Example: To assign the value of an arithmetic expression to another shell variable, use **let**:

let C=$((A+B))

Operators

<table>
<tr><td>- +</td><td>unary minus and plus</td></tr>
<tr><td>! ~</td><td>logical and bitwise negation</td></tr>
<tr><td>* / %</td><td>multiplication, division, remainder</td></tr>
<tr><td>+ -</td><td>addition, subtraction</td></tr>
<tr><td><< >></td><td>left and right bitwise shifts</td></tr>
<tr><td><= >= < ></td><td>comparison</td></tr>
<tr><td>== !=</td><td>equality and inequality</td></tr>
<tr><td>&</td><td>bitwise AND</td></tr>
<tr><td>^</td><td>bitwise exclusive OR</td></tr>
<tr><td>|</td><td>bitwise OR</td></tr>
<tr><td>&&</td><td>logical AND</td></tr>
<tr><td>||</td><td>logical OR</td></tr>
<tr><td>= *= /= %= += -= <<= >>= &= ^= |='</td><td>assignment</td></tr>
</table>

Looping Statements

until *TEST-COMMANDS*; **do** *CONSEQUENT-COMMANDS*; **done**

Execute the CONSEQUENT-COMMANDS until the TEST-COMMANDS section has a non-zero exit status.

while *TEST-COMMANDS*; **do** *CONSEQUENT-COMMANDS*; **done**

Execute CONSEQUENT COMMANDS as long as the final command in TEST-COMMANDS has an exit status of zero.

for *NAME [in WORDS ...]*; **do** *COMMANDS*; **done**

Execute COMMANDS for each member of the WORDS set with NAME bound to the current member.

Conditional Statements

Conditional statements are statements which affect the flow of the execution. The common characteristic is that they evaluate conditions present and may take action based on those conditions. The two most common are the **if** statement and the **case** statement:

if [*CONDITION*] **then**
STATEMENTS;
[elif *CONDITION-JR* then
STATEMENTS-JR;]
[else *ALTERNATE STATEMENTS*]
fi

This command executes the **STATEMENTS** if the final command in the **CONDITION** sequence has an exit status of zero.

If the exit status of the **CONDITION** is non-zero, the **elifs** are executed in turn, again evaluating the exit status of the final command and either executing the **CONDITION-JR** commands or not, depending on the exit status of **STATEMENTS-JR**.

If **ALTERNATE-CONSEQUENTS** exist and the final **TEST-COMMAND** has a non-zero exit status, the **ALTERNATE-CONSEQUENTS** are executed.

Example: To test whether the script file ***~/startx*** exists (**-e** flag) and run it if it does:

```
if [ -e ~/startx ]; then
        . ~/startx
fi
```

case WORD in [PATTERN [| PATTERN]...) COMMANDS ;;]... esac

The case command is used to selectively execute commands. Conceptually, it's a lengthy if statement with a lot of conditions. If WORD matches PATTERN the COMMANDS associated with PATTERN are executed.

Example: To test the value of the first argument passed in and execute various scripts based on its value:

```
case $1 in
    0 ) . script1;;
    1 ) . script2;;
    2 ) . script3;;
esac
```

The bash Shell

The **test** command can also be used to evaluate common characteristics of files and strings:

---

test -[bcdfhLpSt] *FILE*

---

test -[gkruwxOG] *FILE*

---

test -e -s -nt -ot -ef *FILE*

---

test *EXPR*

Evaluate the expression and return a status of 0 (true) or 1 (false), depending on the value of the expression. It can be used to test properties of files, evaluate some properties of strings, and in numeric comparisons.

File Tests

-b *FILE*	Is file a block special device?
-c *FILE*	Is file a character special device?
-d *FILE*	Is file a directory?
-e *FILE*	Does file exist?
-f *FILE*	Is file a regular file?
-G *FILE*	Are you & file in a common group?
-H *FILE*	Is file a hard link?
-L *FILE*	Is file a symbolic link?
-O *FILE*	Do you own file?
-p *FILE*	Is file a named pipe?
-r *FILE*	Do you have read permission?
-S *FILE*	Is file a socket?

-t [*FD*]	Is file opened on a terminal?
-w *FILE*	Do you have write permission?
-x *FILE*	Do you have execute permission

Access Permission tests

Note: All the tests in this section fail if the specified file does not exist.

-g *FILE*	Is the set-group-id bit set?
-k *FILE*	Is the sticky bit set?
-r *FILE*	Is the file readable?
-u *FILE*	Is the set-user-id bit set?
-w *FILE*	Is the file writable?
-x *FILE*	Is the file executable?
-O *FILE*	Is the file owned by the current user?
-G *FILE*	Is the file owned by the current group?

File Characteristic tests

-e *FILE*	Does the file exist?
-s *FILE*	Is the file size greater than zero?
FILE1 **-nt** *FILE2*	FILE1 is newer than FILE2? (T/F)
FILE1 **-ot** *FILE2*	FILE1 is older than FILE2? (T/F)
FILE1 **-ef** *FILE2*	True if FILE1 and FILE2 are hard linked (they have the same device and inode numbers).

String tests

-z *STRING*	Is string zero length?
-n *STRING*	Is string non-zero length?
STR1=*STR2*	True if STR1 is the same as STR2.
STR1 != *STR2*	True if STR1 is not the same as STR2.

Numeric tests

Note: All arguments must be numeric.

ARG1 **-eq** *ARG2*	ARG1 equal to ARG2.
ARG1 **-ne** *ARG2*	True if ARG1 is not equal to ARG2.
ARG1 **-lt** *ARG2*	True if ARG1 is less than ARG2.
ARG1 **-le** *ARG2*	True if ARG1 is less than or equal to ARG2.
ARG1 **-gt** *ARG2*	True if ARG1 is greater than ARG2.
ARG1 -ge ARG2	True if ARG1 is greater than or equal to ARG2.

Logical connectives

! *EXPR*	True if EXPR is false (Logical not).
EXPR1 **-a** *EXPR2*	True if EXPR1 and EXPR2 are true (Logical and).
EXPR1 **-o** *EXPR2*	True if either EXPR1 or EXPR2 are true (Logical or).

Shell Functions

Shell functions are a way to invoke a group of commands by typing a single name.

[**`function'**] **NAME** () { *COMMAND-LIST*; }

Example: The following function prints out the square of its argument:

function printsquare()

```
{
echo "The square of $1 is (($1*$1))";
}
```

Directory Manipulation

pushd [DIR | +N | -N]

Save the current directory on a list and then "cd" to DIR. With no arguments, exchanges the top two directories.

+N	Brings the Nth directory (counting from the left of the list printed by "dirs") to the top of the list by rotating the stack.
-N	Brings the Nth directory (counting from the right of the list printed by "dirs") to the top of the list by rotating the stack.
DIR	Makes the current working directory be the top of the stack, and then CDs to DIR. You can see the saved directory list with the "dirs" command.

popd [+N|-N]

Pop the directory stack and cd to the new top directory.

+N	Remove the Nth directory (counting from the left of the list printed by "dirs"), starting with zero.
-N	Removes the Nth directory (counting from the right of the list printed by "dirs"), starting with zero.

dirs [+N | -N] [-L]

Display the list of currently remembered directories.

+N	Display the Nth directory (counting from the left of the list, starting with 0).

-N	Display the Nth directory (counting from the right of the list, starting with 0).
-L	Expand the ~ usually used to abbreviate the home directory into a full path in order to produce a longer listing.

Shell Builtins

The following commands are built in to the bash shell and accessible via the command line or for use in scripting:

:	Expand arguments and perform redirections, but nothing else.
. filename	Execute the shell commands contained in the specified filename.
break	Exit from a for, while, or until loop.
cd	Change the current working directory.
continue	Resume the execution of the loop (for, while, or until) in which the continue command is contained at the next iteration.
echo [*arg*,...]	Print to standard output the specified arguments separated by spaces.
eval [*arg*, ...]	Concatenate the arguments into a single command, read the result, and execute it.
exec command	When an executable command is specified, it replaces the shell. When no command is specified, redirections may be used to affect the current shell environment.
exit	Exit the shell.
export *arg*,...	Pass the arguments as variables to the child processes in the environment.
getopts	Parse options to shell scripts or functions.
hash	Remember the full pathnames of commands specified as arguments, so that they need not be searched for on subsequent invocations.
kill *process*	Send a signal to a process.

pwd	Print the current working directory.
read var,...	Read a line from the shell input and use it to set the values of specified variables.
readonly	Mark variables as unchangeable.
return value	Exit shell function with specified value.
shift	Shift positional parameters to the left.
test *expr*, [	Evaluate the specified conditional expression.
times	Print out the user and system times used by the shell and its children.
trap	Specify commands to be executed when the shell receives signals.
umask	Set the shell process's file creation mask.
unset	Get rid of the specified shell variable.
wait	Wait until child processes exit and report their exit status.

CHAPTER

9 TERMINAL & KEYBOARD

Introduction

The Unix terminal interface is a masterpiece of generalized programming. It tries to be all things to all hardware and for the most part, it succeeds. Consequently, however, it is a little complicated.

Because the control codes for monitors vary widely from vendor to vendor and model to model, program output used to be hardware-specific. In effect, every time you wanted a program to run on a new piece of hardware, you had to rewrite the program. Obviously, this got cumbersome very quickly.

Linux uses intermediate programs to take the output of application programs and translate it into whatever format the display device wants. In effect, these programs are databases of hardware capabilities and control codes. These programs (**termcap** and **terminfo**) use different formats to store what is essentially the same data:

termcap	A *text* file containing descriptions of the functions of various terminals.
terminfo	A collection of *binary* files which store terminal functionality information.

Throughout this section, you'll be seeing a lot of the word **tty**, which stands for **tele**ty**pe**, though almost no one uses actual teletypes anymore. A **tty** is the device (e.g., ***/dev/tty****) via which you, the typist, communicate with your machine.

The **getty** program starts the process of making your terminal usable. It prints out a login prompt and monitors the tty device for user input. Terminal characteristics may be displayed or modified with **stty**.

TIP One fairly common problem is having your **TERM** environment variable (which should be set to whatever type of terminal you have, e.g., wy150) set wrong. If your display or scrolling is whacked, this is the first thing to check.

TIP If you're having problems with your display and you're sure you've specified the right database entry, the entry itself may be wrong. Most terminals will emulate a **vt100** at the expense of some terminal functionality.

The commands in this section allow you to display and modify your terminal and keyboard configuration. They include:

captoinfo	Convert a termcap entry to a terminfo entry.
clear	Clear the terminal screen.
dumpkeys	Display a copy of keyboard translation table.
getkeycodes	Print scancode-to-keycode translation table.
getty	Monitor a device in hopes of starting a login session.
infocmp	Compare or display terminfo entries.
loadkeys	Load keyboard translation table.
login	Initiate user login.
setterm	Set terminal configuration values.
stty	Display or set tty configuration values.
tic	Compile a terminfo entry.
tput	Access terminal information.
tset	Set terminal information.

Related Files

/usr/lib/kbd/keymaps	Usual directory for keytable files.
/etc/issue	Login banner.
/etc/gettydefs	Getty definitions file.
/etc/conf.getty[.line]	Contains the runtime configuration. Note that uugetty uses /etc/conf.uugetty[.line].
/etc/gettydefs	Contains speed and tty settings to be used by getty.
/usr/lib/kbd/keymaps	Default directory for keymaps.
/usr/src/linux/drivers/char/defkeymap.map	Default kernel keymap.
/var/run/utmp	Database of users currently logged in.
/var/log/wtmp	Stores login & logout history.
/usr/spool/mail/*	Individual mail folder.
/etc/motd	Message of the day (displayed at login).
/etc/passwd	Contains account information.
/etc/nologin	If this file exists, only root may log in.
.hushlogin	If exists, login is quiet.

/etc/securetty	Specifies the ttys from which root may log in.
/usr/share/terminfo	Terminal capability database.

Commands

captoinfo [-vn *width*] [-V] [-1] [-w *width*] *file* . . .

Convert termcap entry to a description of a terminfo entry.

Example: To convert the entire default termcap file and send the results to standard out:

captoinfo

-v	Output the specified (1-10) level of debugging information.
-V	Display version information and exit.
-1	Output fields one per line.
-w	Specify the width of output.

clear

Clear the terminal display screen.

Example: To clear all the characters currently displayed off your screen:

clear

dumpkeys [-hilfn -ccharset --help --short-info --long-info --numeric --full-table --funcs-only --keys-only --compose-only --charset=*charset*]

Write to standard output the current contents of the keyboard mapping tables. Usually used to make backup files before doing potentially dangerous to your settings.

Example: To dump the contents of the keyboard mapping file together with the action symbols and their numeric values:

dumpkeys > keyfile.bak

Example: To generate a more readable (but not loadable) stream of dump-key information:

dumpkeys -l

-h --help	Display program version and usage information.
-i --short-info	Display the following information about the kernel's keyboard driver: • Keycode range supported by the kernel • Number of actions bindable to a key • Ranges of action codes supported by the kernel • Number of function keys supported by kernel • Current function strings associated with a key
-l --long-info	Display the short-info information, plus a list of action symbols supported by loadkeys and dumpkeys, plus the symbol's numeric values.
-n --numeric	Print the action code values in hexadecimal notation.
-f --full-table	First, output a list of all the current key modifiers. Then output a list of the actions associated with each possible key+modifier combination.
--funcs-only	Output only the function key definitions.
--keys-only	Output only the key bindings (do not include string definitions).
--compose-only	Output only the compose key combinations.
-ccharset --charset=charset	Interpret character code values according to the specified character set.

getkeycodes

Print the kernel scancode-to-keycode mapping table.

Example: This command has no options.

getkeycodes

getty [-d *defaults_file*] [-a] [-h] [-r *delay*] [-t *timeout*] [-w *waitfor*] line [*speed* [*type* [*lined*]]]

getty -c gettydefs_file

Get a **tty**. Monitor an input device for user activity and perform the initialization functions necessary to begin a login session. Sets terminal mode, communication speed, and line discipline, then displays the login prompt and accepts the user name.

Getty first parses its command line for applicable options. It then scans the defaults file (usually ***/etc/conf.getty***) for specified runtime values. It then performs a line initialization, if specified. After initialization, the line is closed and reopened. It displays the login prompt and, upon reading a login name, invokes the **login** program.

Getty isn't really a user command; it's almost always run automatically by **init**. You can find the command line in ***/etc/inittab***. There are several variations on getty (**mingetty, mgetty, agetty**) which perform roughly the same function but are optimized for various hardware configurations.

Example: To monitor tty1 for user activity:

getty tty1

Defaults File

Getty looks for the file ***/etc/conf.getty.line*** (or ***/etc/conf.getty***) and, if found, uses it to set the following options:

SYSTEM=*name*	Set the nodename value as specified.
VERSION=*string*	Set the version value to the specified string. If string begins with "/", it is assumed to be the path to a file specifying the VERSION value, */proc/version* by default.
LOGIN=*name*	Specify the login program (/bin/login by default).
INIT=*string*	If defined, string is an expect/send sequence that is used to initialize the line before getty attempts to use it.

ISSUE=*string*	Specify the location of file containing or actual value of the "issue string" which is displayed on startup.
CLEAR=*value*	Specify whether or not to clear the screen before displaying the issue or login prompt (where value=[YES|NO]).
HANGUP=value	Specify whether or not to hang up the line during startup. (value=[YES|NO]).
WAITCHAR=*value*	If value=YES, getty will wait for a single character from its line before continuing.
DELAY=*seconds*	Force getty to wait the specified number of seconds after the WAITCHAR is accepted before continuing.
TIMEOUT=*number*	Force getty to exit if no user name is input before the specified number of seconds elapses.
CONNECT=*string*	If defined, specify an expect/send sequence used in establishing a connection.
WAITFOR=*string*	Specify a string of characters to be waited for before issuing a login prompt.
ALTLOCK=*line*	Tell getty to lock the device specified by line in addition to the device which it is attached to.
ALTLINE=*line*	Use the device specified by line to handle modem initialization.
RINGBACK=*value*	When value=YES, ringback calling is used.
SCHED=*range1 range2 range3 ...*	Specify a range of times in which logins are allowed. ranges are formatted as DOW:HR:MIN-DOW:HR:MIN.

OFF=string	Specify a string to be sent when the line is scheduled to be OFF.
FIDO=string	Specify the path to the FidoNet mailer.
EMSI=value	When value=yes, look for FidoNet EMSI sequences in the input.

Getty recognizes the following escape characters for use in the issue or login banner:

****	Backslash (\).
\b	Backspace (^H).
\c	Placed at the end of a string, this prevents a new-line from being typed after the string.
\f	Formfeed (^L).
\n	New-line (^J).
\r	Carriage-return (^M).
\s	A single space (" ").
\t	Horizontal tab (^I).
\nnn	Outputs the ASCII character whose decimal value is nnn.

Getty recognizes the following @char parameters and substitutes the listed value in any issue or login displays:

@B	The current (evaluated at the time the @B is seen) baud rate.
@D	The current date, in MM/DD/YY.
@L	The line to which getty is attached.
@S	The system node name.
@T	The current time, in HH:MM:SS (24-hour).

@U	The number of currently signed-on users.
@V	The value of VERSION, as given in the defaults file.

kbd_mode [-a | -u | -k | -s]	kbd_mode either displays the current keyboard mode (RAW, MEDIUMRAW or XLATE) or, if one of the following options is used, modifies the keyboard mode as follows: **-s** scancode mode (RAW). **-k** keycode mode (MEDIUMRAW). **-a** ASCII mode (XLATE). **-u** UTF-8 mode (UNICODE).

kbdrate [-s] [-r *rate* ***] [-d*** *delay* ***]***	This command specifies changes to the repeat rate and delay time for IBM keyboards. If called with no options, kbdrate will reset the rate to 10.9 characters per second and the delay to 250 milliseconds.
-s	Run silent (display no messages).
-r *rate*	Specify a new character per second (cps) rate, where rate is one of: 2.0, 2.1, 2.3, 2.5, 2.7, 3.0, 3.3, 3.7, 4.0, 4.3, 4.6, 5.0, 5.5, 6.0, 6.7, 7.5, 8.0, 8.6, 9.2, 10.0, 10.9, 12.0, 13.3, 15.0, 16.0, 17.1, 18.5, 20.0, 21.8, 24.0, 26.7, 30.0.
-d *milliseconds*	Specify the delay in milliseconds. Allowable values are: 250, 500, 750, 1000.

infocmp [-dcnpILCuV1] [-v n] [-s d| i| l| c] [-w width] [-A directory] [-B directory] [termname...]

This command deals with terminfo entries. It either compares two specified entries, prints out a description, or sets new values.

Example: To generate source information for the vt100 terminfo entry:

infocmp -C vt100

Example: To generate a list of the differences between a wy50 and a wy150 terminfo entry:

infocmp -d wy50 wy150

-d	Generate a list of the differences between the two entries.
-c	Generate a list of the capabilities which the two entries have in common.
-n	Generate a list of the capabilities which neither entry has.
-I	Generate a source listing by terminfo name for each terminal named (this is the default).
-L	Generate a source listing by C variable name for each terminal named.
-C	Generate a source listing by termcap name for each terminal named. Output generated by this option may be used as a termcap entry, though the translation process is not perfect and may require some hand-tweaking.
-r	Generate a source listing by termcap name, including capabilities in termcap form for each terminal named.
-s	Sort by one of the following: **d** Retain the order the output fields were stored in the terminfo database. **i** Sort by terminfo name. **l** Sort by long C variable name. **c** Sort by termcap name.

-1	Display fields one per line.
-F	Compare two terminfo files.
-Rsubset	Restrict output to the specified subset (SVr1 | Ultrix | HP | AIX | BSD).
-T	Do not restrict amount of text generated.
-V	Display version information.
-e	Output in the form of a C initializer for a TERMTYPE structure.
-f	Indent complex output strings.
-i	Analyze the initialization (is1, is2, is3), and reset (rs1, rs2, rs3), strings in the entry.

-p	Disregard padding when doing comparisons.
-v n	Output tracing information to standard error.
-w width	Display output in the specified width.

loadkeys [-c --clearcompose] [-d --default] [-h --help] [-m --mktable] [-s --clearstrings] [-v --verbose] [filename...]

Read in the keymap for the kernel from the specified file.

Example: To read in the keymap generated in the **dumpkeys** example (above):

loadkeys keyfile.bak

-d, --default	Load in a default keymap, usually */usr/lib/kbd/keymaps* or */usr/src/linux drivers/char.*
-c, --clearcompose	Empty the kernel accent table.
-v, --verbose	Verbose output.
-s, --clearstrings	Clear the kernel string table.
-m, --mktable	Print to standard output a file which is formatted to be used as the specifier for default key bindings for the kernel. (Typically */usr/src/linux/drivers/char/defkeymap.c*)
-h --help	Display help information.

login [*name*]

login -p

login -h *hostname*

login -f *name*

Login is the program which initiates user access onto the system. If access is granted, **login** sets UID, GID, HOME, PATH, SHELL, TERM, MAIL and LOGNAME.

Example: This is another one of those programs that usually isn't run by a human being. (Typically, it's called by getty).

ROOT **login**

TIP If you have a multi-user system and you want to keep people from logging on for a while, create a file called ***/etc/nologin***.

-p	Tell login to preserve the current environment.
-f	Do not do a second login authentication.
-h	Used by other servers to pass the name of the remote host to login so that it may be placed in utmp and wtmp.

setterm [-term *terminal_name*]

setterm [-reset]

setterm [-initialize]

setterm [-cursor [*on|off*]]

setterm [-keyboard pc|olivetti|dutch|extended]

setterm [-repeat [on|off]]

setterm [-appcursorkeys [on|off]]

setterm [-linewrap [on|off]]

setterm [-snow [on|off]]

setterm [-softscroll [on|off]]

setterm [-defaults]

setterm [-foreground black|red|green|yellow|blue|magenta|cyan|white|default]

setterm [-background black|red|green|yellow|blue|magenta|cyan|white|default]

setterm [-ulcolor black|grey|red|green|yellow|blue|magenta|cyan|white]

setterm [-ulcolor bright red|green|yellow|blue|magenta|cyan|white]

setterm [-hbcolor black|grey|red|green|yellow|blue|magenta|cyan|white]

setterm [-hbcolor bright red|green|yellow|blue|magenta|cyan|white]

setterm [-inversescreen [on|off]]

setterm [-bold [on|off]]

setterm [-half-bright [on|off]]

setterm [-blink [on|off]]

setterm [-reverse [on|off]]

setterm [-underline [on|off]]

setterm [-store]

setterm [-clear [all|rest]]

setterm [-tabs [tab1 tab2 tab3 ...]] where (tabn = 1-160)

setterm [-clrtabs [tab1 tab2 tab3 ...] where (tabn = 1-160)

setterm [-regtabs [1-160]]

setterm [-blank [0-60]]

setterm [-powersave [on|vsync|hsync|powerdown|off]]

setterm [-powerdown [0-60]]

setterm [-dump [1-NR_CONS]]

setterm [-append [1-NR_CONS]]

setterm [-file *dumpfilename* **]**

setterm [-standout [attr]]

setterm [-blength [0-2000]]

setterm [-bfreq *freqnumber*]

This command displays to standard output a character string which will set the specified terminal capabilities. Most of the options are self-explanatory.

Example: To set your terminal keyboard type as Olivetti:

setterm -keyboard olivetti

-term	Use to override the TERM environment variable.
-reset	Display terminal reset string.
-initialize	Display the current terminal initialization string.
-default	Reset the display options to their default values.
-store	Store the current display options as the default.

stty [SETTING]...

stty [OPTION]

If invoked with no options, **stty** displays the baud rate, line discipline number and line settings which differ from those of "**stty sane**." If invoked with options, it will display or set one or more specified values.

Example: If you really messed up your **stty** values and you want things back in a reasonable configuration:

stty sane

Control Key	stty Name	Function
<Ctrl>-\	quit	More enthusiastic version of ^C.
<Ctrl>-?, <Del>	erase	Erase last character.

<Ctrl>-C	intr	Stop running program.
<Ctrl>-D	eof	Signal end of input.
<Ctrl>-Q		Restart output to screen.
<Ctrl>-S	stop	Stop output to screen.
<Ctrl>-U	kill	Erase command line.
<Ctrl>-Z	susp	Suspend executing command.

-a, --all	Display all current settings in human readable form.
-g, --save	Display all current settings formatted to be usable as an argument to another stty command which will restore current settings.

Control Settings

parenb	Tell stty to generate a parity bit in output and expect a parity bit in input. May be negated.
parodd	Tell stty to set odd parity (even if negated). Negatable.
cs5, cs6, cs7, cs8	Tell stty to set character size to 5, 6, 7, or 8 bits.
hup, hupcl	Tell stty to send a hangup signal when the last process closes the tty. May be negated.
cstopb	Tell stty to use two stop bits per character (one if negated). Negatable.
cread	Tell stty to allow input to be received. Negatable.
clocal	Tell stty to disable modem control signals. Negatable.
crtscts	Tell stty to enable RTS/CTS flow control. Negatable.

Input Settings

ignbrk	Tell stty to ignore break characters. Negatable.

brkint	Tell stty to make breaks cause an interrupt signal. Negatable.
ignpar	Tell stty to ignore characters with parity errors. Negatable.
parmrk	Tell stty to mark parity errors (with a 255-0-character sequence). May be negated.
inpck	Enable input parity checking. Negatable.
istrip	Clear high (8th) bit of input characters. Negatable.
inlcr	Translate newline to carriage return. Negatable.
igncr	Tell stty to ignore carriage return. Negatable.
icrnl	Translate carriage return to newline. Negatable.
ixon	Enable XON/XOFF flow control (that is, "CTRL-S'/ `CTRL-Q"). May be negated.
ixoff, tandem	Enable sending of "stop" character when the system input buffer is almost full, and "start" character when it becomes almost empty again. Negatable.
iuclc	This option translates uppercase characters to lowercase. It may be negated.
ixany	This option tells stty to allow any character to restart output. If negated, only the start character can restart output.
imaxbel	If a character arrives when the input buffer is full, this option tells stty to beep but not flush the input buffer.

Output Settings

opost	Postprocess output. Negatable.
olcuc	Translate lowercase characters to uppercase. May be negated.

ocrnl	Translate carriage return to newline. Negatable.
onlcr	Translate newline to carriage return-newline. May be negated.
onocr	No carriage returns in the first column. Negatable.
onlret	Tell stty that newline will also perform a carriage return.
ofill	Tell stty to implement delays with padding characters rather than via timing. Negatable.
ofdel	Specify use of delete characters for fill instead of null characters. Negatable.
nl1, nl0	Specify a newline delay style.
cr3, cr2, cr1, cr0	Specify a carriage return delay style.
tab3, tab2, tab1, tab0	Specify a horizontal tab delay style.
bs1, bs0	Specify a backspace delay style.
vt1, vt0	Specify a vertical tab delay style.
ff1, ff0	Specify a form feed delay style.

Local Settings

isig	This option enables the "interrupt", "quit", and "suspend" special characters. Negatable.
icanon	Enable "erase", "kill", "werase", and "rprnt" special characters. Negatable.
iexten	Enable non-POSIX special characters. Negatable.
echo	Echo input characters. Negatable.
echoe, crterase	Tell stty to echo "erase" characters as backspace-space-backspace. Negatable.

echok	Tell stty to echo a newline after a "kill" character. Negatable.
echonl	Echo newline even if not echoing other characters. Negatable.
noflsh	Disable flushing after "quit" and "interrupt" special characters. Negatable.
xcase	Enable input and output of uppercase characters by preceding their lowercase equivalents with "\", when "icanon" is set. Negatable.
tostop	Halt background jobs that try to write to the terminal. Negatable.
echoprt, prterase	Tell stty to echo erased characters backward, between "\" and "/". Negatable.
echoctl, ctlecho	Control characters output in hat notation ("^C") instead of literally. Negatable.
echoke, crtkill	Echo the "kill" special character by erasing each character on the line as indicated by the "echoprt" and "echoe" settings, instead of by the "echoctl" and "echok" settings. Negatable.

Combination Settings

evenp, parity	Equivalent to "parenb -parodd cs7". Negatable. If negated, same as "-parenb cs8".
oddp	Equivalent to "parenb parodd cs7". Negatable. If negated, same as "-parenb cs8".
nl	Equivalent to "-icrnl -onlcr". Negatable. If negated, same as "icrnl -inlcr -igncr onlcr -ocrnl -onlret".
ek	Reset the "erase" and "kill" special characters to their default values.

sane	Equivalent to: cread -ignbrk brkint -inlcr -igncr icrnl -ixoff -iuclc -ixany imaxbel opost -olcuc -ocrnl onlcr -onocr -onlret -ofill -ofdel nl0 cr0 tab0 bs0 vt0 ff0 isig icanon iexten echo echoe echok -echonl -noflsh -xcase -tostop -echoprt echoctl echoke and also sets all special characters to their default values.
cooked	Equivalent to "brkint ignpar istrip icrnl ixon opost isig icanon", plus sets the "eof" and "eol" characters to their default values if they are the same as the "min" and "time" characters. May be negated. If negated, same as "raw".
raw	Equivalent to: -ignbrk -brkint -ignpar -parmrk -inpck -istrip -inlcr -igncr -icrnl -ixon -ixoff -iuclc -ixany -imaxbel -opost -isig -icanon -xcase min 1 time 0 Negatable. If negated, same as "cooked".
cbreak	Equivalent to "-icanon". Negatable. If negated, same as "icanon".
pass8	Equivalent to "-parenb -istrip cs8". Negatable. If negated, same as "parenb istrip cs7".
litout	Equivalent to "-parenb -istrip -opost cs8". Negatable. If negated, same as "parenb istrip opost cs7".
decctlq	Equivalent to "-ixany". Negatable.
tabs	Equivalent to "tab0". Negatable. If negated, same as "tab3".
lcase LCASE	Equivalent to "xcase iuclc olcuc". Negatable.
crt	Equivalent to "echoe echoctl echoke".
dec	Equivalent to "echoe echoctl echoke -ixany intr ^C erase ^? kill C-u".

Special Characters

The default values of special characters are system-specific. They are set with the syntax "name value" where the value can be given in hat notation (e.g., "^C"), literally, or as an integer (precede with 0x for hexadecimal).

intr	Interrupt signal.
quit	Quit signal.
erase	Erase the last character typed.
kill	Erase the current line.
eof	Terminate input, a.k.a. end of file.
eol	End the line.
eol2	Alternate character to end the line.
swtch	Switch to a different shell layer.
start	Restart the output after stopping it.
stop	Stop the output.
susp	Send a terminal stop signal.
dsusp	Send a terminal stop signal after flushing the input.
rprnt	Redraw the current line.
werase	Erase the last word typed.
lnext	Enter the next character typed literally, even if it is a special character.

Special Settings

***min** N*	Specify the minimum number of characters that will satisfy a read until the time value has expired, at which point "-icanon" is set.
***time** N*	Specify the number of tenths of a second before reads time out if the minimum number of characters have not been read, when "-icanon" is set.
***ispeed** N*	Specify an input speed of N.
***ospeed** N*	Specify an output speed of N.
***rows** N*	Define the number of rows to the tty kernel driver.
***cols** N, **columns** N*	Define the number of columns to the tty kernel driver.
size	Display the number of rows and columns that the kernel thinks the terminal has.
***line** N*	Specify a line discipline to use.
speed	Print the terminal speed.
N	Tell stty to use the specified input and output speed: N can be one of: 0 50 75 110 134 134.5 150 200 300 600 1200 1800 2400 4800 9600 19200 38400 "exta" "extb". "exta" is the same as 19200; "extb" is the same as 38400. 0 hangs up the line if "-clocal" is set.

tic [-1CINRTcfrs] [-e *names*] [-o *dir*] [-v[n]] [-w[n]] *file*

Compile the specified source file into a terminfo database entry. By default, output goes to ***/usr/share/erminfo***.

Example: To compile the file obscure into a terminfo entry:

tic obscure

-c	Check only for errors in source file.
-vn	Specify a level of verbose debugging information from 1-10. (Detail increases with n.)
-odir	Specify a target directory for output.
-wn	Specify width of output.
-1	Make output width one column.
-C	Translate source to termcap format.
-I	Translate source to terminfo format.
-L	Force source translation to terminfo format using the long C variable names listed in <term.h>
-N	Disable smart defaults.
-Rsubset	Restrict output to a given subset.
-T	Allow output to be of any size.
-r	Force entry resolution even when translating to termcap format.
***-e** list*	Limit the affected terminal types to those in the (comma separated) specified list.
-f	Format complex output by indenting.
-s	Output summary information about the results of the compile.
file	Source file.

tput [-Ttype] capname [parms ...]

tput [-Ttype] init

tput [-Ttype] reset

tput [-Ttype] longname

tput -S <<

This command may be used to display or set the values of variables which correspond to terminal capabilities as specified in terminfo.

Example: To initialize the current terminal:

tput init

-Ttype	Specify type of terminal.
capname	Indicate a specific terminfo attribute for processing.
parms	If the attribute is a string that takes parameters, the arguments parms will be instantiated into the string. An all-numeric argument will be passed to the attribute as a number.
-S	This option allows you to specify more than one value per invocation of tput. If this option is used, tput becomes interactive and further options are entered via standard input.
init	This option causes tput to attempt the following: 1) output terminal initialization strings as specified in terminfo, 2) reset tty driver, 3) set tabs.
reset	Output terminal's reset (rather than initialization) strings.
longname	Display the long name of the current terminal as specified in terminfo.

tset [-lQqrs] [-] [-e *ch*] [-i *ch*] [-k *ch*] [-m *mapping*] [*terminal*]

reset [-lQqrs] [-] [-e *ch*] [-i *ch*] [-k *ch*] [-m *mapping*] [*terminal*]

This command is used to initialize terminals. It first decides what type of terminal you are using through one of three methods:

1. Terminal type is specified on command line.
2. If not, checks the TERM environment variable.
3. Uses the default type, "unknown".

The command is somewhat interactive. For example, it prompts the user to confirm its guesswork regarding terminal type. Once it has settled on a terminal type, it uses that information to set a bewildering variety of display options (window size, erase character, interrupt...)

Example: To display your terminal initialization shell commands to standard output:

tset -s

-q	Display terminal type but alter nothing.
-e	Set the erase character as specified.
-l	Do not send terminal or tab initialization strings.
-i	Set the interrupt character as specified.
-k	Set the line kill character as specified.
-m	Specify a mapping from a port type to a terminal.
-Q	Suppress display for line kill, erase, and interrupt characters.
-r	Output terminal type to standard error.
-s	Output the shell commands needed to initialize the TERM environment variable.

CHAPTER

10

DISKS

Introduction

The Linux concept of a disk is not particularly intuitive. First, a single physical disk may contain several disk devices (***/dev/hda1, /dev/hda2***, ...). Second, it is fairly rare to deal with disks directly in the course of day-to-day operations. Once a disk has been defined, you usually must put a filesystem on it in order to get any use out of it (see Chapter 11 for more information on the creation and maintenance of filesystems).

Those of you who've been reading these introductory sections have probably noticed a common theme by now: Linux does not care about the name of a particular resource; it is usually much more interested in what its *number* is. Disks are no exception. All Linux devices have two numbers associated with them: the **major device number**, which corresponds to a device driver (program for manipulating the device hardware) within the kernel, and the **minor device number**, which specifies a particular device handled by that driver.

Humans Think of	The Kernel Prefers
Timmy	uid=508
ls	inode=2026
/dev/hda5	major=3, minor=5

Dividing an actual physical disk into usable chunks accessible to Linux is called **partitioning**. The resultant chunks are called **partitions**. There may be more than one partition on a given disk. Partitioning is most easily accomplished with one of the disk formatting programs (e.g., **cfdisk**, **fdisk**...).

Discounting the amount of space required for system bookkeeping (superblock, inode table), partitions may be of any size. Within the partition, however, the disk is arranged into equally sized chunks of space called **blocks**. The size of the blocks differ from system to system but usually is some multiple of 512.

The commands covered in this section include:

badblocks	Test a disk for bad blocks.
cfdisk	Partition a disk.
du	Display information about disk usage.
fdformat	Format a floppy disk.
fdisk	Partition a disk.
quota	Display or set disk quotas.
setfdprm	Set floppy disk parameters.

Related Files

/dev/hd??	Standard paging devices.
/dev/sd??	Standard (SCSI) paging devices.
/etc/fstab	ascii filesystem description table.

Commands

badblocks [-b *block-size*] [-o *output_file*] [-s] [-v] [-w] *device blocks-count* [*start-block*]

This command is used to search for bad blocks on a hardware device. You should specify the device (e.g., ***/dev/hda1***) and the count of the number of blocks on the device.

Example: To check /dev/hda1 for bad blocks:

ROOT

badblocks /dev/hda1 3096

-b block-size	Specify the size of blocks in bytes.
-o output_file	Specify a file to which the list of bad blocks is output. Default is to display to standard out.
-s	Progress indicator. Display the block numbers as they are checked.
-v	Verbose output.
-w	Write-mode test option: badblocks will write a few bytes to each block and then read them back in to verify that everything worked. Of course, this will overwrite data already on the block, so be careful.

cfdisk [-avz] [-c *cylinders*] [-h *heads*] [-s *sectors-per-track*] [-P *opt*] [*device*]

This is an interactive, (ascii) graphic program for partitioning a hard drive. It works in the following manner:

1. It tries to read the geometry of the hard disk.
2. It looks for a current partition table.

TIP When attempting to partition a SCSI drive on an adapter without a BIOS, you should set the cylinders, heads and sectors-per-track on the command line.

Example: This command is interactive. When invoked, you see a screen similar to the following:

ROOT

cfdisk

```
                              cfdisk 0.81

                          Disk Drive: /dev/hda
           Heads: 240   Sectors per Track: 63   Cylinders: 832

 Name        Flags      Part Type  FS Type          [Label]        Size (MB)
-------------------------------------------------------------------------------
 hda1        Boot        Primary   DOS FAT16 (big)  [NO NAME    ]    2997.43
 hda5                    Logical   Linux ext2                         214.11
 hda6                    Logical   Linux ext2                        1638.99
 hda7                    Logical   Linux ext2                         302.70
 hda8                    Logical   Linux ext2                         103.36
 hda9                    Logical   Linux ext2                         819.50
 hda10                   Logical   Linux Swap                          66.45



  [Bootable]  [ Delete ]  [  Help  ]  [Maximize]  [ Print  ]
  [  Quit  ]  [  Type  ]  [ Units  ]  [ Write  ]
```

The following keys are active for the screen above:

b	Toggle the bootable flag of the current partition.
d	Delete the selected partition.
g	Alter the disk geometry. Warning: this option, even more than most in this section, is dangerous.
h	Display the help screen.

m	Maximize the usage of the current partition by recovering the unused space between the partition table and the beginning of the partition.
n	Create a new partition. You will be prompted for size and (assuming the new partition doesn't use up all of the available free space) whether to put the new partition at the beginning or the end of the free space.
p	Print the partition table to the screen or a file. Output is in one of the following forms: r Raw data—exactly what would be written to disk. s Partition table in sector order format. t Partition table in raw format.
q	Quit program without saving changes.
t	Change the filesystem type.
u	Toggle units of the partition size display (megabytes, sectors, cylinders).
W	Save changes to disk.
Up Arrow, Down Arrow	Highlight the previous or next partition.
CTRL-L	Redraw the screen.
?	Display the help screen.

Command Line Options

-a	Tells cfdisk to use an arrow cursor rather than highlighting.
-v	Display version information.
-z	Invoke cfdisk with zeroed partition table.
-c	Specify a number of cylinders.
-h	Specify a number of heads.

-s	Specify the number of sectors-per-track.
-P [r/s/t]	Display the partition table in raw, standard, or table formats.

du [OPTION]... [FILE]...

With no arguments, "du" reports the disk space used by the current directory. The output is in 1024-byte units by default, unless the environment variable "POSIXLY_CORRECT" is set, in which case 512-byte blocks are used (unless "-k" is specified).

Example: To display disk usage information for all files in the / filesystem, not just the directories (**-a** option):

du -a /

-a, --all	Include all files in output, rather than just directories.
-b, --bytes	Output file size in bytes rather than kilobytes.
-c, --total	Display totals after processing.
-D, --dereference-args	Dereference symbolic links.
-h, --human-readable	Append a size letter to the end of each quantity displayed. (M=megabytes, K=kilobytes,...)
-k, --kilobytes	Display size in kilobytes.
-l, --count-links	Count the size of all files even if they have already been counted as a hard link.
-L, --dereference	Dereference symbolic links.
-m, --megabytes	Display size in megabytes.
-s, --summarize	Display totals only for each argument.
-S, --separate-dirs	When outputting the size of a directory, do not include the size of any subdirectories it may have.
-x, --one-file-system	Limit processing to the current filesystem.

fdformat [-n] *device*

Perform a low level format on a floppy disk. The major device number is 2. The device is usually one of the following, (*NOT* ***/dev/fd0*** or ***/dev/fd1***):

/dev/fd0d360 (minor = 4)

/dev/fd0h1200 (minor = 8)

/dev/fd0D360 (minor = 12)

/dev/fd0H360 (minor = 12)

/dev/fd0D720 (minor = 16)

/dev/fd0H720 (minor = 16)

/dev/fd0h360 (minor = 20)

/dev/fd0h720 (minor = 24)

/dev/fd0H1440 (minor = 28)

/dev/fd1d360 (minor = 5)

/dev/fd1h1200 (minor = 9)

/dev/fd1D360 (minor = 13)

/dev/fd1H360 (minor = 13)

/dev/fd1D720 (minor = 17)

/dev/fd1H720 (minor = 17)

/dev/fd1h360 (minor = 21)

/dev/fd1h720 (minor = 25)

/dev/fd1H1440 (minor = 29)

Example: To format a high density floppy in the disk drive:

ROOT

fdformat /dev/fd0H1440

To make **/dev/fd0** or **/dev/fd1** work with this command, you must first run **setfdprm**.

TIP

-n	Do not verify.

fdisk [-b] [-u] [*device*]

fdisk -l [-b] [-u] [*device* ...]

fdisk -s *partition* ...

fdisk -v

The **fdisk** command is used to modify a hard disk's partition table. The command is menu driven, the following options apply:

TIP You'd probably be happier using **cfdisk**.

Example: To invoke **fdisk** on ***/dev/hda***:

ROOT **fdisk /dev/hda**

Once invoked, fdisk is interactive. The following keys are used:

a	Toggle bootable (y/n) flag on the current partition.
d	Delete current partition.
l	List partition types.
m	Display menu.
n	Create a new partition.
p	List all current partitions.
q	Quit without saving changes.
t	Modify type of current partition.
u	Toggle unit of entry between cylinders and sectors.
v	Verify current partition table.
w	Write changes to disk.

-V	Display version information and exit.
-l	List partition tables and exit.
-b	Include a "Begin" column in the partition table listing.
-u	List the partition table sizes in sectors rather than cylinders.
-s partition	Display partition size (in blocks).

quota [-guv | q]

quota [-uv | q] *user*

quota [-gv | q] *group*

Display disk usage and limit information for the specified user or group.

Example: To display disk usage quotas for the user Mary:

quota mary

-g	Display quotas for the group of which the user is a member.
-u	Display user quotas. Same as default.
-v	Display quotas on filesystems where no storage is allocated.
-q	Display information only on filesystems where usage is over quota.

setfdprm [-p] *device name*

setfdprm [-p] *device size sectors heads tracks stretch gap rate spec1 fmt_gap*

setfdprm [-c] *device*

setfdprm [-y] *device*

setfdprm [-n] *device*

Set parameters on a floppy disk as specified by the user or, without any options, as found in /etc/fdprm.

Example: To set the parameters as previously specified in ***/etc/fdprm***:

ROOT **setfdprm /dev/fd0 floppy**

***-p** device name*	Load a new parameter set for the specified device.
***-c** device*	Clear the parameters of the specified device.
***-y** device*	Enable format detection messages for the specified device.
***-n** device*	Disable format detection messages for the specified device.

CHAPTER

11

FILESYSTEMS

Introduction

A **filesystem** is Linux's mechanism for organizing the various types of mass storage (hard disk, floppy disk, CD-ROM) and presenting them to the user. In order to better understand the applicable commands, a cursory description of the structure of a filesystem is presented below:

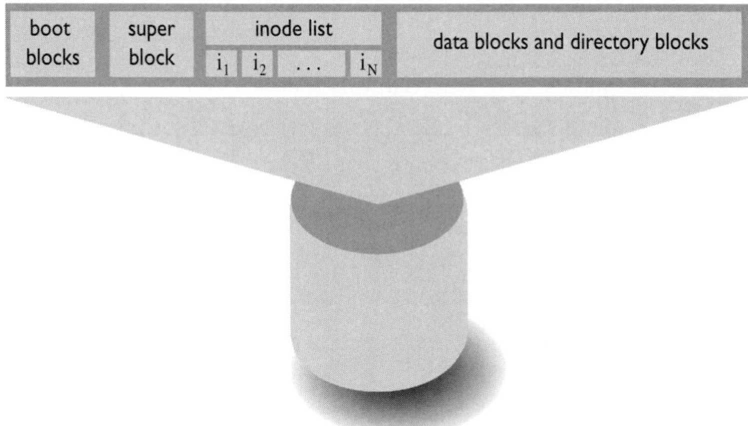

Figure 11-1 **Filesystem Structure**

The **boot block** contains information necessary for Linux to access the filesystem. The **superblock** contains information about the structure of the filesystem itself (length, size and location of the inode tables, usage information, size of the cylinder groups).

The **inode list** is a collection of data structures which contain information about individual files within the system. **Data blocks** are fixed-length sections of disk space used for storing the actual information within the files.

We speak of filesystems being either **mounted** or **unmounted** depending on whether or not the disk space they represent is currently available for use. At boot time, the init process tries to mount those filesystems specified for automounting in the ***/etc/fstab*** file. If you have root privileges, you can mount and unmount those (and any other existing filesystems) at will, provided they are not currently in use.

Filesystems may be of different types, depending on the information they contain. For example, although the most common type is ext2, you might use a filesystem of type msdos to access MS-DOS files.

Important properties of filesystems include:

mount point	The point in the directory tree at which the filesystem is attached (e.g., /tmp, /home, /usr/local).
type	One of: minix, ext, ext2, xiafs, hpfs, msdos, umsdos, vfat, proc, nfs, iso9660, smbfs, ncpfs, affs, ufs, romfs, sysv, xenix, coherent.
device name	The device file which corresponds to a given filesystem (e.g., /dev/hda1, /dev/sda2 ...).

The following commands are covered in this section:

debugfs	Inspect and possibly debug a filesystem.
df	Display information about filesystems.
dumpe2fs	Superblock and group information for an e2fs.
e2fsck	Consistency check on an e2fs.
fsck	Consistency check on a filesystem.
fsck.minix	Consistency check on a minix filesystem.
fuser	Process id's of processes using the specified filesystems.
lsattr	List attributes of files on filesystem.

lsof	List open files.
mke2fs	Make e2fs filesystem.
mkfs	Make filesystem.
mkfs.minix	Make minix filesystem.
mklost+found	Make lost+found directory on current filesystem.
mkswap	Create swap space on a device.
mount	Mount the current filesystem.
rdev	Display root device.
swapoff	Disable swapping.
swapon	Enable swapping.
sync	Write out buffered memory.
tune2fs	Tweak e2fs filesystem parameters.
umount	Unmount a filesystem.

Related Files

/proc	A pseudo file system which utilizes no disk space but is used by the kernel to store information about currently running processes.
/etc/fstab	Contains a listing of your currently defined filesystems.
/usr/src/linux/fs	Defines which types of file systems your kernel recognizes.
/etc/mtab	Table of mounted file systems.
/etc/mtab~	Lock file.
/etc/mtab.tmp	Temporary file.
/etc/exports	File specifying clients which the mount daemon is authorized to serve.

Commands

debugfs [-f *cmd_file*] [-R *command*] [-V] [-w [*device*]]

Examine and debug an ext2 filesystem. Note that this is an interactive command; once invoked, you get a debugfs prompt and can fiddle with it indefinitely. The filesystem should be unmounted before you run **debugfs**. Use with extreme caution; you can destroy the filesystem with this command. Note that the default if for **debugfs** to be run in read-only mode.

Example: To run debugfs on the filesystem in /dev/hda6 in read/write mode:

ROOT **debugfs -w /dev/hda6**

Example: To use debugfs to display the contents of the superblock of /dev/hda6 and exit:

ROOT **debugfs -R show_super_stats /dev/hda6**

To get block numbers and other information prior to invoking **debugfs**, run **dumpe2fs**.

TIP

-w	Open the filesystem in read/write mode. device is the device file corresponding to the ext2 filesystem (e.g., /dev/hdXX).
***-f** cmd_file*	Execute commands in cmd_file.
***-R** request*	Execute command, then exit.
-V	Print version number.

Once invoked, **debugfs** uses the command subset below. Note that in many cases, files may be specified either by pathname or inode number. (The inode is the low-level Linux representation for all types of files, including directories.) Inodes are input as decimal numbers surrounded by angle brackets (“<”, “>”).

***cat** filespec*	Dump the contents of the inode filespec to stdout.
***cd** filespec*	Change the current working directory to filespec.
***chroot** filespec*	Change the root directory to be the directory filespec.
close	Close the currently open file system.
***clri** filespec*	Clear the contents of the inode filespec.
***dump [-p]** inode outfile*	Dump the contents of the file specified by inode outfile. If the -p option is used, debugfs sets the file permissions of outfile to match filespec.
expand_dir directory	Expand the directory.
***find_free_block** [goal]*	Starting at *goal,* find and allocate the first free block.

***find_free_inode** [dir [mode]]*	Find a free inode and allocate it. dir specifies the inode number of the directory which is to be allocated. *mode* specifies the permissions of the new inode.
***freeb** block*	Mark the block number block as not allocated.
***freei** filespec*	Free the inode specified by filespec.
help	Print a list of commands understood by debugfs(8).
***icheck** block ...*	Print a listing of the inodes which use the one or more blocks specified on the command line.
***initialize** device blocksize*	Create an ext2 file system on device with device size blocksize.
***kill_file** filespec*	Deallocate the inode filespec and its blocks.
***ln** filespec dest_file*	Create a link named dest_file, which is a link to filespec. Does not adjust the inode reference counts.
***ls [-l]** filespec*	Print a listing of the files in the directory filespec.
***modify_inode** filespec*	Modify the contents of the inode structure in the inode filespec.
***mkdir** filespec*	Make a directory.
***mknod** filespec [p|[[c|b] major minor]]*	Create a special device file. If a character or block device is to be made, the major and minor device numbers must be specified.
***ncheck** inode_num ...*	Take the requested list of inode numbers, and print a listing of pathnames to those inodes.
***open [-w]** device*	Open a file system for editing.
pwd	Print the current working directory.
quit	Quit debugfs.

rm *pathname*	Delete pathname.
rmdir *filespec*	Remove the directory filespec. This function is currently not implemented.
setb *block*	Mark the block number block as allocated.
seti *filespec*	Mark inode filespec as in use in the inode bitmap.
show_super_stats	List the contents of the superblock.
stat *filespec*	Display the contents of the inode structure of the file specified by filespec.
testb *block*	Test if the block number block is marked as allocated in the block bitmap.
testi *filespec*	Test if the inode filespec is marked as allocated in the inode bitmap.
unlink *pathname*	Remove the link specified by pathname to an inode. Note this does not adjust the inode reference counts.
write *source destination*	Copy the contents of source to destination.

df [option, ...] [*file*,...]

Report the amount of space used and available on filesystem(s).

Example: To print out the current state of the filesystems with size in megabytes (**-h** option):

df -h

```
Filesystem      Size  Used  Avail  Capacity Mounted on
/dev/hda5       167M   45M   114M     28%    /
/dev/hda7       402M  2.9M   379M      1%    /home
/dev/hda6       1.6G  815M   703M     54%    /usr
```

where **Filesystem** is the disk partition corresponding to the mounted filesystem. **Mounted on** gives the entry in ***/etc/fstab*** corresponding to the disk partition. **Size, Used**, and **Avail** are obvious (though normally displayed by block count rather than megabytes).

-a, --all	Also list filesystems of size 0, which are omitted by default.
-h, -human-readable	Append letters to specify units of measurement (e.g., M=megabyte, K=kilobyte).
--inodes	List inode usage information instead of block usage.
-k, --kilobytes	Print size in 1024 byte blocks.
-m, --megabytes	Print size in megabyte blocks.
--no-sync	Do not run the sync system call before getting usage data.
-P, --portability	Use the POSIX output format.
--sync	Invoke the sync system call before getting usage data.
-t *FSTYPE,**--type=**FSTYPE*	List only filesystems of type FSTYPE.
-T,--print-type	Include the filesystem type (nfs, 4.2, ufs, efs, hsfs, cdfs, pcfs) in the listing.
-x *FSTYPE, **--exclude-type=**FSTYPE*	Exclude from the listing filesystems of type FSTYPE.
-v	Ignored; for compatibility with System V versions of "df".

dumpe2fs [-b] [-V] *device*

Print the superblock and blocks group information for the filesystem present on device.

Example: To print out the bad blocks on the filesystem located on ***/dev/sda1***:

dumpe2fs -b /dev/sda1

ROOT

To find out the devices associated with a given filesystem, use **df**.

TIP

-b	Print the blocks which are reserved as bad in the filesystem.
-V	Print the version number of dumpe2fs and exit.

e2fsck [-pacnyrdfvstFSV] [-b *superblock*] [-B *blocksize*] [-l\|-L *bad_blocks_file*] [-C *fd*] *device*

e2fsck is used to check a Linux second extended file system for internal consistency. If errors are found, it can sometimes make repairs. If the system thinks the filesystem was unmounted cleanly, it will not perform a thorough check.

Example: To force a check of the /dev/hda2 filesystem:

e2fsck -f /dev/hda6

-a	Automatically repair the filesystem whenever possible.
-b *superblock*	Use an alternative superblock specified by superblock. Normally used when the original superblock has been corrupted.
-B *blocksize*	Force e2fsck to search for the superblock at the specified blocksize.
-c	Find and mark any bad blocks on the filesystem.
-C *fd*	Write completion information to the specified file descriptor so that the progress of the filesystem check can be monitored.
-d	Print debugging output.
-f	Force checking of the filesystem.
-F	Flush the buffer caches before beginning check.
-l *filename*	Add the blocks listed in the file specified by filename to the list of bad blocks.
-L *filename*	Set the bad blocks list to be the list of blocks specified by filename.

-n	Open the filesystem read-only, and assume an answer of "no" to all questions.
-p	Automatically repair the filesystem, if possible.
-r	No effect; included for backward compatibility.
-s	Force the filesystem to use little endian byte order if it isn't already.
-S	Byte swap the filesystem, regardless of its current byte order.
-t	Include timing statistics for e2fsck.
-v	Verbose mode.
-V	Print version information and exit.
-y	Assume an answer of "yes" to all questions.

fsck [-AVRTNP] [-s] [-t *fstype*] [fs-options] *filesys* [...]

Check and repair a Linux file system. *filesys* is either the device name or the mount point.

Example: To check the /usr/local filesystem without making any repairs:

ROOT **fsck -N /usr/local**

Example: To check the filesystem on /dev/hdb2 and repair only after asking for confirmation:

ROOT **fsck -r /dev/hdb2**

-A	Attempt to check all filesystems in /etc/fstab in one run.
-R	When checking with -A flag, skip the root filesystem.
-T	Don't show the title on startup.
-N	Show what would be done, but don't execute.
-P	Used with -A flag to check the root filesystem in parallel with other filesystems.

-s	Serialize fsck operations.
-V	Verbose.
***-t** fstype*	Specify the type of file system to be checked. If used with -A flag, check only filesystems that match fstype. Otherwise, check only filesystems that do not match fstype.
-fs-options	Any options which are not understood by fsck, or which follow the -- option are treated as file system-specific options to be passed to the file system-specific checker.
-a	Automatically repair the filesystem without prompting for confirmation.
-r	Repair only after asking for confirmation.

fsck.minix [-larvsmf] *device*

Perform a consistency check on a Minix filesystem.

Example: To check the filesystem in /dev/sdb2 and include superblock information in the output:

fsck.minix -s /dev/sdb2

ROOT

-l	List all filenames.
-r	Repair filesystem only after prompting for confirmation.
-a	Automatically repair filesystem without prompting for confirmation.
-v	Verbose.
-s	Include super block information.
-m	Activate MINIX-like "mode not cleared" warnings.
-f	Force file system check.

fuser [-a|-s] [-n *space*] [-signal] [-kmuv] *name* ... [-] [-n *space*] [-signal] [-kmuv] *name* ...

fuser -l

fuser -V

Display the process id's of processes using the specified files or filesystems. In the default mode, the following codes are used to specify the type of access taking place.

c	Current directory.
e	Executable being run.
f	Open file. f is omitted in default display mode.
r	Root directory.
m	Mmap'ed file or shared library.

Example: To check and kill any process accessing the /home filesystem:

ROOT **fuser -k /home**

Example: To display the user names of people accessing a specified file:

ROOT **fuser -u /home/someone/file**

TIP Bookmark this one. You'll need it sooner or later.

-a	Show all files specified on the command line.
-k	Kill any process accessing the file.
-l	Display list of signal names.
-m *file*	List all processes accessing files on filesystem or block device specified by name.
-n *space*	Use a different name space.
-s	Operate silently. Overrides options a, u, and v.

-signal	Use the specified signal instead of SIGKILL.
-u	Append the user name of the process owner to each PID.
-v	Verbose mode.
-V	Display version information.
-	Reset all options and set the signal back to SIGKILL.

lsattr [-Radv] [*files...*]

Lists the attributes of a file on a Linux second extended file system.

Example: To recursively list the attributes in the ***/home*** filesystem:

lsattr -R /home

-R	Recursively list attributes of directories and their contents.
-a	List all files in directories, including those that start with a period (".'').
-d	List any directories as if they were files, rather than listing their contents.
-v	List the version.

lsof [-?abChlnNOPRstUvVX] [-A A] [-c c] [-d d] [-D D] [+|-f] [-F [f]] [-g [s]] [-i [i]] [-k k] [-m m] [+|-M] [-o [o]] [-p s] [+|-r [t]] [-S [t]] [-T [t]] [-u s] [+|-w] [--] [*names*]

List all open files belonging to all active processes. Useful for identifying the process(es) which keep you from unmounting the filesystem which you desperately need to unmount for repairs.

Example: To list all files currently opened by user Jones:

lsof -u jones

Example: To list the process ID's for all users accessing the /usr/local filesystem (and kill them off):

lsof -t /usr/local | kill -9

-? -h	Help for lsof command.
-a	Subject list selection options to a logical AND.
***-A** alternate*	Use alternate as an alternate name list file.
-b	Skip kernel functions that might block.
***-c** char*	List files for processes executing command beginning with characters specified by char.
-C	Disable reporting of path name components from the kernel's name cache.
***-d** s*	List files whose file descriptors are in the set s.
***-D** function*	Specify use of the device cache file. function is one of: ? Report device cache file paths. b Build the device cache file. i Ignore the device cache file. r Read the device cache file. u Read & update the device cache file.
***-F** char_list*	char_list select the fields to be output for processing for another program.
***-g** [pgrp]*	List files for processes whose process group identifiers are in the comma-separated set pgrp.
***-i** [iadr]*	List files whose Internet address matches the address specified in iadr. iadr is of the form: **[protocol][@hostname|hostaddr][:service|port]**
***-k** kernel_name_list_file*	Specifies a kernel name list file instead of /vmunix, /mach, etc.
-l	Prevent conversion of user ID numbers to login names.
***-m** kernel_memory_file*	Allows the user to specify a kernel memory file other than the default.

+/-M	Enable or disable the reporting of portmapper registrations for TCP and UDP ports.
-n	Prevent conversion of network numbers to host names for network files.
-N	This option selects the listing of NFS files.
-o	Display file offset at all times.
***-o** num_digits*	Specifies the number of decimal digits to be printed after the 0t for a file.
-O	Do not take steps to avoid being blocked by kernel operations.
***-p** process_id, process_id, ...*	List files for processes specified by process_id.
-P	Do not convert port numbers to port names for network files.
+/-r [t]	Put lsof in repeat mode. lsof will list open files as specified in other options, pause for time "t", and repeat.
-R	This option directs lsof to list the Parent Process IDentification number in the PPID column.
-s	Always display file size.
-S [secs]	Specifies a time-out value in seconds for kernel functions that might otherwise deadlock.
-t	Produce terse output (process id only). Useful for piping to kill().
***-u** user, user,...*	List files for users whose login names or UIDs have been specified.
-U	List Unix domain sockets.
-v	Version information.

-V	Specify files which lsof was asked to find but could not.
+/-w	Enable or disable warning messages.

mke2fs [-c | -l *filename* **] [-b** *block-size* **] [-f** *fragment-size* **] [-i** *bytes-per-inode* **] [-m** *reserved-blocks-percentage* **] [-o** *creator-os* **] [-q] [-r** *fs-revision evel* **] [-R** *raid_options* **] [-s** *sparse-super-flag* **] [-v] [-F] [-L** *volume-label* **] [-M** *last-mounted-directory* **] [-S] [-V]** *device* **[** *blocks-count* **]**

Create a Linux second extended file system. device is the special file corresponding to the hardware device.

Example: To create a filesystem on ***/dev/hdb2***, checking for bad blocks before formatting:

ROOT

mke2fs -c /dev/hdb2

Example: To re-create a damaged superblock on an already existing filesystem while (hopefully) preserving the existing files:

ROOT

mke2fs -S /dev/sda1

TIP

In order to create a filesystem, you must first partition out some disk space. Use **fdisk** or **cfdisk** for to partition space.

-b *block-size*	Specify the size of blocks in bytes.
-c	Check the device for bad blocks before creating the file system.
-f *fragment-size*	Specify the size of fragments in bytes.
-i *bytes-per-inode*	Specify the bytes per inode ratio.
-l *filename*	Read the bad blocks list from filename.
-m *reserved-blocks-percentage*	Specify the percentage of blocks reserved for the superuser.
-o	Specify a creator operating system other than the default.

-q	Supress output. (Quiet.)
***-s** sparse-super-flag*	Turn on (1) or off (0) the sparse super flag.
-v	Verbose execution.
-F	Force mke2fs to run, even if the specified device is not a block special device.
-L	Set the volume label for the filesystem.
-M	Set the last directory in the new filesystem to be mounted. (Some utilities look at this value to see where the filesystem should be mounted.)
***-r** revision*	Set the filesystem revision for the new filesystem.
***-R** raid_option*	Set raid-related options for the filesystem.
-S	Write superblock and group descriptors only. Useful in error recovery when you want to preserve the inode table.
-V	Print version number.

mkfs [-V] [-t *fstype*] [*fs-options*] *filesys* [*blocks*]

Create a Linux file system on a device. This command is a front end for one of several other commands (e.g., **mke2fs**, **mkfs.minix**) which do the actual work.

Example: To create a minix filesystem mounted at databases:

mkfs -t minix /databases

ROOT

-V	Verbose output.
***-t** fstype*	Specifies the type of filesystem to be built.
-c	Check for bad blocks before creating the filesystem.

-l filename	Read the bad block list from the file specified by filename.
-v	Produce verbose output.

mkfs.minix [-c | -l *filename*] [-n *namelength*] [-i *inode-count*] [-v] *device* [*size-in-blocks*]

Create a Linux MINIX filesystem on a device.

Exit Codes	
0	No errors
8	Operational error
16	Usage or syntax error

Example: To create a minix filesystem with a maximum namelength of 16 on /dev/sda1:

ROOT

mkfs.minix -n 16 /dev/sda1

-c	Check for bad blocks before creating the filesystem.
-n namelength	Specify the maximum length of filenames.
-i inodecount	Specify the number of inodes for the filesystem.
-l filename	Read the bad blocks list from filename.
-v	Make a minix version 2 filesystem.

mklost+found

Create a lost+found directory in the current working directory.

Example: This command has no options.

mklost+found

mkswap [-c] *device* [*size-in-blocks*]

Create a Linux swap space on a device or in a file. Swap space is disk (or, less usefully, file) space used to augment your system's RAM. When you run out of room in memory, the kernel swaps a chunk of the data in memory out to disk. When it's needed, it's swapped back in.

Example: To create a swap area on the device ***/dev/hda8***:

mkswap /dev/hda8

ROOT

TIP

Swap partitions are more efficient than swap devices.

-c	When creating swap partition on a device, check for bad blocks.

mount [-hV]

mount -a [-fFnrsvw] [-t vfstype]

mount [-fnrsvw] [-o options [,...]] *device* | *dir*

mount [-fnrsvw] [-t *vfstype*] [-o options] *device dir*

Attach a filesystem to the directory tree and thereby make it ready for use.

Example: To make the cd-rom in the drive accessible for read:

mount /mnt/cdrom

ROOT

Example: To make the disk space represented by ***/dev/hda8*** accessible for read/write as the ***/tmp*** filesystem:

mount/dev/hda8 /tmp

ROOT

TIP

The filesystems in ***/etc/fstab*** can be mounted automatically at boot time, so if you don't want to have to remount a new filesystem manually, include a line for it in ***/etc/fstab***.

-V	Display version.
-h	Display help message.
-v	Verbose mode.

-a	Mount all filesystems (of the given types specified in ***/etc/fstab***.)
-F	Used with -a.) Fork off a new incarnation of mount for each device. Used for mounting across different devices/different NFS's.
-f	Do everything except for actually executing the system call that mounts the filesystem. Useful in debugging.
-n	Execute without writing in /etc/mtab.
-s	Tolerate sloppy mount options rather than failing.
-r	Mount the file system in read-only mode.
-w	Mount the file system read/write.
-t vfstype	Specifies the file system type.
-o	Allows the user to specify one or more of the following list of options:

async All I/O to the file system should be done asynchronously.

atime Update inode access time for each access. This is the default.

auto Can be mounted with the -a option.

defaults Use default options: rw, suid, dev, exec, auto, nouser, and async.

dev Interpret character or block special devices on the file system.

exec Permit execution of binaries.

noatime Do not update inode access times on this file system.

noauto Can only be mounted explicitly (i.e., the -a option will not cause the file system to be mounted).

nodev Do not interpret character or block special devices on the file system.

noexec Do not permit execution of code on the mounted file system.

nosuid Do not allow set-user-identifier or set-group-identifier bits to take effect.

nouser Forbid an ordinary (i.e., non-root) user to mount the file system. This is the default.

remount Attempt to remount an already-mounted file system.

ro Mount the file system read-only.

rw Mount the file system read-write.

suid Allow set-user-identifier or set-group-iden-tifier bits to take effect.

sync All I/O to the file system should be done synchronously.

user Allow an ordinary user to mount the file system.

Some options to the -o flag are specific to the filesystem. An incomplete list of those options follows:

Mount options for affs

uid=*value* ***and gid=****value*	Set owner and group of the root of the file system.
setuid=*value* ***and setgid=****value*	Set the owner and group of all files.
mode=*value*	Set mode of all files to value && 0777 regardless of original permissions.
protect	Do not allow any changes to the protection bits on the file system.
usemp	Set uid and gid of the root of the file system to the uid and gid of the mount point.
verbose	Print an informational message for each successful mount.

prefix=*string*	Prefix used before volume name, when following a link.
volume=*string*	Prefix (of length at most 30) used before "/" when following a symbolic link.
reserved=*value*	Number of unused blocks at the start of the device.
root=*value*	Give explicitly the location of the root block.
bs=*value*	Specify value for blocksize.

Mount options for ext2

bsddf / minixdf	Set the behavior for the statfs system call to one of the two options.
check / check=normal / check=strict	Set checking level.
check=none / nocheck	Turn off checking.
debug	Print debugging info when invoked.
errors=continue / errors=remount-ro / errors=panic	Define the behavior when an error is encountered.
grpid or bsdgroups / nogrpid or sysvgroups	Specify what group id a newly created file gets.
resgid=n and resuid=n	Specify who benefits from reserved blocks.
sb=n	Specify a block other than 1 as the superblock. Useful when filesystem has been damaged.

Mount options for FAT, the MS-DOS filesystem.

blocksize=512 / block-size=1024	Set blocksize (default 512).
***uid=**value **and gid=**value*	Set the owner and group of all files. (Default: the uid and gid of the current process.)
***umask=**value*	Pretend the (non-existent in FAT) file permissions are equal to value.
check=[r / n / s]	Filename checking = relaxed, normal, or strict. Default = n.
conv=b[inary] / conv=t[ext] / conv=a[uto]	Specifies whether or not to convert text files from MS-DOS format to UNIX format.
debug	Turn on the debug flag.
fat=12 / fat=16	Specify either a 12 bit fat or a 16 bit fat.
quiet	Turn on the quiet flag. Attempts to chown or chmod files do not return errors, although they still fail.

Mount options for nfs

rsize=8192,wsize=8192	By resetting the buffer size, you can dramatically increase the speed of your NFS connection.
hard	Force a program accessing a file on a NFS mounted file server to hang when the server crashes and wait until the server is back on line.
soft	Allows the kernel to time out if the nfs server does not respond.
nolock	Do not use locking. Do not start **lockd**.

mountd [-f *exports-file*] [-d *facility*] [-P port] [-Dhnprv] [--debug facility] [--exports-file=*file*] [--help] [--allow-non-root] [--re-export] [--version]

The **mountd** program is the NFS mount daemon. Before exporting a file system, it checks ***/etc/exports*** for permission. If the request is approved, it creates a file handle for the requested directory and adds an entry to /etc/rmtab. When unmounting, the entry in ***/etc/rmtab*** is removed.

Example: This daemon is usually invoked via script at boot time with a line like:

ROOT

mountd &

To startd mountd from **inetd**, add the following two lines to **/etc/inetd.conf**:

```
mount/1-2 dgram  rpc/udp wait  root  /usr/sbin/rpc.mountd rpc.mountd

mount/1-2 stream rpc/tcp wait  root  /usr/sbin/rpc.mountd rpc.mountd
```

-f or --exports-file	This option specifies the exports file, which lists the clients that this server is authorized to serve, together with the parameters to apply to each mount.
-d or --debug	Debug mode. Tells mountd to log each operation to standard error.
-F or --foreground	Force mountd to stay attached to the terminal.
-h or --help	Display help information.
-n or --allow-non-root	Optionally allow mountd to serve requests that come from non-reserved IP ports.
-P portnum or --port portnum	Specify the port for mountd to listen to.
-p or --promiscuous	Force the server to honor requests from any client on the network.
-r or --re-export	Allow imported file systems to be exported.
-v or --version	Display the version number of the program.

rdev [-rsvh] [-o *offset*] [*image* [*value* [*offset*]]]
rdev [-o *offset*] [*image* [*root_device* [*offset*]]]

Display the ***/etc/mtab*** line for the current root file system. Useful in scripting for identifying which device your filesystem is mounted on.

Example: To identify the device associated with the root filesystem:

rdev

ROOT

-s	Causes rdev to act like swapdev.
-r	Causes rdev to act like ramsize.
-R	Causes rdev to act like rootflags.
-v	Causes rdev to act like vidmode.
-h	Provides help.

/sbin/swapoff [-h -V]

/sbin/swapoff -a

/sbin/swapoff *specialfile* ...

Disable swapping on the specified device or file.

Example: To disable swapping on ***/dev/hd8***:

swapoff /dev/hda8

ROOT

-a	Disable swapping on all devices specified as swap devices in ***/etc/fstab***.
-h	Display help information.
-V	Display version information.

/sbin/swapon [-h -V]

/sbin/swapon -a [-v]

/sbin/swapon [-v] [-p *priority*] *specialfile* ...

/sbin/swapon [-s]

Swapon enables swapping/paging on the specified devices or files. The **swapon** command is typically executed during multiuser initialization.

Example: To enable swapping on ***/dev/hda8***:

ROOT

swapon /dev/hda8

-h	Display help information.
-V	Display version information.
-s	Summarize swap usage by device.
-a	Make all devices marked "sw" in /etc/fstab available.
-p priority	Specify priority from 0-32767 for swapon.

sync

Write any data buffered in memory out to disk.

Example: This command has no options.

sync

tune2fs [-l] [-c *max-mount-counts*] [-e *errors-behavor*] [-i *interval-between-checks*] [-m *reserved-blocks-percentage*] [-r *reserved-blocks-count*] [-s *sparse-super-flag*] [-u *user*] [-g *group*] [-C *mount-count*] [-L *volume-name*] [-M *last-mounted-directory*] [-U UUID] *device*

Allows the user to adjust some parameters on the Linux second extended filesystem specified by device. Do not use on a mounted filesystem.

Example: To specify the user informix as the beneficiary of any reserved blocks:

tune2fs -u informix /dev/hda2

ROOT TIP

Taking the time to add labels (e.g., /, /home, /usr ...) to your disk partitions makes them easier to identify when partitioning new space with **cfdisk**.

-c *max-mount-counts*	Specify the maximum number of mounts between two filesystem checks.
-e [continue / remount-ro / panic]	Specify the action for the kernel to take upon detection of an error.
-g *group*	Set the user group which can benefit from the reserved blocks. group can be a numerical gid or a group name.
-i *interval-between-checks[d/m/w]*	Specify the maximum time between two filesystem checks in days, weeks or months. A value of zero will disable checking.
-l	Display the contents of the superblock.
-m *reserved-blocks-percentage*	Specify the percentage of reserved blocks.
-r *reserved-blocks-count*	Specify the count of reserved blocks.
-s *sparse_super_flag*	Set or reset the sparse_superblock flag. Used to save space on enormous filesystems.
-u *user*	Specify the user who can benefit from reserved blocks.
-C *mount-count*	Specify the number of times the filesystem has been mounted.
-L *volume-label*	Specify the volume label of the filesystem.

***-M** last-mounted-directory*	Specify the last-mounted directory for the filesystem.
***-U** UUID*	Specify the UUID of the filesystem.

umount [-hV]

umount -a [-nrv] [-t *vfstype*]

umount [-nrv] *device* | *dir* [...]

Remove the specified filesystem from the directory hierarchy, thereby rendering it unavailable for use. Note that this command cannot be run successfully when any portion of the filesystem is in use. To identify who is using some portion of the filesystem, use the **lsof** command.

Example: To unmount the /home filesystem:

ROOT **umount /home**

Example: To unmount all the filesystems specified in /etc/mtab:

ROOT **umount -a**

-V	Version.
-h	Help.
-v	Verbose.
-n	Unmount without writing in /etc/mtab.
-r	If unmounting fails, try to remount in read-only mode.
-a	Run umount on all filesystems listed in /etc/mtab.
-t vfstype	Act only on filesystems of type vfstype.

CHAPTER

12

PRINTERS & PRINT QUEUES

Introduction

The print system in Linux is spread across several programs, devices, and configuration files.

The Print Process

After it leaves your application, **lpr** takes the print job and preprocesses it according to any command-line options and/or printer specific configuration requirements. The resultant file and a paired file containing processing instructions are placed in a directory associated with the printer, called a **spool directory** or **print queue** (usually ***/var/spool/lpd/****). Print jobs stored in these directories are said to be **spooled** or **queued**. Multiple jobs may wait in these directories until the printer is ready to handle them. Once the file is successfully spooled, **lpr** notifies the **printer daemon, lpd**, that there is a new job awaiting processing.

The printer daemon filters the file according to the instructions left for it by **lpr** and passes the output to an actual printer device, typically ***/dev/lp??***. The printer daemon handles all information exchange with the printer hardware. It is possible to bypass the daemon and **cat** stuff directly to the printer device, but it's not good form.

In addition, you should be aware that **lpd** uses printer-specific parameters stored in the ***/etc/printcap*** (a printer capabilities database, not unlike termcap and terminfo in function) to translate the generic print data into printer-specific sequences of control characters.

The commands covered in this section include:

lpc	Control the line printer system.
lpd	The line printer daemon.
lpq	Query the specified print spool.
lpr	Send a file to the print queue.
lprm	Remove a file from the print queue.
pr	Print a file.
tunelp	Modify printer characteristics.

Related Files

/dev/lp*	Line printer devices.
/dev/printer	Socket for local requests.
/etc/hosts.equiv	One of two files which may specify printer access.
/etc/hosts.lpd	One of two files which may specify printer access.
/etc/printcap	Printer description file.
/etc/passwd	Personal identification.
/etc/printcap	Printer capabilities data base.
/usr/sbin/lpd*	Line printer daemons.
/var/spool/*	The spooling directory, as determined from printcap.
/var/spool/*/minfree	Specifies number of disk blocks to leave free s.t. the queue can't completely fill the disk.
/var/spool/output/*	Directories used for spooling.
/var/spool/output/*/cf*	Daemon control files.
/var/spool/output/*/df*	Data files specified in "cf" files.
/var/spool/output/*/tf*	Temporary copies of "cf" files.
/var/spool/*/lock	The lock file to obtain the currently active job.

Commands

lpc [command [argument ...]]

This command is used by root to manage the line printer system. If called with no arguments, lpc will supply an interactive prompt, otherwise it will interpret command line arguments as interactive commands. Note that it is effective only on printers specified in /etc/printcap.

Example: To invoke **lpc** from the command line and then use it to disable the print queue associated with lp1:

ROOT

lpc

lpc> disable lp1

? [command ...], help [command ...]	Output a short description of the specified command, or, if none specified, a list of available commands.
abort { all l printer }T	Terminate spooling daemon on the local host and disable printing on the specified printer.
clean { all l printer }	Remove any control files, temporary files, or data files that may exist on the local printer queue(s).
disable { all l printer }	Prevent new printer jobs from being entered by lpr.
down { all l printer } message ...	Bring the specified printers down. (Turn off the queue, disable printing, put message in the printer status file.)
enable { all l printer }	Allow new jobs to be entered into the spool queue.
exit, quit	Exit from lpc.
restart { all l printer }	Tries to restart the printer daemon, possibly (if user is superuser) killing the current daemon.
start { all l printer }	Start a spooling daemon and enable printing for the listed printer(s).
status { all l printer }	Display the status of queues and daemons on the local machine.

***stop** { all | printer }*	After current job completes, halt the spooling daemon and disable printing.
***topq** printer [jobnum ...] [user ...]*	Put the jobs (in the order listed) at the top of the print queue.
***up** { all | printer }*	Activate everything and start a new print daemon.

lpd [-l] [port#]

lpd is the line printer daemon. Normally, this command is invoked at boot time from the **rc** file. It consults the ***/etc/printcap*** file to learn about existing printers, then handles print requests. Its duties include handling print requests, transferring files to the spooling area, and removing jobs from the queue.

Example: This daemon is usually invoked by an rc script. To start **lpd** with logging, put a line like the following in a script:

lpd -l &

ROOT

-l	Log all valid print requests (primarily used for debugging).
port#	Specify the Internet port number used to meet with other processes.

The daemon relies on automatically generated cf (configuration) files which specify output formatting information. The files begin with "cf" and use the following set of control characters prepended to each line to tell lpd what to do:

J	Job Name. String to be used for the job name on the burst page.
C	Classification. String to be used for the classification line on the burst page.
L	Literal. The line contains identification information from the password file and causes the banner page to be printed.
T	Title. String to be used as the title for pr(1).
H	Host Name. Name of the machine where lpr was invoked.

P	Person. Login name of the person who invoked lpr. This is used to verify ownership by lprm.
M	Send mail to the specified user when the current print job completes.
f	Formatted File. Name of a file to print which is already formatted.
l	Like "f" but passes control characters and does not make page breaks.
p	Name of a file to print using pr(1) as a filter.
t	Troff File. The file contains troff(1) output (cat phototypesetter commands).
n	Ditroff File. The file contains device independent troff output.
r	DVI File. The file contains Tex l output DVI format from Standford.
g	Graph File. The file contains data produced by plot(3).
c	Cifplot File. The file contains data produced by cifplot.
v	The file contains a raster image.
r	The file contains text data with FORTRAN carriage control characters.
1	Troff Font R. Name of the font file to use instead of the default.
2	Troff Font I. Name of the font file to use instead of the default.
3	Troff Font B. Name of the font file to use instead of the default.
4	Troff Font S. Name of the font file to use instead of the default.
W	Width. Changes the page width (in characters) used by pr(1) and the text filters.
I	Indent. The number of characters to indent the output by (in ascii).
U	Unlink. Name of file to remove upon completion of printing.
N	File name. The name of the file which is being printed, or a blank for the standard input (when lpr is invoked in a pipeline).

lpq [-l] [-P*printer*] [*job #* ...] [*user* ...]

Looks at the spooling area and reports on the status of the indicated job. If no job is specified, **lpq** reports on the whole queue. All arguments other than -P and -l are interpreted as user names or print job numbers.

Example: To get verbose information on the current print jobs for lp10:

lpq -Plp10 -l

-P	Tells lpq to look only at the specified printer.
-l	Long list. With this option, lpq will print information about each file in the job. (Normally, output is restricted to a single line.)

lpr [-Pprinter] [-#num] [-C *class*] [-J *job*] [-T *title*] [-U *user*] [-i [*numcols*]] [-1234 *font*] [-wnum] [-cdfghlnmprstv] [*file* ...]

lpr sends a request to a spooling daemon to print the specified files when a printer becomes available.

Example: To print two copies (#2) of the file stuff.out to printer lp1:

lpr -Plp1 -#2 stuff.out

Non-standard text files can be printed using the following options:

-c	Print data which is in cifplot format.
-d	Print data which is in tex DVI format.
-f	Assume the first character of each line is a FORTRAN carriage control character.
-g	Print data which is in standard plot format.
-l	Allow printing of control characters; do not recognize page breaks.
-n	Print data which was formatted by ditroff.
-p	Use pr(1) to format the files (equivalent to print).

-t	Print data which was formatted by troff.
-v	Print raster image data formatted for printers like the Benson Varian.

These options apply to the handling of the print job:

-P	Send output to the specified printer.
-h	Do not include the burst page in the output.
-m	Send mail when job completed.
-r	Remove file upon completion.
-s	Use symbolic links rather than copying files to the spool directory.
***-#**num*	Print the specified number of copies.
***-[1234]**font*	Mount the specified font on font position i.
***-C** class*	Use the specified classification on the burst page.
***-J** job*	Use the specified job name on the burst page.
***-T** title*	Use the specified title instead of the file name.
***-U** user*	Print the specified user name on the burst page.
***-i** [numcols]*	Indent the output the specified number of columns.
-wnum	Use the specified page width.

lprm [-P*printer*] [-] [*job # ...*] [*user ...*]

Remove the specified jobs from the print queue.

Example: To remove job 43 from printer lp1:

lprm -Plp1 43

Job numbers may be obtained via the **lpq** command.

TIP

-Pprinter	Specify the queue from which the file is to be removed.
-	Remove all jobs owned by the current user. If user is superuser, remove all files in the specified queue.
user	Remove all jobs belonging to the specified user (valid only for superuser).
job #	Remove the specified job from the queue. (Job numbers may be obtained via lpq.)

pr [OPTION]... [*FILE*]...

Format and print a file. The formatting includes a 5 line header (2 blank lines, a line with the date, the file name, and the page count, and then 2 more blank lines), a 5 blank line footer. Line widths are truncated to 72 columns.

Note that this command does not by itself send files to a printer, only to standard output.

Example: To print the file skinny.txt with a width of 50 columns (-w option):

pr -w 50 skinny.txt

+FIRST_PAGE[:LAST_PAGE]	Specify the start page, or, if LAST_PAGE is included, a page range.
-COLUMN	Produce output of the specified COLUMN width.
-a	Print columns across, rather than down.
-c	Include control characters in the output.
-d	Format output double-spaced.
-e[IN-TABCHAR[IN-TABWIDTH]]	Expand tabs to spaces on input.

-f, -F	Separate output pages with a form feed.
-h HEADER	Use the specified header string rather than the file name as a header.
***-i**[OUT-TABCHAR[OUT-TABWIDTH]]*	Replace spaces with tabs on output.
-j	Merge lines of full length.
***-l** PAGE_LENGTH*	Use the specified page length.
-m	Merge print several files. Print one file per column. May be used with -s[SEPARATOR].
***-n**[NUMBER-SEPARATOR[DIGITS]]*	Precede each column with a line number.
***-N** LINE_NUMBER*	Use the specified value as the starting line number.
***-o** N*	Set the left margin at the specified number of spaces.
-r	Suppress warning messages when a file cannot be opened.
***-s**[SEPARATOR]*	Use the specified separator between columns.
-t	Suppress header and footer information. Do not pad bottoms of pages with blanks.
-T	Suppress header and footer information. Suppress form feeds.
-v	Output unprintable characters in backslash octal notation.
***-w** PAGE_WIDTH*	Use the specified page width.

tunelp *<device>* **[-i** *<IRQ>* **| -t** *<TIME>* **| -c** *<CHARS>* **| -w** *<WAIT>* **| -a [on|off] | -o [on|off] | -C [on|off] | -r | -s | -q [on|off]]**

tunelp allows the user to set parameters for the specified line printing devices.

Example: To set the printer driver /dev/lp1 to use IRQ 10 (**-i** options):

tunelp /dev/lp1 -i 10

-i *<IRQ>*	Use the specified IRQ for the specified parallel port.
-t *<TIME>*	Specify the time (in jiffies) to wait if the printer doesn't take a character for the number of tries dictated by the -c parameter.
-c *<CHARS>*	Specifies the number of times to try to output a character before going to sleep. 120 is a reasonable value for most printers, but 250 is the default because some printers require that much.
-w *<WAIT>*	Busy loop counter for the strobe signal. Increase for use with printers which demand a long strobe, also may help when printing via long cables.
-a *[on/off]*	Toggle whether or not to abort on error. (Default is off.)
-o *[on/off]*	Check for "out of paper" and other errors when using open() call.
-C *[on/off]*	Extra careful error checking. Very useful for printers which will accept jobs even when powered off.
-s	Return the current printer status.
-r	Reset the port.
-q *[on/off]*	Toggle printing the current IRQ setting.

CHAPTER

13

DAEMONS

Introduction

Daemons are the invisible workhorses of the Linux world. A **daemon** is a program run in the background (that is, not attached to any particular terminal) that performs some system task. Typically, that system task is to service a request by some user program for a piece of information (e.g., **rwhod**), access to some system resource (e.g., **lpd**), or to facilitate communication between two systems or two parts of the same system (e.g., **telnetd, talkd**).

The word "daemon" should be pronounced the same as "demon" but lots of people say "day-mon" or "die-mon" and no one laughs. In general, I try to stick with whichever pronunciation my boss prefers. The word originates in Greek mythology and refers to a supernatural agent somewhere above a human but below a god in the order of things. Classical daemons are distinct from demons in that they are capable of both good and evil, which also fits in pretty well with my experience of the Linux variety.

By convention, the individual "d" at the end of each daemon name *is* pronounced, and people *will* look at you funny if you mess this up. For example, the program "**named**" is pronounced "name-dee".

If you are working with your system at the user level, you may go for months without having to mess with daemons. If you are managing a medium-sized or large network, you may do nothing else. Either way, the actual mechanics of configuring the various daemons are beyond the scope of this book.

TIP

Lots of times, configuration files are found in the ***/etc*** directory. If you're hunting a particular configuration file, you might try this:

ls -l /etc/*.conf | grep <yourcommand>

These days, most commercial Linux distributions configure the big daemons for you as part of the installation process. This is both good, in that configuring daemons can be an enormous pain in the butt, and bad, in that if you don't have a feel for Linux daemonology you'll never have a complete understanding of how your system works.

Daemons are usually started without human intervention. This usually happen in one of three ways:

- invoked by an **rc** script at boot time
- invoked by **init** at boot time
- invoked by the **inetd** daemon as needed, sometimes via **tcpd**

The examples in this chapter will reflect that fact. In the case where the daemon might profitably be invoked by **inetd**, I'll give you a line to put in the ***inetd.conf*** file. Note that **inetd** relies on the **/etc/services** file for information about what ports to monitor for what service requests.

TIP

Obviously, the daemon programs may not be in the same place on your system as they are on mine. Before modifying your ***inetd.conf***, do a sanity check on program location.

An **Internet port** is a logical network connection associated with a particular service. Note that these are distinct from the actual physical ports into which you might plug a serial line. An Internet port is born when the network programmers of the world get together and decide that thus-and-such port number will be associated with thus-and-such service from now on. There's nothing special about the port numbers, just that everyone agrees on what they are and what they will stand for. The ***/etc/services*** file contains the port/service associations for your machine.

The ultimate aim of daemon configuration is to get them to a state where they start up and shut down as needed without any human intervention whatsoever. To this end, the **inetd** program (itself a daemon) has been created. Inetd monitors certain ports for Internet service requests and invokes the daemons associated with those ports as needed. To put a daemon under the control of inetd, you must add a line in the following format to the ***/etc/inetd***.conf file:

```
service  socket_type   protocol  wait user  program  arguments
```

where

- **service** is a network service defined in ***/etc/services.***
- **socket_type** is one of (stream | dgram | raw | rdm | seqpacket).
- **protocol** is a valid protocol (e.g., tcp, udp) as specified in ***/etc/protocols.***
- **wait** is either wait or nowait.
- **user** is the name of the user as whom the service is run.
- **program** the program to be executed when inetd receives a request on the associated socket.
- **arguments** are the arguments associated with the program to be run.

The daemons described in this chapter are:

fingerd	Services finger requests.
erd	Services finger requests.
ftpd	Services ftp requests.
gated	Handles network routing.
gdc	Program to control gated.
identd	TCP/IP identification protocol.
imapd	Remote mail access.
inetd	Invokes other daemons, as necessary.
klogd	Kernel log daemon.
lpd	Services line printer requests.
mountd	NFS mount daemon.
named	Internet domain name service.
pppd	Handles point-to-point protocol communication.
rexecd	Remote command execution.

rlogin	Remote system login.
rcmd	Remote command execution.
rshd	Remote command execution.
rwhod	Services rwho/ruptime.
syslogd	System log daemon.
talk	Communication between two users.
tcpd	Access control for Internet services.
telnetd	Services telnet requests.
tftpd	Services tftp requests.
yppasswdd	Changes password

Related Files

/usr/tmp/gated/dump	Gated writes status info to this file.
/etc/gated.conf	Gated's configuration file.
/etc/gated.pid	File where gated writes its process id.
Comm/etc/gated.conf+	A new gated configuration file to be installed by gdc.
/etc/gated.conf-	An old gated configuration file which has been saved by gdc.
/etc/gated.conf--	A really old configuration file twice replaced by gdc.
/etc/printcap	Printer description file.
/var/spool/*	Printer spool directories.
/dev/lp*	Line printer devices.
/dev/printer	Socket for local requests.

/etc/hosts.equiv	Lists machine names allowed printer access.
/etc/hosts.lpd	Lists machine names allowed printer access, but not under same administrative control.
/etc/named.conf	Default name server configuration file.
/var/run/named.pid	Process id of named.
/var/tmp/named_dump.db	Dump of the name server database.
/var/tmp/named.run	Named debug output.
/var/tmp/named.stats	Nameserver statistics data.

Commands

fingerd [-wul] [-pL *path*]

Returns a human-readable status report on either the system or a particular person. Options to this command should be specified in ***/etc/inetd.conf.***

Example: This daemon is usually invoked by **inetd** (which uses tcpd to provide access control and logging services). To start **fingerd**, add the following line to your inetd.conf file:

ROOT
```
finger stream tcp nowait root /usr/sbin/tcpd in.fingerd
```

-w	Tells fingerd to include a welcome banner which contains some system information (uptime, OS nae, release) with output.
-u	Reject all requests of the form "finger @host".
-l	Log information about requests.
-p	Specify an alternate location for fingerd to find the finger program.

ftpd [-d] [-v] [-l] [*-ttimeout*] [*-Tmaxtimeout*] [-a] [-A] [-L] [-i] [-o] *-uumask*]

ftpd is the File Transfer Protocol server.

Example: This daemon is usually invoked by **inetd** via the **tcpd** daemon (which provides logging and access control). To start **ftpd** with logging (-**l**) and access control (-**a**), add the following line to your ***inetd.conf*** file:

ROOT
```
ftp stream tcp nowait root /usr/sbin/tcpd in.ftpd -l -a
```

-d, -v	Sends debugging information to the syslog.
-l	Log information about each ftp session to the syslog.
-a	Enable use of the ftpaccesss configuration file.
-A	Disable use of the ftpaccess configuration file.
-L	Log all commands sent to the ftpd server to the syslog.

-i	Log all files received to the xferlog.
-o	Log all files transmitted to the xferlog.
-u	Specify a default umask.

gated [-c] [-C] [-n] [-N] [-t *trace_options*] [-f *config_file*] [*trace_file*]

Gated is a routing service which handles a variety of routing protocols. It may be configured to some or all of the protocols which it is capable of handling.

Example: It's a good idea to invoke this command via **gdc**. But to invoke from the command line as a background process (&), type:

gated &

ROOT

-c	Tells gated to parse the configuration file, report any syntax errors, and exit.
-C	Tells gated to parse the configuration file for syntax errors.
-n	Prohibit gated from modifying the kernel forwarding table.
-N	Tell gated not to run as a daemon.
-t *trace_options*	Allows the user to specify a comma-separated list of trace options on the command line.
-f config_file	Specify a non-default configuration file.

gdc [-q] [-n] [-c *coresize*] [-f *filesize*] [-m *datasize*] [-s *stacksize*] [-t *seconds*] *command*

This command is the **gated** controller, a user interface for controlling the **gated** routing daemon. You can use it to stop, start, signal, maintain configuration files, and generate or maintain core dumps.

ROOT TIP

Example: To invoke **gated** and send all output to the system log:

gdc -q start

In order for these controls to take effect, you must start **gated** with **gdc**.

-n	Do not check the kernel forwarding table.
-q	Quiet operation. Log any output to the system log.
***-t** seconds*	Allow the user to specify how long gdc will wait for gated to complete startup, shutdown, and other operations.
***-c** coresize*	Specify an upper limit on the size of core dumps which may be generated by gated. Typically used to increase the system default when it is too small to be useful.
***-f** filesize*	Specify a maximum file size which a gated started with gdc can produce.
***-m** datasize*	Specify an upper limit on the size of the data segment of a gated started with gdc.
***-s** stacksize*	Specify the maximum size of a stack of a gated started by gdc.

The following actions may be specified at the command line:

checkconf	Check ***/etc/gated.conf*** for syntax errors.
checknew	Check ***/etc/gated.conf+*** for syntax errors.
newconf	Replace ***/etc/gated.conf*** with ***/etc/gated.conf+***.
backout	Move the old configuration file (***/etc/gated.conf-***) back into place as the current active gated.conf. Also rotates the current /etc/gated.conf to ***/etc/gated.conf+***
BACKOUT	Same as backout (above), but will overwrite any existing /etc/gated.conf+
modeconf	Set all configuration files to mode 664, owner=root, group=gdmaint.
createconf	If ***/etc/gated.conf+*** does not exist, create a zero length file with the file mode set to 664, owner=root, group=gdmaint.

running	Test to see if gated is currently running.
start	Start gated.
stop	Stop gated.
restart	Stop and restart gated.
rmcore	Delete any gated core dump file.
rmdump	Delete any gated state dump file.
rmparse	Delete any parse error file generated by checkconf or checknew.

/usr/sbin/in.identd [-i|-w|-b] [-t<*seconds*>] [-u<*uid*>] [-g<*gid*>] [-p<*port*>] [-a<*address*>] [-c<*charset*>] [-C[<*keyfile*>]] [-o] [-e] [-l] [-V] [-m] [-N] [-d] [-F<*format*>] [*kernelfile* [*kmemfile*]]

identd is an implementation of the IDENT user identification protocol. It works by looking up specific TCP/IP connections and returning the user name of the process owning the connection.

Example: This daemon is usually invoked by **inetd**. To start **identd** with logging (**-l** option) and without letting it display operating system information (**-o** option), add the following line to your ***inetd.conf*** file:

```
auth stream tcp nowait nobody /usr/sbin/in.identd in.identd -l -o
```

-i	Use this flag when starting the daemon from inetd with the nowait option—it will make inetd start one identd daemon for each connection request.
-w	Use this flag when starting the daemon from inetd with the wait option—it will start a single copy of identd upon receiving the first connection request and handle subsequent requests without having to do the necessary nlist lookup in the kernel file at startup time. This is the preferred mode of operation.
-b	Run the daemon in standalone mode without assistance from inetd.

-t<seconds> — Tells **identd** to timeout after the specified number of seconds.

-u<uid> — Tells **identd** to switch to the specified user id number after binding itself to the TCP/IP port when using -b mode of operation.

-g<gid> — Tells identd to switch to the specified group id number after binding itself to the TCP/IP port when using -b mode of operation.

-p — Specify an alternative port number to bind to when operating in -b mode.

-a<address> — Specify the local address to bind the socket to when operating in -b mode.

-V — Display version information and exit.

-l — Use the system logging daemon.

-o — Tell identd not to reveal the operating system it is run on. Security feature.

-d — Tell identd to return "UNKNOWN-ERROR" rather than "NO-USER" or "INVALID-PORT" errors. Security feature.

-c — Add the optional character set designator to the reply generated.

-C[<keyfile>] — Tells **identd** to return encrypted tokens rather than user names. The tokens are created using DES keyed off the first line of the specified keyfile.

-n — Tells **identd** to return user numbers rather than user names.

-N — When this flag is invoked, identd will check for a ".noident" file in the home directory of each user which identd is about to identify. If the file exists, identd will return HIDDEN-USER rather than user information.

-m — Allow multiple requests to be processed per session.

-d	Debugging mode. This option violates the protocol and may create security holes. Use with caution.
-F<format>	Display information in the specified format. Format is one of %u user name %U user number %g (primary) group name %G (primary) group number %l list of all groups by name %L list of all groups by number %p process ID of running process %c command name %C command and arguments
-v	Verbose output.
-f<config-file>	Use the specified configuration file rather than the default. Currently useless, as there are no configuration files involved.

/usr/etc/imapd

Supports the IMAP4 remote mail access protocol, typically on port 143.
Example: This daemon is usually invoked by **inetd**. To start **imapd:**

```
imap stream tcp nowait root /usr/sbin/tcpd imapd
```

inetd [-d] [-q *queuelength*] [*configuration file*]

Inetd is the mother of daemons. It doesn't directly provide any user services, but it calls other daemons which do. Inetd was created because many daemons are needed only occasionally. However, in order to be of use, daemons have to monitor ports for service requests. In order to do the monitoring, they take up system resources. If you have a lot of services configured, that can be a significant burden. Inetd alleviates that problem by monitoring the ports for other daemons and calling them as needed. **Inetd** should be started at boot time by ***/etc/rc.local***.

ROOT

Example: To invoke **inetd**, create a script with the following line:

inetd &

-d	Invoke inetd in debug mode.
***-q** queuelength*	Specify the length of a socket listen queue (default 128).

klogd [-c n] [-d] [-f *fname*] [-il] [-n] [-o] [-p] [-s] [-k *fname*] [-v]

klogd is the kernel log daemon. It intercepts and logs Linux kernel messages.

Example: This daemon is usually invoked by **init,** perhaps with a line like the following (**&** runs it in the background):

ROOT

klogd &

-c n	Specify the default log level of console messages.
-d	Debug mode.
-f file	Log to the specified file rather than syslog.
-i, -I	Send a signal to the currently executing klogd daemon.
-n	Do not automatically background.
-o	One-shot mode. Read and log all messages in the kernel message buffers, then exit.
-p	Paranoid mode. Load kernel module symbol information whenever an Oops string is found in the kernel message stream.
-s	Use the system call interface to access the kernel message buffers.
-k file	Use the specified file as the source of kernel symbol information.
-v	Display version information and exit.

lpd [-l] [*port#*]

lpd is the line printer daemon. It handles the manipulation of spooled files and any actual printing. It gets printer information from printcap. The original invocation listens only for requests; it forks off child processes to handle any requests received.

Example: This daemon is usually invoked by an rc script. To start **lpd** with logging, put a line like the following in a script:

lpd -l & ROOT

-l	Turn logging of requests on.
port#	Allow the user to specify an internet port number on the command line rather than letting the process obtain the port number from getservbyname.

Daemons

/usr/sbin/rpc.mountd [*-f exports-file*] [**-d** *facility*] [**-P** port] [-Dhnprv] [--debug *facility*] [--exports-file=*file*] [--help] [--allow-non-root] [--re-export] [--version]

mountd is the NFS mount daemon. Before exporting a file system, it checks ***/etc/exports*** for permission. If the request is approved, it creates a file handle for the requested directory and adds an entry to /etc/rmtab. When unmounting, the entry in ***/etc/rmtab*** is removed.

Example: This daemon is usually invoked via script at boot time with a line like:

mountd & ROOT

To startd mountd from **inetd**, add the following two lines to **/etc/inetd.conf**:

```
mount/1-2 dgram  rpc/udp wait  root  /usr/sbin/rpc.mountd rpc.mountd
mount/1-2 stream rpc/tcp wait  root  /usr/sbin/rpc.mountd rpc.mountd
```

-f or --exports-*file*	Specify an export file other than the default, /etc/exports.
-d or --debug	Enable verbose logging of each transaction to standard error.
-F or --*foreground*	Run mountd in the foreground.

-h* or *--help	Display help information and exit.
-n* or *--allow-non-root	Permit mount requests that do not originate from reserved IP ports.
-P** portnum* **or *--port *portnum*	Specify a port for inetd to listen on. Typically, the port number is specified in /etc/services.
-p* or *--promiscuous	Tell mountd to service any host on the network.
-r* or *--re-export	Allow re-export of imported NFS of SMB filesystems.
-v* or *--version	Display version information and exit.

named [-d *debuglevel*] **[-p** *port#*] **[-(b|c)** *config_file*] **[-f -q -r] [-u** *user_name*] **[-g** *group_name*] **[-t** *directory*] **[-w** *directory*] [*config_file*]

Named is the Internet domain name server. It resolves host names into IP addresses. Named gets configuration information from ***/etc/named.conf***.

Example: This daemon is usually invoked by **inetd**. To start **named** with some debugging information:

ROOT

named -d 1 &

-d *debuglevel*	Specify the level of debugging information.
-p *port#*	Tell named to use the specified remote port number.
-(b|c) *config_file*	Specify an alternate configuration file (default is /etc/named.conf).
-f	Tell named to run in the foreground.
-q	Trace all incoming queries if NAMED has been compiled with QRYLOG defined.
-r	Recursion off. Allow name resolution only from local (primary or secondary) zones.

***-u** user_name*	Tell named to run as the specified user after initialization.
***-g** group_name*	Tell named to run as the specified group after initialization.
***-t** directory*	Tell named to chroot into the specified directory after processing any command line arguments.
***-w** directory*	Specify a working directory for the server.

/usr/sbin/rpc.nfsd [-f exports-file] [-d facility] [-P port] [-R dirname] [-Fhlnprstv] [--debug facility] [--exports-file=file] [--foreground] [--help] [--allow-non-root] [--re-export] [--public-root dirname] [--port port] [--log-transfers] [--version] [numservers]

Daemons

The **nfsd** program is an NFS service daemon which handles client filesystem requests.

Example: This daemon is usually started at system boot time. To start **nfsd** form with re-exported of filesystems which have themselves been imported (**-r** option), add the following line to a script:

nfsd -r &

ROOT

-f or --exports-file	Tell nfsd to use the specified exports file.
-d facility or --debug facility	Enable verbose debugging.
-F or --foreground	Tell nfsd to run in the foreground.
-h or --help	Display help information and exit.
-l or --log-transfers	Attempt to log all files transferred by the NFS server.
-n or --allow-non-root	Permit servicing of NFS requests that do not originate from reserved IP ports.
-P portnum or --port portnum	Tell nfsd to listen on the specified port rather than port 2049.

-p or --promiscuous	Allow nfsd to serve any host on the network.
-r or --re-export	Allow filesystems which have themselves been remotely mounted on the host system to be re-exported.
-R or --public-root	Specify the directory associated with the public file handle.
-v or --version	Display version information.

pppd [*tty_name*] [*speed*] [*options*]

pppd is the Point-to-Point protocol daemon. PPP is a method for transmitting datagrams over serial connections.

Example: To start **pppd** on tty10 with baud rate 14400:

ROOT

pppd tty10 14400

<tty_name>	Specifies a tty to use for communication. May be /dev/<something>.
<speed>	Specify a baud rate for data transfer.
active-filter filter-expression	Specify a packet filter used to determine which packets are link activity.
asyncmap *<map>*	Set the async character to <map>.
auth	Require authentication before transmitting packets.
call *name*	Read options from the file /etc/ppp/peers/name.
connect script	Use the specified executable or shell command to set up the serial line.
crtscts	Tell pppd to use hardware flow control to control the flow of data on the serial port.
defaultroute	Add a default route to the system routing tables, using the peer as the gateway, when IPCP negotiation is completed.

disconnect scrip	Run the specified script when **pppd** closes the link.
escape xx,yy,...	Escape the specified list of characters when transmitting. Characters are specified as a comma-separated list of hexadecimal codes.
file name	Read command line options from the specified file.
lock	Tell **pppd** to create a uucp-style lock file for the serial device to ensure exclusive access.
mru n	Specify a Maximum Receive Unit (MRU) of n. The MRU value is the upper limit on the size of packets received.
mtu n	Specify a Maximum Receive Unit (MRU) of n. The MRU value is the upper limit on the size of packets transmitted.
passive	Allow **pppd** to passively wait for a connection.
<local_IP_address>: <remote_IP_address>	Specify the local and/or remote interface IP addresses.
chap-interval n	Rechallenge the peer every n seconds.
chap-max-challenge n	Specify an upper limit on the number of challenges.
chap-restart n	Specify retransmission interval for challenges of n seconds.
debug	Enable connection debugging.
default-asyncmap	Disable asyncmap negotiation.
default-mru	Disable Maximum Receive Unit negotiation.
demand	Tell **ppp** to initiate the link only on demand.
***domain** d*	Append the domain name d to the local host name for authentication purposes.

holdoff *n*	Specify the number of seconds to wait before re-initialization after a link is terminated.
idle *n*	Tell pppd to disconnect if the link is idle for n seconds.
ipcp-accept-local	Tell pppd to accept the peer's idea of our local IP address.
ipcp-accept-remote	Tell pppd to accept the peer's **ide** of its remote IP address.
ipcp-max-configure *n*	Set the maximum number of IPCP configure-request transmissions to n (default 10).
ipx	Enable the IPXCP and IPX protocols.
ipx-network *n*	Set the IPX network number in the IPXCP configure request frame to n, a hexadecimal number (without a leading 0x).
ipx-node *n:m*	Set the IPX node numbers (local:peer).
ipx-router-name <string>	Specify the name of the IPX router.
kdebug *n*	Enable debugging code in the kernel-level PPP driver. The argument n is a number which is the sum of the following values: 1 to enable general debug messages, 2 to request that the contents of received packets be printed, and 4 to request that the contents of transmitted packets be printed.
lcp-echo-failure *n*	Instruct **pppd** to presume the peer is dead when n LCP echo-requests are sent without receiving a valid LCP echo-reply.
lcp-echo-interval *n*	Tell **pppd** to send an LCP echo-request fram?? to the pee?? every n seconds.
lcp-max-configure *n*	Set the maximum number of LCP configure-request transmissions to n (default 10).

lcp-max-terminate *n*	Specify a maximum number of LCP terminate-request transmissions.
lcp-restart *n*	Specify an LCP restart interval.
local	Do not use the modem control lines.
login	Use the system password database for authenticating the peer using PAP, and record the user in the system wtmp file.
maxconnect *n*	Terminate the connection after the specified number of seconds.
modem	Tell **pppd** to use the modem control lines (default).
ms-dns *<addr>*	Allow **pppd** to supply a Microsoft Domain Name Server address to clients.
ms-wins *<addr>*	Allow pppd to supply a Windows Internet Name Server address to clients.
name name	Specify a local system name (for authentication purposes).
netmask *n*	Specify an IP netmask of n.
noaccomp	Disable any use of Address/Control compression.
noauth	Do not require peer authentication.
nobsdcomp	Disable any use of BSD-Compress compression.
noccp	Disable any use of CCP (Compression Control Protocol).
nocrtscts	Disable hardware flow control over the serial port.
nodefaultroute	Disable the default route option.
nodeflate	Disables any use of deflate compression.

nodetach	Do not detach from the controlling terminal.
noip	Disable IPCP negotiation and IP communication.
noipx	Disable the IPXCP and IPX protocols.
nomagic	Disable magic number negotiation.
nopcomp	Disable protocol field compression negotiation.
nopersist	Exit immediately when a connection terminates.
nopredictor1	Do not accept or agree to Predictor-1 compression.
noproxyarp	Disable proxyarp.
pass-filter filter-expression	Specify a packet filter to apply to data packets to determine which packets will be allowed to pass.
persist	Try to re-open a terminated connection rather than exiting.
predictor1	Compress frames using Predictor-1 compression.
refuse-chap	Do not allow authentication with CHAP.
refuse-pap	Do not allow authentication with PAP.
require-chap	Require the peer to authenticate itself using CHAP [Challenge Handshake Authentication Protocol] authentication.
require-pap	Require the peer to authenticate itself using PAP [Password Authentication Protocol] authentication.
silent	Do not transmit LCP packets to initiate a connection.

usehostname	Force the use of the specified hostname as the local system name.
user name	Specify a user name to be used for authenticating on the peer.
vj-max-slots n	TCP/IP header compression and decompression code to n where 2<=n<=16. Specify the number of connection slots to be used by the Van Jacobson.
xonxoff	Use software flow control to control the flow of data on the serial port.

rexecd

Rexecd is the remote execution server. It provides remote program execution capabilities with name/password authentication.

Example: This command has no options. To start rexecd:

rexecd ROOT

rlogind [-ahlLn]

This program is the server for the **rlogin** program. It provides remote login access based on privileged port numbers from trusted hosts. As the use of this daemon can be something of a security hole, you should configure and use it with caution.

Example: To start **rlogind**, allowing use of the .rhosts file for access control (-h option), add the following line to your ***inetd.conf*** file:

```
login stream tcp nowait root /usr/sbin/tcpd in.rlogind
```
ROOT

-a	Ask the host for verification.
-h	Allow use of superuser ".rhosts" files.
-l	Do not allow authentication base on the user's .rhosts file.
-L	Do not allow authentication base on .rhosts hosts.equiv files.
-n	Disable keep-alive messages.

rshd [-ahlnL]

This program is the server for the **rcmd** and **rsh** programs. It provides remote execution capabilities with authentication based on privileged port numbers for trusted hosts. Obviously, the use of this daemon can constitute a huge security hole. Configure and use it with caution.

Example: To start **rshd** with logging (**-L**), add the following line to your ***inetd.conf*** file:

ROOT

```
shell stream tcp nowait root /usr/sbin/tcpd in.rshd -L
```

-l	Prevents authentication based on the user's .rhosts file.
-h	If user is superuser, this option may override the -l option and allow authentication based on .rhosts file.
-n	Disable transport-level keepalive messages.
-L	Log all successful accesses to syslogd as auth.info messages.

rwhod [-bpa]

Rwhod maintains the database used by **rwho** and **ruptime**.

Example: To start **rwhod** allowing both broadcast and point-to-point interfaces:

rwhod -a

-b	Use only broadcast interfaces (e.g., ethernets).
-p	Use only point to point interfaces.
-a	Use all interfaces.

syslogd [-d] [-f *config file*] [-h] [-l *hostlist*] [-m *interval*] [-n] [-p *socket*] [-r] [-s *domainlist*] [-v]

This program provides facilities for logging and kernel message trapping. Logging may be either local or remote.

Example: This daemon is usually invoked at boot time by one or another of the rc scripts. To start **syslogd** with timestamping at 20-minute intervals (**-m** option):

syslogd -m &

-d	Debug mode.
***-f** config file*	Specify an alternate configuration file.
-h	Allow syslogd to forward any remote messages to defined forwarding hosts.
***-l** hostlist*	Specify a host which should be logged only by hostname rather than fully qualified domain name.
***-m** interval*	Mark timestamps to the system log at regular intervals.
-n	Do not auto-background.
***-p** socket*	Specify an alternate UNIX domain socket rather than /dev/log.
-r	Allow syslogd to receive messages from the network via an Internet domain socket.
***-s** domainlist*	Specify domain names to be stripped off before logging.
-v	Display version information and exit.

Daemons

talkd

This daemon is the program which notifies user B that user A wants to have a conversation via **talk**.

Example: This command has no options. **Talkd** is usually started by **inetd**, which uses tcpd to do the actual invocation. To start **talkd**, add the following line to your ***inetd.conf*** file:

```
talk  dgram  udp  wait  root /usr/sbin/tcpd in.talkd
```

tcpd

This daemon is used to provide access control and logging for standard TCP/IP services. It monitors incoming requests for **telnet, finger, ftp,**

exec, rsh, rlogin, tftp, talk, comsat, etc., and services their requests, logging and booting people out as necessary. **Inetd** uses this program to invoke other tcp daemons.

Example: This daemon is usually invoked by **inetd**. To use **tcpd** to invoke ftpd, add the following line to your **inetd.conf** file:

ROOT
```
ftp stream tcp  nowait root /usr/sbin/tcpd in.ftpd -l -a
```

/usr/sbin/in.telnetd [-hns] [-a *authmode*] [-D *debugmode*] [-L loginprg] [-S tos] [-X *authtype*] [-edebug] [-debug port]

Telnetd is the daemon which services telnet requests.

Example: This daemon is usually invoked by **inetd**. To start **telnetd**:

ROOT **telnetd &**

-a authmode	Specify the authentication mode.

debug	Turns on authentication debugging code.
user	Only allow connections when the remote user can provide user authentication information.
valid	Only allow connections when the remote user can provide user authentication information.
other	Equivalent to "valid".
none	Do not require authentication.
off	Disable the authentication code.

-D debugmode	Specify one of the following debug modes:

options	Prints information about the negotiation of telnetoptions.
report	Prints the options information, plus some additional information about what processing is going on.

	netdata	Displays the data stream received by **telnetd**.
	ptydata	Displays data written to the pty.
	exercise	Has not been implemented yet.

-edebug	Enable encryption debugging code.
-h	Disable printing of host information until the login verification is completed.
-L loginprg	Specify a login program other than the default.
-n	Disable TCP keep-alives.
-s	Allow only SecurID logins.
-S *tos*	Set type-of-service to tos.
-X *authtype*	Disable the use of the specified type of authentication.

tftpd [directory ...]

Supports the trivial file transfer protocol.

Example: This daemon is usually invoked by **inetd**. To start **tftpd:**

tftpd &

ROOT

rpc.yppasswdd [-D *directory*] [-e *chsh*|*chfn*]

rpc.yppasswdd [-s *shadow*] [-p *passwd*] [-e chsh|chfn]

When using NIS, change passwords across the network with **yppasswd**. **Yppasswdd** is the server daemon.

Example: To start **yppasswdd**:

ROOT

yppasswdd &

***-D** directory*	Specify a directory where the passwd and shadow passwd files may be found.
***-p** passwdfile*	Tell rpc.yppasswdd to use a source file other than /etc/passwd.
***-s** shadowfile*	Tell rpc.yppasswdd to use a source file other than /etc/passwd.
-e [chsh|chfn]	Enable users to change either their shell or GECOS field.
-m	No effect. Included for compatibility.
-v --version	Display version information and exit.

CHAPTER 14

MACHINE INFORMATION

Introduction

This section contains a grab bag of commands which will provide information about your system's hardware and network position.

arch	System architecture information.
hostname	Set or display hostname information.
hwclock	Set or display hardware clock information.
uname	Machine and operating system information.

Related Files

/etc/hosts	Contains hostname to IP address mappings.
/etc/adjtime	Contains historical information about clock adjustments.

Commands

arch

Output the machine architecture. Output is along the lines of "i386", "i486", "i586", "i686", "alpha", "sparc", "arm", "m68k"...

Example: This command has no options.

arch

hostname [NAME]

If no arguments, hostname displays the name of the current host system. Otherwise, it sets the hostname as specified or displays the specified information.

Example: To set your system name to "odin":

hostname odin

-a, --alias	Show alias name of the host.
-d, --domain	Display DNS domain name.
-F, --file filename	Read hostname from specified file rather than /etc/hosts.
-f, --fqdn, --long	Display fully qualified domain name.
-h, --help	Display help message.
-i, --ip-address	Display host's IP address.
-s, --short	Display short host name.

-V, --version	Display version information.
-v, --verbose	Verbose output.
-y, --yp, --nis	Display NIS domain name.

hwclock --show

hwclock --set --date=newdate

hwclock --systohc

hwclock --hctosys

hwclock --getepoch

hwclock --setepoch --epoch=year

hwclock --adjust

hwclock --version

Display or set the values of the hardware clock. Note that this value is distinct from system time. The hardware clock is entirely independent from software, whereas the system time is mediated by a system interrupt.

Example: To display the time as understood by your hardware clock:

hwclock --show

It is required that you invoke **hwclock** with one of the following options:

--show	Display time to standard output.
--set	Set the clock to the time specified at the --date option.
--hctosys	Set the system time from the hardware clock.
--systohc	Set the hardware clock from the system time.
--adjust	Adjust the hardware clock time.
--getepoch	Display the hardware clock's epoch value. (The epoch value is the number of years since 0 A.D. to which a value of 0 in the hardware clock would refer.)
--setepoch	Set the hardware clock's epoch value to the specified value.
--version	Display the version of hwclock to standard output.

The following are optional:

--date=*date_string*	Specifies the time to which to set the hardware clock. hwclock --set --date="06/27/99 10:15:09"
--epoch=*year*	Specify the value for the epoch year.
--utc	Tells hwclock to keep itself in coordinated universal time.
--directisa	On an ISA machine, tells hwclock to use explicit I/O instructions to access the hardware clock.
--test	Do everything except actually update the hwclock.
--debug	Display debug information.

uname [OPTION]...

Display information about the machine and operating system to standard output. Displays some or all of the following information:

system name, node name, release,

operating system version, machine

Example: To display information about your operating system release:

uname -r

-a, --all	Display all the possible information.
-m, --machine	Display the hardware type.
-n, --nodename	Display the network node hostname.
-p, --processor	Display the processor type.
-r, --release	Display the operating system version.
-s, --sysname	Display the operating system name.
-v	Display the operating system version.

CHAPTER

15

KERNEL

Introduction

Kernel is the word we use to refer to the Linux program itself. The kernel controls access to the hardware and other system resources. The kernel is the single most important program on a system, and thus access to it is, of necessity, highly restricted. The programs described in this section provide the means of interactive access to the kernel.

One of the nice things about Linux is that the source code for the kernel is included in the distribution, specifically in the directory ***/usr/src/linux.*** If you don't like something, change it.

Some parts of the kernel can be compiled separately and linked as needed. These programs are known as **modules**. The linking process depends on the kernel's internal data structure for resolving variable and function names, known as the **symbol table**, being exported for outside use.

TIP

The module names generally make sense. If you're trying to figure out what module is associated with, say, the reverse address resolution protocol, try typing:

modprobe -l | grep rarp

The commands covered in this section include:

depmod	Create a module dependency list.
modprobe	Load or list loadable modules.
insmod	Install a module.
kerneld	Run kernel program in user space.
ksyms	Display kernel symbols.
lsmod	List installed modules.
bdflush	Flush dirty buffers to disk.
rmmod	Remove specified module.

Related Files

/etc/conf.modules	depmod & modprobe configuration file

Commands

depmod [-a]

depmod [-a *version*]

depmod module1.o module2.o ...

modprobe module.o [symbol=*value* ...]

modprobe -t *tag pattern*

modprobe -a -t *tag pattern*

modprobe -l [-t tag] *pattern*

modprobe -r *module*

modprobe -c

The **depmod** and **modprobe** commands are used to manage a modular Linux kernel.

The **depmod** command is used to create a Makefile-esque dependency (modules.dep) file based on the symbols it finds in the set of modules mentioned in the command line. The resultant file can be used by modprobe to automatically load the relevant modules.

Modprobe will load modules in one of two ways:

- It will attempt to load all the modules in a list and stop as soon as one of them successfully loads (useful for loading a single device driver)
- It can load all the modules in a list (useful at boot time)

Example: To create a list of all modules on the system:

ROOT **depmod -a**

Example: To load the module cdrom.o:

ROOT **modprobe cdrom.o**

-a	Work on all modules.
-r	Automatically load a stack of modules.
-l	List available modules.
-t	Limit activity to modules of the specified type.
-c	Display configuration information.
-d	Debug mode.

insmod [-fkmpsxXv] [-o *module_name*] *object_file* [symbol=value ...]

Install a loadable module in the running kernel. This command works by resolving all symbols from the kernel's symbol table, which must be exported.

Example: To install the module rarp.o:

ROOT **insmod /lib/modules/preferred/ipv4/rarp.o**

-f	Force the load even if the running kernel and the kernel version for which the module was compiled do not match.
-k	Set the auto-clean flag on the module.
-m	Output a load map.
-o	Explicitly name the module rather than deriving the name from the base name of the source object file.

-p	Probe the module to see if it could be successfully loaded.
-s	Output everything to syslog(3) instead of the terminal.
-v	Verbose operation.
-X,	Export all the module's external symbols.
-x	Do not export all the module's external symbols.

kerneld [debug] [keep] [delay=<*seconds*>] [type=<*message number*>]

Perform kernel tasks (such as loading and unloading modules) in user space. Typically, this daemon is used for loading and unloading modules.

Example: To invoke kerneld in debug mode:

kerneld debug ROOT

debug	Debug mode.
keep	Ignore all requests for unloading modules.
delay=<seconds>	Delay the removal of modules for the specified number of seconds (60 by default).
type=<message type>	Listen for all messages whose type is less than or equal to <message type>.

ksyms [-a] [-h] [-m]

Display exported kernel symbols (e.g., program variables, function names).

Example: To display the kernel symbol table:

ksyms -a ROOT

-a	Display all symbols, including those from the kernel proper.
-h	Suppress the column header.
-m	Display module information.

lsmod

Display information about loaded modules.

Example: To display information (Module Name, Memory Pages, Used by) about the loaded modules on a system:

lsmod

bdflush [opt]

Flush dirty (used since last flush) buffers back to disk.

Example: To flush the used buffers back to disk:

ROOT

bdflush

-d	Display kernel parameters.
-h	Display help information.
-s *<seconds>*	Call sync every <seconds> seconds.
-f *<seconds>*	Call flush every <seconds> seconds.
-0	Max fraction of LRU list to examine for dirty blocks.
-1	Max number of dirty blocks to write each time bdflush activated.
-2	Number of clean buffers to be loaded onto free list by refill_freelist.
-3	Dirty block threshold for activating bdflush in refill_freelist.
-4	Percentage of cache to scan for free clusters.
-5	Time for data buffers to age before flushing.
-6	Time for non-data (dir, bitmap, etc) buffers to age before flushing.
-7	Time buffer cache load average constant.
-8	LAV ratio (used to determine threshold for buffer fratricide).

rmmod [-as] *module*

Remove the specified module from the running kernel.

Example: To remove the rarp module from the running kernel:

rmmod rarp

-a	Attempt to remove all unused modules.
-s	Direct output to the system log rather than the terminal.

PART

2

MANIPULATING DATA & TEXT FILES

CHAPTER

16

DISPLAYING FILES

Introduction

There are a variety of ways to get the contents of a file on screen. Most people seem to agree that **less** is the most versatile paginator; consequently, you rarely see the others these days. Also included here are a few of the more specialized text display programs (e.g., **tac, rev**) that come in handy from time to time.

The commands covered in this section are designed to display the contents of an ASCII file, in whole or in part, to the screen. They include:

cat	Send contents of a file to standard output.
head	Display the top of a file to standard output.
less	Display a file, with scrolling.
look	Display lines which begin with a given string.
rev	Display lines from last character to first.
tac	Display lines in reverse order.
tail	Display the bottom of a file to standard output.

Commands

cat [OPTION] [*FILE*]...

Copies the specified file (or standard input) to standard output.

Example: To display the contents of the file ***/etc/passwd*** to standard output:

cat /etc/passwd

TIP Frequently used on the left side of a pipe to send the contents of a file to some other program as input, e.g.:

cat database.dat | sort -rn

-A, --show-all	Equivalent to "-vET".
-b, --number-nonblank	Include line numbers for output (nonblank lines only). Number all nonblank output lines, starting with 1.
-e	Equivalent to "-vE".
-E, --show-ends	Display a "$" after the end of each line.
-n, --number	Include line numbers in output.
-s, --squeeze-blank	Condense any sequence of two or more blank lines into a single blank line.
-t	Same as "-vT".
-T, --show-tabs	Output <TAB> characters as "^I".
-u	No effect; included for Unix compatibility.
-v, --show-nonprinting	Output control characters in "^whatever" format, excepting only line feed and tab.

head [OPTION]... [*FILE*]...

head -NUMBER [OPTION]... [*FILE*]...

Display the first part of the specified file(s) to standard output.

Example: To print the first 300 bytes (**-c** option) of textfile.txt to standard output:

head -c 300 textfile.txt

-c *BYTES*, ***--bytes=****BYTES*	Output the specified number of bytes rather than initial lines. Byte count may be specified in blocks (b), kilobytes (k), and megabytes (m).
-n N, --lines=*N*	Output the specified number of lines (default is 10).
-q, --quiet, --silent	Do not include file names in output.
-v, --verbose	Include file names in output.

less -?

less --help

less -V

less --version

less [-[+]aBcCdeEfgGiImMnNqQrsSuUVwX]

[-b *bufs***] [-h** *lines***] [-j** *line***] [-k** *keyfile***]**

[-{oO} *logfile***] [-p** *pattern***] [-P** *prompt***] [-t** *tag***]**

[-T *tagsfile***] [-x** *tab***] [-y** *lines***] [-[z]** *lines***]**

[+[+]cmd] [--] [*filename***]...**

The preferred method for displaying text files. This program's name is an illustration of one of the big truisms in computer science—when you've been programming for twenty hours, almost anything is funny. The gag is that this program is an improvement on a program called "more" that also displayed stuff to standard output. "less" is "more". Get it? Hahahaha. Ha. The big improvement over "more" is that you can scroll backward as well as forward within the file.

Example: To paginate a lengthy display, pipe it to less:

grep -n [AaEeIiOoUu] | less

Less is interactive; once invoked, there are a variety of ways to specify how far and in what direction you wish to scroll. The following may be preceded by an integer, hereafter N, which specifies some number of lines.

h or H Help:	Display a summary of the interactive commands.
SPACE, ^V, f, ^F	Scroll forward N lines (one window by default).
z	Like space, but with the option to specify a new window size.
ESC-SPACE	Scroll forward a full screen, ignoring possible end of file.
RETURN, ^N, e, ^E, j, ^J	Scroll forward N lines.
d, ^D	Scroll forward N lines, default .5 screen.
b, ^B or ESC-v	Scroll backward N lines, default 1 window.
w	Like ESC-f, but with if N specified, it becomes the new window size.
y, ^Y, ^P, k, ^K	Scroll backward N lines, default 1.
u, ^U	Scroll backward N lines, default .5 screen.
ESC-) or RIGHTARROW	Scroll horizontally right N characters, default 8.
ESC-(or LEFTARROW	Scroll horizontally left N characters, default 8.
r or ^R or ^L	Redraw the screen.
R	Repaint the screen, discarding any buffered input.
F	Scroll forward, and keep trying to read when the end of file is reached.
g, <, ESC-<	Go to line N in the file, default 1.
G or > or ESC->	Go to line N in the file, default the end of the file.
p or %	Go to a position N percent into the file.

{	If a left curly bracket appears in the top line displayed on the screen, the { command will trace through the file to the matching right curly bracket.
}	If a right curly bracket appears in the bottom line displayed on the screen, the } command will trace through the file to the matching left curly bracket.
(	Like {, but applies to parentheses rather than curly brackets.
)	Like }, but applies to parentheses rather than curly brackets.
[	Like {, but applies to square brackets rather than curly brackets.
]	Like }, but applies to square brackets rather than curly brackets.
ESC-^F	Followed by two characters, acts like {, but uses the two characters as open and close brackets.
ESC-^B	Followed by two characters, acts like }, but uses the two characters as open and close brackets.
m	Followed by any lowercase letter, marks the current position with that letter.
', X^X	Followed by any lowercase letter, returns to the position which was previously marked with that letter.
/pattern, ESC-/pattern	Search forward in the file for the N-th line containing the pattern.
^N or !	Search for lines which do NOT match the pattern.
^E or *	If the specified pattern is not found in the current file, continue looking in the next file listed.
^F or @	Begin searching for pattern in the first line of the first file listed (regardless of which file is currently displayed).

^K	Keep current position, but highlight any text matching pattern.
^R	Don't interpret regular expression metacharacters.
?pattern, ESC-? pattern	Search backward in the file for pattern.
n	Continue previous search.
N	Continue previous search, but in reverse direction.
ESC-n	Continue search, but crossing file boundaries.
ESC-N	Repeat previous search, but in the reverse direction and crossing file boundaries.
ESC-u	Undo search highlighting.
:e [filename]	Look at a new file.
^X^V, E	Same as :e.
:n	Switch to the next file in the command line list.
:p	Switch to the previous file in the command line list.
:x	Switch to the first file in the command line list.
=, ^G, :f	Display information about the current file (name, line num...).
-[option]	While the program is running, set the specified option.
-+[option]	Reset the specified option to its default setting.
--[option]	Reset the specified option to the opposite of its default setting.
_[option]	Display the current value of the specified option.

+cmd	Run specified command each time a new file is examined.
V	Display the version number.

Command Line Options

-?, --help	Display an online summary of commands.
-a	Start search after last line displayed on screen.
-bn	Use only the specified number of buffers on each file.
-B	Force **less** to limit use of buffers to number specified by -bn.
-c	Redraw from top line down (as opposed to bottom up).
-C	Same as -c, but clear the screen first.
-d	Suppress the dumb terminal error message.
-e	Automatically exit upon reaching end-of-file for 2nd time.
-E	Automatically exit upon reaching end-of-file for 1st time.
-f	Force **less** to open directories, device special, and other non-text files.
-g	Highlight only the particular string found by the last search command.
-G	Do not highlight strings found by search commands.
-hn	Scroll backward to upper limit of n lines.
-i	Treat uppercase and lowercase letters as identical in searches.
-I	Like -i, but searches ignore case even if the pattern contains uppercase letters.
-jn	If found, position search target at screen line n.

-kfilename	Use specified file as a lesskey file.
-m	Prompt verbosely.
-M	Prompt extremely verbosely.
-n	Do not print line numbers.
-N	Number the displayed lines.
-ofilename	Copy input to the specified file while outputting to display.
-Ofilename	Same as -o; overwrite existing file, if necessary.
-ppattern	Same as +/pattern.
-P	Prompt.
-q	Be somewhat quieter than the default.
-Q	Run in total silence; never ring the terminal bell.
-r	Include raw control characters in output.
-s	Squeeze. Condense 2 or more blank lines into a single blank line.
-S	Truncate long lines rather than folding to next line.
-ttag	Edit the file containing tag.
-Ttagsfile	Use the specified file instead of "tags".
-u	Output backspace and carriage returns as printable characters.
-U	Output backspace, carriage returns and tabs as printable characters.
-V, --version	Output version number.
-w	Use blank lines to represent lines past end-of-file (as opposed to ~).
-xn	Set tab stop every nth position.

-X	Do not send termcap initialization strings to the terminal.
-yn	Scroll forward to a maximum of n lines.
[z]n	Set the default scrolling window size to be n lines.
-"	Set the filename quoting character.
--	Delimiter only; used to mark the end of options.
+	Delimiter; anything which follows is taken as an initial argument to less.

look [-dfa] [-t *termchar*] *string* [*file*]

Display any lines in the specified file which contain a prefix of string.

Example: To display all lines that start with the string "Example":

look Example disp.txt

-d	Use alphanumeric characters only in comparisons.
-f	Tread upper- and lowercase letters as equivalent.
-a	Specify use of the alternate dictionary /usr/dict/web2
***-t** char*	Specify that an occurrence of character char terminates any comparisons.

rev [file]

Copy the lines of file to standard output in reverse order.

Example: This command has no options. If your input file was:

```
abcd
efgh
ijkl
```

then

rev infile

would yield

```
dcba
hgfe
lkji
```

tac [OPTION] *FILE*

Copy lines to standard output in reverse order. Typically used to reverse files containing records separated by some separator (new line by default). Opposite of "cat". Ha-ha.

Example: If your input file was:

```
abcd
efgh
ijkl
```

then

tac infile

would yield

```
ijkl
efgh
abcd
```

-b, --before	Attach the separator to the beginning of the record which it precedes in the file.
-r, --regex	Treat the separator string as a regular expression.
-s SEPARATOR, --separator=SEPARATOR	Use the specified characters as the record separator (instead of newline).

tail [OPTION]... [*FILE*]...

tail -NUMBER [OPTION]... [*FILE*]...

tail +NUMBER [OPTION]... [*FILE*]...

Print the last portion of a file for standard output.

Example: To print the last 20 lines of textfile.txt:

tail -n 20 textfile.txt

***-c** BYTES, **--bytes=**BYTES*	Output the specified number of bytes, rather than lines. Bytes may be specified in blocks (b), kilobytes (k), or megabytes (m).
-f, --follow	Keep looking for additional characters at the end of a (presumably growing) file.
-n N, --lines=N'	Output the last N lines (default 10).
-q, -quiet, --silent	Do not include file name headers in output.
-v, --verbose	Include file names in output.

CHAPTER

17

COMPARING & MERGING FILES

Introduction

The commands in this section operate on the contents of files, usually text files. In most cases they are capable of including or excluding patterns, as specified by regular expressions. See the chapter on "Finding Stuff" for more information about regular expressions.

TIP The dash character, "-", is usually used to specify standard input as one of the input files.

comm	Compare 2 sorted files; outputs common lines.
cmp	Compare 2 files, usually binaries.
diff	Show the difference between 2 files.
diff3	Show the differences between 3 files.
sdiff	Merge 2 files

Commands

comm [OPTION]... *FILE1 FILE2*

Compares two files and prints the results in three-column output:

unique to file1   unique to file2   common lines.

The files must be sorted before **comm** can be used.

Example: To compare the entries in two database files, t1old.db and t1new.db:

comm t1old.db t1new.db

cmp OPTIONS... *FROM-FILE* [*TO-FILE*]

-1	Suppress printing of column 1.
-2	Suppress printing of column 2.
-3	Suppress printing of column 3.

cmp compares two files and outputs the first byte & line number where they differ.

TIP Use **cmp**, rather than **diff**, to compare binary files.

Example: To compare file1.txt and file2.txt, skipping the initial 1024 bytes, and including the characters in the display:

cmp --ignore-initial=1024 -c file1 file2

-c	Include the differing characters in the display.
--ignore-initial=BYTES	Skip over the specified number of bytes before beginning to compare.
-l	Include the offsets and octal values of any differing bytes in the output.
--print-chars	Include the differing characters in the output.
--quiet, -s, --silent	Don't output anything.
--verbose	Include offsets and octal values of any differing bytes in the output.
-v, --version	Output the version number.

diff OPTIONS... *from-file to-file*

Display the differences between the two files specified on the command line.

Example: To display the difference between a file recently modified and an older version of the same file:

diff source.c source.old

Example: To display the differences between a file recently modified and an older version of the same file, excluding any changes to VAR1:

diff -exclude=VAR1 source.c source.old

-LINE_CNT	Include the specified number of lines of context when outputting differences. Obsolete.
-a	Treat all files (including binaries) as text.
-b	Do not report differences in amount of white space.
-B	Do not report differences in number of blank lines.
--binary	Perform comparisons in binary mode.
--brief	Report only if differences exist; do not list differences.
-c	Output using context format.
-C LINES, --context[=*LINES****]***	Output using context format, including the specified number of lines with each difference.
--changed-group-format=*FORMAT*	Use FORMAT to output a line group containing differing lines from both files in if-then-else format.
-d	Use a different (usually slower) algorithm which may return fewer changes.

-D *NAME*	Make merged "#ifdef" format output, conditional on the preprocessormacro NAME.
-e, --ed	Format output as an "ed" script.
--exclude=*PATTERN*	When performing a recursive comparison on subdirectories, ignore any whose names match PATTERN.
--exclude-from=*FILE*	When performing a recursive comparison on subdirectories, ignore any whose names match the patterns contained in FILE.
--expand-tabs	Convert tabs to some number of spaces.
-f	Format output similar to an ed script, but has changes ordered as they appear in the file.
-F *REGEXP*	Output, along with some surrounding lines (for context), any value that matches REGEXP.
--forward-ed	Format output similar to an ed script, but has changes ordered as they appear in the file.
-h	No effect; included for backward compatibility.
-H	Process files using heuristics; may speed processing of large files.
--horizon-lines=*LINES*	Do not discard the last LINES lines of the common prefix and the first LINES lines of the common suffix.
-i	Treat upper- and lowercase letters as equivalent.

***-I** REGEXP*	Ignore changes that just insert or delete lines that match REGEXP.
***--ifdef=**NAME*	Make merged if-then-else output using NAME.
--ignore-all-space	Ignore any white spaces (including <TAB>s) when comparing lines.
--ignore-blank-lines	Ignore any changes that involve entirely blank lines.
--ignore-case	Treat upper- and lowercase letters as equivalent.
--ignore-matching-lines=REGEXP	Ignore differences that involve lines matching REGEXP.
--ignore-space-change	Ignore changes in the amount of white space.
--initial-tab	Prefix a tab instead of a space when formatting output.
-l	Paginate output using "pr".
***-L** LABEL*	Substitute LABEL for the filename when outputting in context format.
***--label=**LABEL*	Substitute LABEL for the filename when outputting in context format.
--left-column	When outputting in side-by-side format, output only the left column of two common lines.
***--line-format=**FORMAT*	Use the specified FORMAT to output all input lines.
--minimal	Use a different algorithm to find a (possibly) smaller group of changes.

-n	Format output in RCS format.
-N, --new-file	When comparing directories, if a file exists in one, pretend it is (at least) present in other directories.
--new-group-format=*FORMAT*	Output a group of lines taken from just the second file in if-then-else format.
--new-line-format=*FORMAT*	Use FORMAT to output a line taken from just the second file in if-then-else format.
--old-group-format=*FORMAT*	Use FORMAT to output a group of lines taken from just the first file in if-then-else format.
--old-line-format=*FORMAT*	Use FORMAT to output a line taken from just the first file in if-then-else format.
-p	When diff-ing C files, include the function name in any output.
-P	When comparing directories, if a file appears only in the second directory of the two, treat it as present but empty in the other.
--paginate	Pass the output through "pr" to paginate it.
-q	Report only whether the files differ, not the details of the differences.
-r	When comparing directories, recursively compare any subdirectories found.
--rcs	Output RCS-format diffs; like "-f", except that each command specifies the number of lines affected.

--recursive	When comparing directories, recursively compare any subdirectories found.
--report-identical-files	Report when two files are the same.
-s	Report when two files are the same.
-S *FILE*	Specify a start file to use when comparing directories.
--sdiff-merge-assist	Include extra information (of use only to sdiff) in output.
--show-c-function	When diff-ing C files, include the function name in any output.
--show-function-line=REGEXP	When outputting in context or unified format, include some of the last preceding line that matches REGEXP.
--side-by-side	Format output side-by-side.
--speed-large-files	Use heuristics to speed handling of large files.
--starting-file=FILE	When comparing directories, start with the specified FILE.
--suppress-common-lines	When outputting in side-by-side format, do not print common lines.
-t	Expand any tabs to spaces.
-T	Prefix any output with a tab rather than a space.
--text	Treat all tiles (including binaries) as text.

-u	Output using the unified output format.
--unchanged-group-format=*FORMAT*	Use FORMAT to output a group of common lines taken from both files in if-then-else format.
--unchanged-line-format=*FORMAT*	Use FORMAT to output a line common to both files in if-then-else format.
--unidirectional-new-file	When comparing directories, if a file appears only in the second directory of the two, treat it as present but empty in the other.
-U *LINES,* ***--unified[=****LINES]*	Output in unified output format, displaying LINES lines of context.
-v, --version	Output the version number of "diff".
-w	Ignore white space when comparing lines.
-W COLUMNS, --width=*COLUMNS*	Specifies an output width of COLUMNS when using side-by-side format.
-x *PATTERN*	When comparing directories, skip over files and subdirectories whose names match PATTERN.
-X *FILE*	When comparing directories, skip over files and subdirectories whose names match any pattern contained in FILE.

diff3 OPTIONS... MOD1 ORIGINAL MOD2

Compare 3 files. Any of the three may be standard input (specified by "-").

Example: To show the overlapping changes between three text files:

diff3 -overlap-only f1.c f2.c f3.c

-a	Treat all files as text.
-A	Incorporate all changes from ORIGINAL to MOD2 into MOD1.
-e	Generate an "ed" script that incorporates all the changes from ORIGINAL to MOD2 into MOD1.
-E	Generate an "ed" script as in -e option, but include bracket lines from overlapping changes' first and third files.
--ed	Output an "ed" script that incorporates any changes from ORIGINAL to MOD2 into MOD1.
--easy-only	Like "-e" option, but include only non-overlapping changes.
-i	Include commands at the end of any "ed" script.
--initial-tab	Prefix any output with a tab rather than spaces.
***-L** LABEL, **--label=**LABEL*	Use the specified LABEL for any brackets output by the -A, -E, or -X options.
-m, --merge	Apply the edit script to the MOD1 file and send the result to standard output.
--overlap-only	Like the -e option, but output only changes which overlap.
--show-all	Incorporate into MOD1 any changes from ORIGINAL to MOD2. Show overlaps with bracket lines.

--show-overlap	Like "-e", except bracket lines from overlapping changes' first and third files.
-T	Prefix any output with a TAB rather than spaces.
--text	Treat all files (including binaries) as text.
-v, --version	Display the version number.
-x	Like "-e", except output only the overlapping changes.
-X	Like "-x", except surround changes with a bracket.
-3	Like "-e", except output only the nonoverlapping changes.

sdiff -o *OUTFILE* OPTIONS... *FROM-FILE TO-FILE*

Merge two files and output the results to OUTFILE.

Example: To interactively merge the files source1 and source2 into the file result:

sdiff -o result source1 source2

-a	Treat all files (including binaries) as text.
-b	Do not consider changes in the amount of white space.
-B	Do not consider changes involving blank lines.
-d	Use a different algorithm which (may) return a smaller set of changes.
-H	Use a heuristic designed to speed handling of large files.
--expand-tabs	When outputting, expand tabs to spaces.

-i	Treat uppercase and lowercase letters as equivalent.
-I *REGEXP*	Do not consider addition/subtraction of lines which match REGEXP.
--ignore-all-space	Ignore white space when comparing lines.
--ignore-blank-lines	Ignore changes that just insert or delete blank lines.
--ignore-case	Treat uppercase and lowercase letters as equivalent.
--ignore-matching-lines=REGEXP	Do not consider addition/subtraction of lines which match REGEXP.
--ignore-space-change	Ignore changes in amount of white space.
-l, --left-column	Output only the left column of two common lines.
--minimal	Use different algorithm which finds a smaller set of changes.
-o *FILE*, ***--output=****FILE*	Send merged output to FILE.
-s, --suppress-common-lines	Suppress output of common lines.
--speed-large-files	Use a heuristic designed to speed handling of large files.
-t	When outputting, expand tabs into spaces.
--text	Treat all files (including binaries) as text.
-v, --version	Display the version number.

-w COLUMNS, --width=COLUMNS	Output using the specified column width.
-W	Do not consider horizontal white space when comparing lines.

CHAPTER

18

DATA FILES

Introduction

The commands in this section do bulk modification of the contents of text files. They are intended for work on data files—output from spreadsheets, databases, etc.—rather than regular natural language text. In general, these commands can:

- Chop files horizontally or vertically
- Sort the file contents
- Compress or expand spaces in a file
- Reformat the file to a new width

A **delimiter** is a character (e.g., a space, a colon, a bar, or just about anything else) that indicates the end of a word. For example, the space is one delimiter for regular English sentences. The colon (":") is the delimiter for the ***/etc/passwd*** file.

If you're looking for something more along the lines of a general purpose editor of text files, see Chapter 20.

column	Format input into columns.
colrm	Remove the specified columns.
csplit	Split file into sections.
cut	Remove the specified columns from a file.

expand	Expand tabs into spaces.
fmt	Format file to a specified width.
fold	Format file to a specified width.
merge	Merge two descendants of a file.
paste	Merge files horizontally.
sort	Sort file contents.
split	Break big files into smaller files.
tr	Translate characters.
unexpand	Compress spaces into tabs.
uniq	Segregate duplicate lines within a file.

Commands

colrm [*startcol* [*endcol*]]

Remove the specified columns from a file. Reads from standard input. Startcol must be specified. If no endcol is specified, **colrm** will remove all columns up to the end of the line. Otherwise, **colrm** will remove all the columns from startcol to endcol.

Example: To remove the first three characters from each line in a testfile:

cat testfile | colrm 1 3

column [-tx] [-c *columns*] [-s *sep*] [*input_file* ...]

This program formats the input data into multiple columns. Typically, you will be formatting a file; however, if no file is specified, **column** will read from standard input.

Example: To create a table from a text file delimited by "|"s:

column -t -s \| datafile.txt > table.txt

Useful for formatting data created by databases and spreadsheets. TIP

-c	Format output for a display the specified number of columns wide.
-s	Specify character(s) used to delimit columns.
-t	Format output as a table.
-t	Determine the number of columns the input contains and create a table. Columns are delimited with whitespace, by default, or pretty-printing displays.
-x	Force column to fill columns before filling rows. (Default is to fill rows before columns.)

csplit [OPTION]... *PATTERN...*

Split the input set into output files according to the criteria set by PATTERN. The output filenames are constructed of a prefix ("xx" by default) and a suffix (00-99 by default).

Example: To split up a file into 100 line segments:

csplit -k testfile 100 {*}

Example: To split up file into segments delimited by the word "Chapter":

csplit -k testfile /Chapter/ {*}

Use with the -k option; otherwise, you usually don't get anything.

PATTERN types

line_num	Copy to output all lines from input up to but not including line_num.
{repeat_count}	Used with the other options to specify the number of times to repeat the splitting. May be either an integer or, to repeat until the input is depleted, an asterisk.

/reg_exp/[[+l-]offset]	Copy to output all lines from input all lines up to, but not including, the line containing a match for regular_expression. Optionally, include (+ offset) or exclude (- offset) the specified number of lines ahead of or behind the match line.
%reg_exp%[offset]	Discard all input up to the line that matches reg_exp.

***-f** PREFIX, **--prefix=**PREFIX*	Use the specified prefix when constructing output filenames.
***-b** SUFFIX, **--suffix=**SUFFIX*	Use the specified suffix when constructing output filenames.
***-n** DIGITS, **--digits=**DIGITS*	Construct output filenames that are DIGITS digits long.
-k, --keep-files	In case of error, keep the output files. (Default is to remove them.)
-z, --elide-empty-files	Do not generate zero length output files.
-s, -q, --silent, --quiet	Suppress printing of output file sizes.

cut [OPTION]... [*FILE*]...

Write to standard output the specified parts of the input set. The RANGEs are specified as integers separated by a dash (e.g., 1-9). There may be more than one range specified (e.g., 1-9, 12-43). Separate multiple ranges with commas.

Example: To print to standard output the first three fields in a file delimited by the vertical bar symbol:

cut -f 1,2,3 -d \| testfile

Example: To print to standard output the first five characters of each line in the file testfile:

cut -c 1-5 testfile

***-b** RANGE, **--bytes=**RANGE*	Output only the bytes specified in RANGE
***-c** RANGE, **--characters=**RANGE*	Output only output the characters specified by RANGE.
***-f** RANGE, **--fields=**RANGE*	Output only output the fields specified by RANGE. By default, fields are delimited by TABS.
***-d** DELIM, **--delimiter=**DELIM*	Optionally, specify a field delimiter other than <TAB>.
-s, --only-delimited	When used with -f, ignore lines which do not contain the field delimiter character.

expand [OPTION]... [*FILE*]...

Used to turn <TAB>s into spaces. Reads from standard input (default) or a file.

-TAB1[,TAB2]... ***-t** TAB1[,TAB2]...* ***--tabs=**TAB1[,TAB2]...*	Set the tab stops. If only one TAB is specified, it will space any succeeding tab stops at equivalent intervals. Otherwise, multiple <TAB> stops may be set at the specified columns.
-i, --initial	Convert only tabs that precede non-space or non-tab characters.

fmt [OPTION]... [*FILE*]...

Reformat input set to produce lines of (at most) a certain width. (Default = 75.) Preserves blank lines and spaces by default.

Example: To format textfile into a file 65 lines wide and send the results to standard output:

fmt -w 65 textfile

-c, --crown-margin	Tells fmt to preserve the indentation of the first two lines within a paragraph and align the left margin of any subsequent lines with the second line.
-t, --tagged-paragraph	Like -c, except that if indentation of the first and second lines of the paragraph match, the first line is treated as a one-line paragraph.
-s, --split-only	Split lines only, never join.
-u, --uniform-spacing	Reduce spacing between words to one space and between sentences to two spaces.
-WIDTH, -w *WIDTH*, ***--width=****WIDTH*	Force "fmt" to fill lines to specify width. By default, fmt leaves a little room at the end of the line.
-p *PREFIX*, ***--prefix=****PREFIX*	Format only lines beginning with PREFIX.

fold [OPTION]... [*FILE*]...

Write each input file (or standard input) to standard output, breaking any lines longer than 80 characters.

Example: To write textfile to standard output in 40 byte length lines:

fold -b 40 textfile

TIP Use the -b option when you're concerned with size rather than appearance. A <tab> takes up one byte, but looks like several spaces.

-b, --bytes	Count bytes rather than columns.
-s, --spaces	Try to break only at word boundaries.
-w *WIDTH*, ***--width=****WIDTH*	Use lines of width WIDTH rather than the default of 80.

merge [options] *mod1_file original_file mod2_file*

Say mod1_file and mod2_file are both modified versions of original_file. **merge** incorporates into mod1_file all of the changes that turned original_file into mod2_file. **merge** has problems when both mod1_file and mod2_file worked on the same chunk of lines. In that case, both sets of modifications are included, together with a message indicating what was done.

Example: To merge the changes you made to your homework last night with the changes you made last Sunday:

merge homework.yestrdy homework.c homework.sun

-A	In case of conflicting modifications, mod2_file wins.
-E, -e	Specify varying levels of information in case of conflicts.
-L label	Specify a label to be used instead of the corresponding filename, in case of conflict.
-p	Rather than overwrite mod1_file, send results to standard output.
-q	Suppress warning about conflicts.

paste [OPTION]... [*FILE*]...

Merge the specified files horizontally.

Example: Say you have 3 files, f1, f2, and f3. f1 contains 1 line: "abc". f2 contains 1 line: "def". f3 contains 1 line: "ghi". In that case,

paste f1 f2 f3

would yield:

abc def ghi

-s, --serial	Paste the lines of each file on a separate line rather than merging them onto a single line.
-d *DELIM-LIST*, ***--delimiters*** *DELIM-LIST'*	Use the listed delimiter(s) instead of <TAB> to separate the merged files.

sort [OPTION]... [*FILE*]...

Sort (or at least compare) the lines in the input set. Write the results to standard output by default. May also be used to merge files or check if they are already sorted.

Example: To sort the contents of file1 and file2 numerically, merging them into file3:

sort -nr file1 file2 > file3

-c	Check to see whether the files are already sorted.
-m	Merge the files while sorting.
-b	Ignore leading blanks.
-d	Ignore all characters except letters, digits, and blanks when sorting.
-f	Treat lowercase and uppercase characters as if they were the same.
-g	Sort numerically, but also allow floating point numbers.
-i	Ignore non-printable characters.
-M	Order any 3-letter month abbreviations (Jan., Feb., ...) by month rather than alphabetically.
-n	Sort numerically.
-r	Reverse the results of the sort.
***-o** OUTPUT-FILE*	Send results to OUTPUT-FILE rather than standard output.
***-t** SEPARATOR*	Use character SEPARATOR as the field separator when finding the sort keys in each line.

tr [OPTION]... *SET1* [*SET2*]

tr (translate) copies standard input to standard output, while making one of the following modifications to the data stream:

1. Translate (and optionally squeeze) specified characters.
2. Squeeze repeated characters.
3. Delete characters.
4. Delete characters, then squeeze repeated characters from the result.

The idea is that a character in the ordered set SET1 is translated into the corresponding character in SET2.

Example: To convert all uppercase letters in a file into lowercase letters and store in the file uppercase.txt:

cat sourcefile | tr '[:upper:]' '[:lower:]' > uppercase.txt

Backslash escapes	A backslash followed by a character not listed below causes an error message.

\a	Control-G
\b	Control-H
\f	Control-L
\n	Control-J
\r	Control-M
\t	Control-I
\v	Control-K
\OOO'	The character with the value given by OOO, which is 1 to 3 octal digits

Ranges	Specify a range by giving the first and last characters specified by a dash (e.g., A-Z, 0-9).
Repeated characters	The notation "[C*N]" in SET2 expands to N copies of character C (e.g., [a*6] = aaaaaa).
Character classes	Some predefined character classes are available:

Data Files

alnum	Letters and digits.
alpha	Letters.
blank	Horizontal whitespace.
cntrl	Control characters.
digit	Digits.
graph	Printable characters, not including space.
lower	Lowercase letters.
print	Printable characters, including space.
punct	Punctuation characters.
space	Horizontal or vertical whitespace.
upper	Uppercase letters.
xdigit	Hexadecimal digits.

-d, --delete	Delete any input characters found in SET1. When given just the "--delete" ("-d") option, "tr" removes any input characters that are in SET1.
-s, --squeeze-repeats	Replace each character in SET1 that is repeated with a single instance of that character.

unexpand [OPTION]... [*FILE*]...

Copies standard input to standard output while replacing any sequences of spaces that are equal to a <TAB> with (you guessed it) a <TAB>.

Example: To compress any sequences of five spaces in textfile into a <TAB>:

unexpand -i 5 -a textfile

-TAB1[,TAB2]..., ***-t** TAB1[,TAB2]...,* ***--tabs=**TAB1[,TAB2]...*	Set the tab stops. If only one TAB is specified, it will space any succeeding tab stops at equivalent intervals. Otherwise, multiple <TAB> stops may be set at the specified columns.
-i	Specify the width of a single tab. (Default is 8.)
-a, --all	Convert all applicable strings, not just the initial ones.

uniq [OPTION]... [*INPUT* [*OUTPUT*]]

uniq goes through a sorted file and discards any repeats it finds.

Example: Say your company has engaged in a partnership with a bunch of idiots who are supposed to ship you a data file each month. You're supposed to load it into your database and do stuff with it. The guys who shipped you the file say that the field which occurs from characters 5 to 10 is the primary key, but they use some awful Precambrian excuse for a database and Informix won't let you load their file because what they're trying to call a primary key isn't unique. The following will make your problem go away:

uniq +4 -w 6 -u datafile > datafile.good

The +4 option tells **uniq** to ignore the first four characters. The **-w 6** specifies that only six characters need be unique. The **-u** option tells the program to discard any duplicates, and the > character redirects the results from standard output to the file datafile.good.

***-N, -f** N, **--skip-fields=**N*	Skip N tab-delimited fields on each line before checking for uniqueness.
***+N, -s** N, **--skip-chars=**N*	Skip N characters before checking for uniqueness.
-c, --count	Add a count of the number of times each line occurred to the output.
-i, --ignore-case	When comparing lines, treat uppercase and lowercase as equivalent.

-d, --repeated	Print only the duplicated lines.
-u, --unique	Print only the unique lines.
***-w** N**, --check-chars=**N*	Compare only N characters on each line (instead of the whole line.)

CHAPTER 19

DOCUMENT FORMATTING

Introduction

The commands and systems in this section are concerned with document formatting. For the most part, this means embedding control sequences in regular ASCII text files which are interpreted as printable symbols by some document formatting system (e.g., **TeX**, **groff**).

TeX

The TeX document formatting system is the creation of Donald Knuth, one of the big names in computer science. Among other things, he is the author of the Art of Computer Programming series. Legend has it that the TeX system was created when Knuth realized he needed a typesetting system that could display the equations in the series. He took a quick eight years off to write TeX, then got right back to work. A popular extension to the TeX system is LaTeX, which provides extensions that enable you to structure the documents.

Document Formatting with Tex

1. Create an ASCII document containing the embedded control codes with <your favorite text editor>. By convention, these documents are stored with a .tex extension.
2. Compile the document into a device independent intermediate file with **tex** (or **latex**).
3. View and print the resulting .dvi file with **xdvi**.
4. Depending on your printer type, use one of the dvi printer commands (**dvips**, **dvilj**) to print the dvi file.

If you're so inclined, you can type in the following example file to get a feel for how TeX works. If not, pretend you did, as the file is used repeatedly in the examples below (see Figure 19.1).

```
\documentclass[12pt]{article}
\begin{document}

\section{A Short Introduction to \LaTeX}
Note how the use of the \begin{verbatim} \LaTeX
\end{verbatim} control sequence in the section
heading generated the \LaTeX symbol.  There are a
wide variety of control sequences available,
including most of the mathematical symbols and
associated greek letters and the standard
typographical symbols.  \LaTeX reserves the
following symbols: \textbf{\$, \&, \#, \%, \_, \{,
\}} which must be preceded with a backslash in the
course of normal typing.

\section{Document Classes}
Documents have classes (e.g. letter, article, book)
which must be defined with the
\begin{verbatim}
\documentclass{}
\end{verbatim}
specifier at the head of your document.

\section{Sample Equation}
In this section we'll see how to create a sample
equation.  In general you're going to be using
function specifiers
\begin{verbatim}
\sqrt{}
```

```
\frac{}
\end{verbatim}
with their operators encased in the curly braces.


\begin{center}
\begin{equation}
x = -b \pm \sqrt{ \frac{b^{(2)}}{4ac}}
\end{equation}
\end{center}

For further documentation, let me refer you to the
\emph{TeXbook}, written by the creator of \LaTeX,
Donald Knuth, and \emph{\LaTeX user's guide and
Reference Manual} by Leslie Lamport.

\end{document}
```

Figure 19-1 The file example.tex

groff

The **groff** (GNU roff) system is Linux's version of the nroff/troff document formatting system. Groff is a front end for **nroff** and **troff**. **nroff** and **troff** were developed at Bell Labs and together make up the standard document formatting system on Unix. For example, the **man** pages are created with this system.

Like TeX, **groff** uses embedded control codes to specify the format of the end-result document. Unlike TeX, **groff** can produce plain ascii files as output.

Where TeX commands can occur anywhere on the line, groff formatting commands are the first things you see on a given line, as shown in the following example (Figure 19.2).

```
.TH example
.SH name
example - simple groff example
.SH SYNOPSIS
example [options] file
.SH DESCRIPTION
.B example
does nothing.

.SH OPTIONS
.TP 5
```

```
.B --help
Displays help message on how to do nothing.
.TP 5
.B --version
Displays information on which version of nothing you
are doing.
.SH BUGS
Occasionally does things.
.SH SEE ALSO
```

Figure 19-2 The file example.man

Groff source files are compiled with the **groff** command and may be displayed to either an ASCII display or an X display (**gxditview**). See the examples with the commands for details.

Ghostscript is Linux's version of the PostScript (tm) typesetting system. Postscript is a **vector-based** language, which means that images are broken up into mathematically representable arcs, lines, and whatnot. The resultant files are system independent and scalable.

The commands covered in this section include:

colcrt	Display underlines on tables on non-graphic displays.
eqn	Groff equation formatter.
gs	Ghostscript typesetting language.
grog	Guess groff options.
gxditview	Display groff files on X terminal.
tbl	Groff table formatter.
tex	Compile TeX source file.
troff	Document formatter (see groff).
xdvi	Display .dvi file (see tex) on X Window.

Related Files

/usr/local/share/ghostscript/M.N/*	Startup files, utilities, font definitions.
/usr/local/share/ghostscript/fonts/*	Additional font definitions.
/usr/local/share/ghostscript/M.N/examples/*	Demo files.
/usr/local/share/ghostscript/M.N/doc/*	Ghostscript documentation.

Commands

colcrt [-] [-2] [*file* ...]

This command is a hack to display underlines, tables, and other half-line intensive output on terminals which can't display underlines. It works by double spacing the output and putting dashes on the empty line beneath the word that's supposed to be underlined.

Example: Colcrt might be used to display the tbl.n table file as follows:

tbl tbl.n | nroff -ms | colcrt - | less

-	Do not underline. Typically used in displaying tables.
-2	Print all half-lines whether they're empty or not. Leads to a uniform appearance but eats up space.

eqn [-rvCNR] [-*dcc*] [-T*name*] [-M*dir*] [-fF] [-*sn*] [-*pn*] [-*mn*] [*files...*]

eqn is used in conjunction with **troff** to compile equation descriptions into **troff** format.

Document Formatting

Example: To compile the file eqn.src:

eqn eqn.src

-C	Enables enq to recognize .EQ and .EN even when followed by a character other than a space or newline.
-N	Do not allow newlines within delimiters.
-v	Display version information.
-r	Limit to one size reduction.
***-m**n*	Specify minimum point size.
***-T**name*	Specify device name to which output will be sent.
***-M**dir*	Tell eqn to search dir for eqnrc before the default directories.
-R	Tell eqn not to load eqnrc.
***-f**F*	Equivalent to a gfont F command.
***-s**n*	Equivalent to a gsize n command.
***-p**n*	Tell eqn to make superscripts and subscripts n points smaller than the surrounding text rather than the default of 70% of the size of the surrounding text.

gs [options] [*files*] ...

gs stands for ghostscript. Ghostscript is the Linux version of the PostScript (tm) typesetting language. This program can be used either for printing or display of documents to a monitor. Initial input is from source files as specified on the command line, but you may optionally enter further commands interactively.

Example: To print the ghostscript file example.gs to the printer hplj:

gs -sDEVICE=hplj example.gs

-- filename *arg1* ***...***	With this option, the specified filename is taken as an argument (as usual), but all remaining arguments are immediately defined as an array in userdict named ARGUMENTS.
-Dname=*token*, ***-dname=****token*	Add a name to systemdict with the given definition.
-D*name*, ***-d****name*	Allow the user to define a name in systemdict with value=null.
-Sname=*string*, ***-sname=****string*	Allow the user to add a name to systemdict with the specified string as the value.
-q	Quiet operation.
-gnumber1xnumber2	Specify a device width.
-r*number*, ***-r****number1xnumber2*	Specify a device resolution.
-I*directories*	Tell ghostscript that the specified directories are part of the search path for library files.
-	Specify to take standard input from a file or pipe.
-dDISKFONTS	Tell ghostscript to load individual character outlines from disk as they are encountered, rather then when the font is loaded. Runs slower, but you can fit more fonts into RAM.
-dNOCACHE	Disable caching of characters. Used in debugging.
-dNOBIND	Disables the "bind" operator. Useful only for debugging.
-dNODISPLAY	Disable initialization of output device.

-dNOPAUSE	Disable pause and prompt at page breaks.
-dNOPLATFONTS	Disable access to fonts provided by the platform (e.g., X-Windows).
-dSAFER	Safe mode. Disable deletefile and renamefile operators, make all files read-only. Typically used when interacting with a spooler.
-dWRITESYSTEMDICT	Override default to leave systemdict writable.
-sDEVICE=device	Use the specified device as the initial output device.
-sOutputFile=filename	Send output to the specified file or pipe.

groff [-tpeszaivhblCENRSVXZ] [-w*name*] [-Wname] [-m*name*] [-F*dir*] [-T*dev*] [-f*fam*] [-M*dir*] [-dcs] [-rcn] [-n*num*] [-o*list*] [-P*arg*] [*files...*]

This command is the front end to the **groff** document formatting system. Typically, it invokes **troff** and some postprocessor. The particular postprocessor to be used should be specified in the device description file by the postpro command. The possible devices are:

ps	PostScript (default device)
dvi	TeX dvi format
X75	75 dpi X11 previewer
X100	100 dpi X11 previewer
ascii	typewriter-like device
latin1	typewriter-like device using ISO Latin-1 character set
lj4	HP LaserJet4 or compatible device

Example: To display the groff example file example.man listed in the introduction to this chapter, type:

groff -Tascii -man example.man

-h	Display help information.
-e	Preprocess with eqn.
-t	Preprocess with tbl.
-p	Preprocess with pic.
-s	Preprocess with soelim.
-R	Preprocess with refer.
-v	Force programs run by groff to display version number.
-V	Display the pipeline to stdout rather than executing it.
-z	Suppress output from troff with the exception of error messages.
-Z	Suppress postprocessing of troff output.
-P*arg*	Pass the specified argument to the postprocessor.
-l	Send output to printer. Note that the print command to be executed is found in the device description file.
-L*arg*	Pass the specified argument to the spooler.
-T*dev*	Tell groff to prepare output for the specified device.
-X	Enable previewing gxditview rather than the usual postprocessor.
-N	Do not allow newlines with eqn delimiters.
-S	Run in safe(r) mode.
-a	Generate ASCII output.

-b	Display a backtrace with each warning or error.
-i	Tell troff to read from standard input when it is done processing files.
-v	Display version information.
***-w**name*	Enable the specified warning.
-W	Disable the specified warning.
-E	Disable error messages.
-z	Suppress formatted output.
-C	Enable compatibility mode.
***-d**cs*, ***-d**name=s*	Define c or name to be a string s; c must be a one-letter name.
***-f**fam*	Specify fam is the default font family.
***-m**name*	Read in the file tmac.name rather than searching for it in /usr/lib/groff/tmac.
-R	Don't load troffrc.
***-n**num*	Specify a starting page number.
***-o**list*	Output only the pages specified in list, a comma-separated list of page ranges.
***-r**cn*, ***-r**name=n*	Set number register c or name to n.
***-T**device*	Tell troff to prepare output for the specified device rather than ps.
***-F**dir*	Search the specified directory for subdirectories devname, the DESC file, and font files before searching the default (/usr/lib/groff/font).
***-M**dir*	Search the directory for macro files before the normal /usr/lib/groff/tmac.

grog [files...]

Guess options for the **groff** command. **grog** will look at files and guess which of the options are needed to print a file.

Example: To get the system to make an educated guess as to which options are required to print the example.man file shown in the introduction:

grog example.man

gxditview [-toolkitoption ...] [-option ...] [*filename*]

This command is used to display **groff** output on an X display. It is somewhat interactive and graphical. The left mouse button brings up the following menu:

Next Page	Display the next page. (also n, <space>, <Enter>)
Previous Page	Display the previous page. (also p, <Backspace>, <Del>)
Select Page	Select a numbered page.
Print	Print the gtroff output.
Open	Open a new file.
Quit	Exit from gxditview.

Example: To display the sample file generated above with gxditview:

gxditview example

-help	Display help information.
-page	Display the specified page number of the document.
-backingStore *backing-store-type*	Cache the window contents for quick display.
-printCommand *command*	Specify a default print command.

***-resolution** res*	Display at the specified resolution.
***-filename** string*	Specify a default filename.

X Toolkit Options

***-bg** color*	Specify a background color.
***-bd** color*	Specify a border color.
***-bw** number*	Specify border width.
***-fg** color*	Specify a foreground (text) color.
***-fn** font*	Specify font.
-rv	Reverse video—swap foreground and background settings.
***-geometry** geometry*	Specify a preference for window size.
***-display** host:display*	Specify host X server.
***-xrm** resourcestring*	Use the specified resource string.

tbl [-Cv] [*files...*]

This command compiles descriptions of tables into troff commands.

Example: Typically invoke automatically by groff. To compile the file tbl.src:

tbl tbl.src

-C	Recognize .TS and .TE even when followed by a character other than space or newline.
-v	Display version number.

tex

The **tex** command compiles (sort of) TeX source file into a displayable and printable .device independent (dvi) file.

Example: To compile the file example.tex into the device independent intermediate file example.dvi:

tex example.tex

-ipc, -ipc-start	Write output to a socket as well as a .dvi file. With -ipc-start, also open a server program to read the output.
-mktex=*FILETYPE*, ***-no-mktex=****FILETYPE*	Turn on or off the mktex, script associated with FILETYPE. The only values that make sense for FILETYPE are tex and tfm.
-mltex	If INITEX, enable MLTeX extensions such as \charsubdef. Implicitly set if the program name is mltex.
-output-comment=*STRING*	Use specified string as the DVI file comment.
-shell-escap,	Enable the \write18{SHELL-COMMAND} feature.

troff [-abivzCER] [-w*name*] [-W*name*] [-dcs] [-f*fam*] [-m*name*] [-n*num*] [-o*list*] [-rcn] [-T*name*] [-F*dir*] [-M*dir*] [files...]

The **troff** command is used to format documents. Typically, it is invoked by **groff** (see above).

-a	Generate ASCII output.
-b	Display a backtrace with each warning or error.
-i	Tells troff to read from standard input when it is done processing files.
-v	Display version information.

-wname	Enable the specified warning.
-W	Disable the specified warning.
-E	Disable error messages.
-z	Suppress formatted output.
-C	Enable compatibility mode.
-dcs, -dname=s	Define c or name to be a string s; c must be a one letter name.
-ffam	Specify fam is the default font family.
-mname	Read in the file tmac.name rather than searching for it in /usr/lib/groff/tmac.
-R	Don't load troffrc.
-nnum	Specify a starting page number.
-olist	Output only the pages specified in list, a comma-separated list of page ranges.
-rcn, -rname=n	Set number register c or name to n.
-Tdevice	Tell troff to prepare output for the specified device rather than ps.
-Fdir	Search the specified directory for subdirectories devname, the DESC file, and font files before searching the default (*/usr/lib/groff/font*).
-Mdir	Search the directory for macro files before the normal /*usr/lib/groff/tmac*.

xdvi [+[page]] [-s *shrink*] [-S *density*] [-nogrey] [-gamma *g*] [-p *pixels*] [-margins *dimen*] [-sidemargin *dimen*] [-topmargin *dimen*] [-offsets *dimen*] [-xoffset *dimen*] [-yoffset *dimen*] [-paper *papertype*] [-altfont *font*] [-nomakepk] [-mfmode *mode-def*] [-l] [-rv] [-expert] [-

mgs[n] *size*] **[-hush] [-hushspecials] [-hushchars] [-hushchecksums] [-safer] [-fg** *color*] **[-bg** *color*] **[-hl** *color*] **[-bd** *color*] **[-cr** *color*] **[-bw** *width*] **[-grid1** *color*] **[-grid2** *color*] **[-grid3** *color*] **[-bw** *width*] **[-display** *host:display*] **[-geometry** *geometry*] **[-icongeometry** *geometry*] **[-iconic] [-font** *font*] **[-keep] [-copy] [-thorough] [-nopostscript] [-noscan] [-allowshell] [-noghostscript] [-interpreter path] [-nogssafer] [-gspalette palette] [-underlink] [-browser WWWbrowser] [-base base URL] [-debug bitmask] [-version]** [*dvi_file*]

This is the program used to display dvi files on the X Window system. A .dvi file is an intermediate file which is used as a halfway point between the .tex source file and printed output. When displayed, the .dvi file is pretty much what you see is what you get.

Example: To display the file example.dvi (see the tex entry for information on creating .dvi files):

xdvi example.dvi

TIP

In my experience, the displayed .dvi files tend to be overlarge. Shrink them with the **-s** <factor> option.

Document Formatting

+page	Specify the first page to show (+ = last page).
-allowshell	Enable the shell escape in PostScript specials.
-altfont *font*	Specify a font to use when the normal font is missing.
-background *color*	Specify background color.
-base *base_URL*	Specify a base URL to which external URL links in the file are relative.
-bd *color*, ***-bordercolor*** *color*	Specify the color of the window border.
-bg *color*	Specify the color of the background.
-borderwidth *width*, ***-bw***	Specify width of the border.

***-browser** WWWbrowser*	Specify WWW browser used to handle external URLs.
-copy (.copy)	Always use the copy operation when writing characters to the display.
-cr** color **(.cursorColor)	Specify the color of the cursor.
***-debug** bitmask*	If nonzero, xdvi prints additional information on standard output.
***-density** density*	Specify the density used when shrinking bitmaps for fonts.
***-display** host:display*	Specify host and screen used for displaying the .dvi file.
-expert	Prevent the buttons from appearing.
***-fg** color*	Determines the color of the text (foreground).
***-foreground** color*	Same as -fg.
***-font** font*	Set the font for use in the buttons.
***-gamma** gamma*	Control the interpolation of colors in the greyscale anti-aliasing color palette.
***-grid1** color*	Specify the color of level 1 grid.
***-grid2** color*	Specify the color of level 2 grid.
***-grid3** color*	Specify the color of level 3 grid.
***-geometry** geometry*	Specify initial geometry of the window.
***-gspalette** palette*	Specify palette to be used when using Ghostscript for rendering PostScript specials.
***-hl** color*	Specify color of page border.
-hush	Suppress all suppressible warnings.

-hushchars	Suppress warnings about undefined characters.
-hushchecksums	Suppress warnings about checksum mismatches between the .dvi file and the font file.
-hushspecials	Suppress warnings about \special strings which it cannot process.
-icongeometry geometry	Specify an initial position for the icon.
-iconic	Start the xdvi window in the iconic state.
-interpreter filename	Use filename as the Ghostscript interpreter.
-keep	Do not move to home position when moving to a new page.
-l	List the names of the fonts to be used.
-margins dimen	Specify size of top margin & side margin.
-mfmode *mode-def*	Specify a mode-def string (used in searching for fonts).
-mgs *size*	Same as -mgs1.
-mgs[n] *size*	Specify the size of the magnifying glass window. Size is either an integer (from a square window) or in the form widthx-height.
-noghostscript	Inhibit the use of Ghostscript for displaying.
-nogrey	Turn off greyscale anti-aliasing.
-nogssafer	Run Ghostscript without -dSAFER. -dSAFER is intended to cripple possibly malicious Ghostscript programs by disabling such options as deletefile.

-nomakepk	Turn off automatic generation of font files.
-nopostscript	Turn off rendering of PostScript<tm> specials.
-noscan	Do not do a preliminary scan of the .dvi file.
-offsets *dimen*	Specify size of horizontal & vertical offsets of the output on the page.
-p *pixels*	Define size of fonts to use, in pixels/inch.
-paper *papertype*	Specify size of printed page.
-rv	Display page with white characters on a black background.
-s *shrink*	Specify initial shrink factor (default = 3).
-S *density*	Same as -density, q.v.
-safer	Turn on all available security options.
-sidemargin *dimen*	Specify the side margin.
-thorough	Display slower but with a stronger guarantee of correctness.
-topmargin *dimen*	Specify top & bottom margins.
-underlink	Underline http links (the default).
-version	Display version information.
-xoffset *dimen*	Specify size of horizontal offset of page output.
-yoffset *dimen*	Specify size of vertical offset of the output on the page.

CHAPTER

20

THE VI EDITOR

Introduction

The **vi** program is the default text editor on most Unix systems. If you're new to **vi**, you may be under the impression that the phrase "text editor" is semantically equivalent to "word processor." If so, allow me to gently disillusion you. The **vi** editor is designed to manipulate ASCII files, such as program source code, shell scripts, and other plain text files.[1]

TIP

When you're just getting started, **vi** will irritate you. Badly. Prepare for this fact. I once saw a guy with a 140 IQ—normally a very civilized sort—bang on his keyboard like a mountain gorilla because he slipped up and deleted two days worth of work.

Modes of Operation

Vi doesn't use the function keys much, which will probably confuse those of you coming in from the commercial word processing world. Virtually all of the vi features are accessed via some combination of the normal alphanumeric keys. Vi uses **modes** to distinguish between the times a key will just put a letter on the keyboard and the times a key will invoke some other vi function.

1. If you want something with a million fonts, font sizes, embedded images, etc., allow me to refer you to the good people at Corel, who have—God bless them—ported over an absolutely sammich version of WordPerfect for use right on your very own Linux system. Mine cost about $60.00. I paid up cheerfully and with sincere gratitude in my heart.

In **edit mode** (reached from **command mode** by typing one of the following **a, i, A, I, o, O ...**), whatever you type in will appear on the screen.

In **command mode**, (reached from edit mode by pressing the **<Esc>** key), the various keys have a confusing variety of functions.

TIP Whatever mode you're in is probably wrong. Try hitting the **<Esc>** key. If that doesn't work, try **i** for insert.

TIP Another very common mistake is leaving your caps lock on. Since uppercase and lowercase characters may have very different functions in command mode, you can mess up a file in a hurry just by hitting that one key. After a while you get to where you recognize the symptoms, but when you're just getting started it can be confusing—just something to keep in mind.

Line Ranges

Many of the commands specified below can be applied to a range of lines rather than the whole file. To specify a line range:

1. Get into command mode.
2. Type a colon.
3. Type a start line and an optional comma and stop line.

The chapter is broken up into the following sections:

Just Enough to Get By	Quick start for beginners.
Starting and Stopping vi	What it sounds like.
Position Within a File	Scrolling and motion.
Searching and Replacing	Also includes pattern matching examples.
Adding and Deleting Text	Invoking edit mode, also deleting.
Yanking and Putting	Not unlike copy & paste.
Shell Interaction	Shell functions available in an edit session.

Related Files

~/.exrc	Specify startup options.

Sections

Just Enough to Get By

As the heading suggests, in this section I attempt to present a subset of the vi commands large enough to enable you to accomplish basic tasks, but small enough that a beginner can remember most of them. Note that the topics covered in this section are covered in more detail in other sections.

Opening & Closing

You **open** a file by typing "vi <filename>" on the command line:

vi chapter29.txt

You **close** a file by getting into command mode (use the <Esc> key), typing a colon ":" and then typing **wq** (write quit). If you don't want to save changes to the file, type **q** (quit). If it gives you any trouble, type **wq!** (enthusiastic quit).

Inserting Text

You insert new text by getting into edit mode. There are a lot of ways to get into edit mode. An incomplete list is presented below:

Key	Function
i	Insert new text at current cursor position.
A	Append new text to the end of the current line.

Deleting Text

Delete text by getting into command mode (press **<Esc>**) and using one of the following keys:

Key	Function
x	Delete a character.

dw	Delete a word.
dd	Delete a line.

Moving Around

Get into command mode by pressing **<Esc>**. The following keys are active:

Key	Function
h	Left one space.
j	Down one line.
k	Up one line.
l	Right one space.

Undo

The undo key is "**u**". Get into command mode (press **<Esc>**) and then press "**u**". This will undo all the changes back to the last time you entered edit mode. You may press undo repeatedly, each time undoing an edit session.

Searching

Search for text by:

1. Get into command mode (press **<Esc>**).
2. Press the forward slash "/". A forward slash character should appear in the lower left corner of your screen.
3. Type the string you wish to search for.

Starting and Stopping vi

Vi can be invoked from the command line as follows:

Command	Effect
vi -r *file*	Recover a buffer saved when vi terminates.
vi +n *file*	Open file on line n.
vi + *file*	Open a file at the last line of file.

vi +/*pattern file*	Open file at the first instance of pattern.
vi *file file*...	Open multiple files. Once inside vi, to get to the next, you type :n from command mode.
view *file*	Open file in read-only mode.

The following commands will either get you out of vi, write any changes you may have made, or both:

Key	Function
:w *file*	Write to the specified file.
:w! *file*	Write to specified file regardless of file permissions.
:wq	Write and quit.
:wq!	Write and quit regardless of access mode.
:x, ZZ	Quit & save any changes.
:q	Quit.
:q!	Quit without saving changes.
Q	Quit vi and start ex.

Position Within A File

Note that for these control keys to be active, you must be in command mode.

By Character	Key	Function
	h	Left one space
	j	Down one line
	k	Up one line
	l, <space>	Right one space

By Line	Key	Function
	0	First position of current line
	^	First nonblank of current line
	$	Last position of current line
	+	First character of previous line
	-	First character of next line
	H	Top line of screen
	nH	n lines after top line
	M	Middle line of screen
	L	Bottom line of screen
	nL	n lines before bottom line

By Screen	Key	Function
	<Ctrl>-f	Forward one screen
	<Ctrl>-b	Backward one screen
	<Ctrl>-d	Forward one half screen
	<Ctrl>-u	Backward one half screen

Line Numbers	Key	Function
	<Crtrl>-g	Display line number and file
	:n	Go to line number n

Searching & Replacing

Searching	Key	Function
	%	Move to matching parentheses, brace, or bracket
	/pattern	Find next instance of pattern
	/	Repeat previously specified pattern search
	/pattern+n	Go to the nth line after the next instance of pattern
	?	Search backward for pattern
	?pattern?-n	Go to nth line before pattern

REPLACING

s/pattern/replacement	Substitute replacement for *first* instance of pattern on each line found.

s/pattern/replacement/g	Substitute replacement for *all* instances of pattern on each line found.

It's usually a good idea to specify a line range when doing pattern replacements. Just indicate the lines you want the changes to apply to, separated by commas. For example: TIP

:1,15

To specify control characters in a pattern search, use the key combination **<Ctrl>-v**, followed by whatever the letter is that corresponds to the control character you're after. TIP

Example: To chop out the first 5 spaces from the beginning of each line (indicated with ^)starting with line 100 and ending with line 200:

:100,200 s/^   //g

Example: To substitute the word "good" for the word "excellent" from the first line of the file to the bottom of the file (**$**):

:1,$ s/excellent/good/g

Vi recognizes the following in the context of pattern specification:

Specifying Position	**Character**	**Stands for**
	.	Matches any single character.
	^	The beginning of a line
	$	The end of a line
	\<	Beginning of a word
	>	End of a word
	b	Empty string at edge of a word
	B	Empty string not at edge of a word

Pattern Repetition	**Character**	**Action**
	?	Match the preceding item at most once.
	*	Match the preceding any number of times (including none).
	+	Match the preceding one or more times.
	{*n*}	Match the preceding exactly n times.
	{*n*,}	Match the preceding n or more times.
	{,*m*}	Match the preceding 0-m times.
	{*n*,*m*}	Match the preceding at least n but no more than m times.

Character Classes	**Notation**	**Stands for**
	[:alnum:]	Alphanumeric characters [0-9A-Za-z]
	[:alpha:]	Alphabetic characters [A-Za-z]
	[:cntrl:]	Control characters

[:digit:]	Digits
[:graph:]	Graphic characters
[:lower:]	Lowercase characters
[:print:]	Printable characters
[:punct:]	Punctuation characters
[:space:]	Whitespace (space, tab ...)
[:upper:]	Uppercase characters
[:xdigit:]	Hexadecimal digits

Adding and Deleting Text

The control characters in this section either put you into edit mode at one position or another or they delete text.

Invoking Edit Mode	Character	Effect
	a	Append after cursor
	A	Append at end of line
	i	Insert before cursor
	I	Insert at end of line
	o	Open a line below the current line
	O	Open a line above the current line

Deleting Text	Character	Effect
	d^	Delete back to line beginning
	d}	Delete up to next paragraph
	d/*pattern*	Delete up to specified pattern
	dd	Delete current line

dG	Delete to end of file
dL	Delete up to last line on screen
dn	Delete up to next occurrence of previously specified pattern
dw	Delete word
x	Delete a character
X	Delete previous character

Yanking and Putting

Yanking and putting are more or less the same as the copying and pasting operations found in GUI word processors. You first select some section of text (with one of the yank commands, below). The text is stored in a buffer either explicitly specified or implied. You then select a new position to place it and use one of the put commands to put it there.

In the descriptions below, **buffer** is the text buffer specified by a single letter from a to z.

Yank	Character	Action
	y	Copy current line to new buffer
	yy	Copy current line
	"<*buffer*><*count*>yy	Yank count lines to specified buffer
	"<*buffer*>d	Delete into specified buffer
	ye	Copy to end of word

Put	Character	Action
	"<buffer>p	Put contents of specified buffer
	p	Put most recently deleted line after cursor
	P	Put most recently deleted line before cursor

Shell Interaction

Rather than force you to quit out of vi when you need to do something shell related, vi has a variety of mechanisms to enable you to do shell stuff without interrupting your edit session.

Character	Action
:!*command*	Run the specified command
:!!	Repeat last command
:start,stop! *command*	Send the specified range of lines to command. Replace the lines with output of command
:count! *command*	Send count lines to command and replace with output
:<Ctrl>-Z	Suspend edit session
:r *file*	Read in contents of specified file
:r !*command*	Read in output of command
:sh	Invoke a subshell
:so *file*	Source (execute) commands in file

CHAPTER

21

ARCHIVING & COMPRESSION

Introduction

The commands in this section deal with the compression, storage, and extraction of system files. Typically, you'll want to compress and store at the same time—no need to take up 200M of storage space when 100M will do.

TIP

One of the biggest differences between a professional systems administrator and some schmuck who knows a few commands is that the systems administrator has a good backup strategy.

A **full backup** saves every file within some specified set. An **incremental backup** backs up only those files which have been changed since some previous backup. The idea behind making incremental backups is that the bulk of the files on the system never change, so it's unnecessarily expensive in terms of time and disk space to keep copying them over and over. The downside is that when you're mixing full & incremental backups, it's more complicated to restore the system to its original state after a disaster.

Of the compression utilities listed here, the two most popular are probably **compress** and **gzip**. **Compress** (.Z file extension) used to go out with all Unix distributions, so you see it around a lot. **Gzip** (.gz file extension) is more efficient and happens to have fewer license restrictions, so it's probably the best choice for day-to-day work.

Backup Levels

The Unix world has adopted the concept of numeric backup levels to describe which files are being saved in a given backup.

Level	Meaning
0	Full backup of all files.
1	Backup of all files modified since the last time a level 0 backup was performed.
2	Backup of all files modified since the most recent level 1 backup.

TIP At some point in your life, your computer will crash and you will lose all the data on it. Whether this is a temporary inconvenience or the first step down the road to suicide is entirely dependent on your level of preparation. Right now, *right this second*, you should think about what you have on your machine that you can't afford to lose. Is it being backed up? If not, go do something about it.

TIP Once you've settled on a backup strategy, you can automate most of it with **cron**. All you'll have to do is switch out the tapes (or whatever) every so often.

TIP Though it is technically possible to use the archiving commands in this section as a normal user, for the most part you're going to be running them as root.

The commands covered in this chapter include:

compress	Compress file with Lempel-Ziv encoding.
cpio	Archive files
dump	Save an entire filesystem
gzexe	Compress an executable file in place
gzip	Compress a file
gunzip	Uncompress a gzipped file
restore	Restore filesystem saved with dump

shar	Create a shell archive
uncompress	Expand compressed file
uuencode	Encode a file for mail transmission
uudecode	Decode a file encoded with uuencode
zcmp	Compare two zipped files
zdiff	Compare two zipped files
zgrep	Search the contents of zipped file(s)
zmore	Display the contents of zipped file(s)
znew	Convert from compress format to zip format

Related Files

/dev/rmt*	Default tape unit to dump to
/etc/dumpdates	Dump date records
/etc/fstab	Dump table: file systems and frequency
/etc/group	To find group operator

Commands

compress [-f] [-v] [-c] [-V] [-r] [-b *bits*] [*name* ...]

uncompress [-f] [-v] [-c] [-V] [*name* ...]

Compress makes files smaller via adaptive Lempel-Ziv encoding, **uncompress** (and **zcat**) reverse the effects of compress. Usually the resultant files are replaced with a similarly named file with a .Z extension. Access permissions, ownership, and modification times are retained.

Example: To compress the file bigfile.txt, type:

compress bigfile.txt

-c	Send results to standard output without changing the files.
-r	Recursive operation. Compress the contents of any directories found.
-V	Display version information.
-b	bits encoding
-v	Verbose operation

cpio {-o|--create} [-0acvABLV] [-C bytes] [-H format][-M ***message*****] [-O [[*****user@]host:*****]*****archive*****][-F[[user@]host:]archive][-file=[[user@]host:]archive] [--format=*****format*****][--sparse][--message=*****message*****][--null] [--reset-access-time] [--verbose][--dot] [--append] [--block-size=blocks] [--dereference][--io-size=bytes] [--help] [--version] < name-list [> archive]**

cpio {-i|--extract} [-bcdfmnrtsuvBSV] [-C *****bytes***] [-E file] [-H *****format*****] [-M *****message*****] [-R [*****user*****][*****:.*****][*****group*****]][-I [[*****user@]host:*****]*****archive*****] [-F [[*****user@]host:*****]*****archive*****][--file=[[*****user@]host:*****]*****archive*****] [--make-directories][--nonmatching] [--preserve-modification-time][--numeric-uid-gid] [--rename] [--list] [--swap-bytes] [--swap][--dot] [--unconditional] [--verbose] [--block-size=blocks][--swap-halfwords] [--io-size=bytes] [--pattern-file=*****file*****][--format=*****format*****] [--owner=[*****user*****][*****:.*****][*****group*****]][--no-preserve-owner] [--message=*****message*****] [--help] [--version][-no-absolute-filenames] [-only-verify-crc] [-**

quiet][pattern...] [< *archive*]

---

cpio {-p|--pass-through} [-0adlmuvLV] [-R [user][:.][group]][--null] [--reset-access-time] [--make-directories] [--link][--preserve-modification-time] [--unconditional] [--verbose][--dot] [--dereference] [--owner=[user][:.][group]] [--sparse][--no-preserve-owner] [--help] [--version] *destination-directory< name-list*

The **cpio** command works on archives. An archive file may be on the hard drive, floppy drive, or tape. Generally speaking, cpio accepts a list of files to be processed from standard input (unless otherwise specified), processes them, and sends the resultant archive to standard output or some device. There are three modes of operation:

Copy-out mode—copy the list of input files into an archive. Typically, the list of input files are generated via the **find** command. Once generated, the archive goes to standard output.

Copy-in mode—copy files out of an archive or list the archive contents. The archive is read from standard input. If shell pattern matching characters are included in the command line, only those files which match the specified pattern will be disinterred; otherwise, all files are extracted.

Copy-pass mode—copy files from one directory tree to another. The list of files to be copied is read from standard input and the target directory is passed as an argument.

Example: To archive the current directory, list out all the files in it, pipe them to cpio, and redirect the output to the file directory.cpio:

ls | cpio -ov > directory.cpio

Example: To extract (-i option) the archive created in the previous example, redirect the contents of the archive to the program:

cpio -iv < directory.cpio

-0, --null	Specify that the input list will be terminated by a null character rather than a newline.
-a, --reset-access-time	Reset the access times of files after reading them so it looks like they haven't been read.
-A, --append	In copy-out mode, append to an existing archive.

-b, --swap	Swap halfwords of words and bytes of halfwords in the data. Used in converting between big-endian and little-endian machines.
-B	Specify a block size of 5120 bytes rather than the 512 byte default.
--block-size= *BLOCKSIZE*	Specify a block-size value of BLOCKSIZE * 512 bytes.
-c	Tell cpio to use the portable (ASCII) archive format.
-C *IOSIZE*, ***--io-size=*** *IOSIZE*	Specify an I/O block size of IOSIZE bytes.
-d, --make-directories	Enable directory createion as appropriate.
-E *FILE*, ***--pattern-file=*** *FILE*	Tell cpio to read patterns specifying filenames for listing/extraction from FILE.
-f, --nonmatching	Tell cpio to copy only files which do not match any of the specified patterns.
-F, --file=archive	Tell cpio to send output to the specified archive file rather than standard input or output.
--force-local	Specify that the archive name given is a local file, even if it contains a colon.
-H FORMAT, --format= FORMAT	Specifies use of one of the following formats: bin—Obsolete binary format. odc—Old (POSIX.1) portable format. newc—New (SVR4) portable format, which supports file systems having more than 65536 i-nodes. crc—New (SVR4) portable format with a checksum added. tar—Old tar format. ustar—POSIX.1 tar format. Also recognizes GNU tar archives. hpbin—Obsolete HPUX binary format. hpodc—Portable format used by HPUXs cpio.
-i, --extract	Specify copy-in mode.

***-I** archive*	Specify an archive filename to be used rather than standard input.
-k	No effect. Included for backward compatibility.
-l, --link	Tell cpio to link files rather than to copy them whenever possible.
-L, --dereference	Tell cpio to copy the file to which a symbolic link points rather than the link itself.
-m, --preserve-modification-time	Tell cpio to retain the archived modification times when creating files.
***-M** MESSAGE, **--message=**MESSAGE*	Display the specified message when you fill up a backup medium. Basically a prompt to switch tapes. Instances of the string %d will be replaced in the printed message by the volume number.
-n, --numeric-uid-gid	Display numeric UID and GID information rather than the user- and group- ids when displaying verbose information.
--no-absolute-filenames	When this option is used, all files will be created relative to the current directory even if the archive specifies an absolute file name.
--no-preserve-owner	Tell cpio to set the ownership on any extracted files to the UID of whoever is doing the extracting.
-o, --create	Specify copy-out mode.
***-O** archive*	Specify an archive file to be used rather than standard output.
--only-verify-crc	Tell cpio to verify the cyclic redundancy check value of archived files without extracting anything.
-p, --pass-through	Specify copy-pass mode.
--quiet	Suppress printing of the block count.
-r, --rename	Allow interactive renaming of files.

-R [user][:.][group], --owner [user][:.][group]	Tell cpio to set the ownership of all files created to the specified user.
-s, --swap-bytes	Swap the bytes of each halfword (2 bytes) in the files.
-S, --swap-halfwords	Swap the halfwords of each word (4 bytes) in the files.
--sparse	Tell cpio to write files containing large blocks of zeroes as sparse files.
-t, --list	Display a table of contents of the input.
-u, --unconditional	Tell cpio to replace all files, specifically without prompting the user before replacing newer files with older files.
-v, --verbose	Display a list of files processed. If uses with -t, generates an ls -l style table of contents listing.
-V --dot	Tell cpio to display a dot (.) for each file processed.
--version	Display version information and exit.

dump [0123456789BbhfusTdWn [argument ...]] filesystem

dump [0123456789BbhfusTdWn [argument ...]] directory

The **dump** command is used to back up filesystems. In the case where the size of the output is larger than the capacity of the storage medium, the output is broken into multiple volumes.

Example: To do a full backup of the /home filesystem:

dump /home

0-9	Specify a dump level. Dump level 0 is a full backup of all files regardless of modification time. Dump levels greater than zero tell dump to back up all files that have been modified since the last dump of a lower level (including new files).
B *records*	Specify the number of dump records per volume (interpreted as the size in kilobytes).
b *blocksize*	Specify the number of kilobytes per dump record.
h *level*	Honor the user "nodump" flag only for dumps at or above the given level.
f *file*	Specify the file to which output is sent. The file may be a special device file (e.g., /dev/rmt12, /dev/rsd1c), an ordinary file or standard output (specified as "-").
d *density*	Specify tape density.
n	Whenever dump requires operator attention, notify all operators in the group "operator" with a wall.
s *feet*	Attempt to calculate the amount of tape needed at a particular density.

TIP

When using the s option, try to err on the side of caution. Better to waste a few feet of tape space than render your entire dump useless.

u	Tell dump to update the file /etc/dumpdates after a successful dump.
T *date*	Use the specified date as the starting time for the dump instead of the time determined from looking in */etc/dumpdates*.
W	After consulting the files */etc/dumpdates* and */etc/fstab*, dump tells the operator what file systems need to be dumped.
w	Like W, but prints only those filesystems which need to be dumped.

gzexe [name ...]

This nifty little program allows you compress executable files in place and have them automatically uncompress and execute when you run them. This does, of course, slow down the execution.

-d	Decompress the specified file rather than compressing them.

TIP To compress a large, rarely used executable:

gzexe big_ol_program

gzip [-acdfhlLnNrtvV19] [-S *suffix*] [*name* ...]

gunzip [-acfhlLnNrtvV] [-S *suffix*] [*name* ...]

Gzip is a utility for compressing and storing files by means of Lempel-Ziv coding. Typically, the compressed file is replaced by a similarly named file with the extension ".gz". By default, access modes and modification time are preserved. Also by default, the original source file is removed.

Example: To compress the file bigfile.c into a smaller file called bigfile.gz:

gzip bigfile.c

Example: To uncompress the file created in the previous example:

gunzip bigfile.gz

--stdout, --to-stdout, -c	These options send any output to standard out, but do not change the original files.
--decompress, --uncompress, -d	Reverse the compression process.
--force, -f	Force gzip to perform the specified action without prompting, if possible.
--help, -h	Display a help message, then exit.

--list, -l

Display the following information for each compressed file:

- size of compressed file
- size of uncompressed file
- ratio of compressed to uncompressed
- name of the uncompressed file

when used with the **--verbose**, the following is also displayed:

- compression method (deflate, compress, lzh, pack)
- the 32 bit cyclic redundancy check of the uncompressed file
- the time stamp of the uncompressed file

when used with the **--quiet** option, the title and totals line are not displayed.

--license, -L

Display license information and exit.

--no-name, -n

Tell gzip not to save (when compressing) or restore (when uncompressing) the original file name and time stamp.

--name, -N

Tell gzip to both save (when compressing) or restore (when uncompressing) the original file name and time stamp.

--quiet, -q

Tell gzip not to display any warnings.

--recursive, -r

Tell gzip to recursively traverse the directory tree, compressing any files it finds.

--suffix SUF, -S SUF

Tell gzip to substitute the specified suffix for ".gz".

--test, -t

Tell gzip to test the integrity of a compressed file.

--verbose, -v	Verbose output. Include name and percentage reduction for each file compressed.
--version, -V	Display version number and compilation options.
--fast, --best, -N	Allow the user to make trade-offs between efficiency of compression (--best, or a numeric value of -1) and speed of the compression process (--fast, -9). The default is -6.

restore key [name ...]

Restore the filesystems saved with **dump**.

Example: To restore the home filesystem saved with **dump** in the example above:

ROOT **restore /home**

r	Restore (rebuild a file system).
C	Read the backup and compare its contents with files present on the disk.
R	Restore requests a particular tape of a multi-volume set on which to restart a full restore (see the r key above).
x	Read the specified files from the given media.
t	List the names of the specified files if they occur on the backup.
i	Interactive restoration. When restoring interactively, restore provides a shell-like interface for use in selecting files to be restored. The following commands apply:
add [arg]	Add current directory or file to the list of files to be extracted.
cd arg	Change the current working directory as specified.
delete [arg]	Delete the current file or directory from the list of files to be extracted.

extract	Extract all listed files from the dump.
help	Display help information.
ls [arg]	List the current or specified directory.
pwd	Print working directory.
quit	Exit immediately.
setmodes	All the directories that have been added to the extraction list have their owners, modes, and times set; nothing is extracted from the dump.
verbose	When set, causes ls command to list the inode numbers of all entries.
b blocksize	Specify blocksize in kilobytes.
D filesystem	Specify name of filesystem used by -C option in comparison.
f archive	Specify archive to be used rather than */dev/rmt*
h	Extract actual directory rather than referenced files.
m	Extract by inode numbers rather than by file name.
N	Do not extract files, only print file names.
s filenumber	Specify the number of the file on a multi-file tape dump. Numbering starts at 1.
T tmpfiledir	Specify a directory to use for temp file storage.
v	Verbose operation. List files as they are restored.
y	Always continue on error, regardless of bad blocks.

shar [OPTION] ... *FILE* ...

shar -S [OPTION] ...

This command creates shell archives. They are in text format and thus mailable. To use a shell archive, execute it with ***/bin/sh***. You may specify the files to be archived either on the command line or in a file.

Example: To create an archive of all the text files in the current directory and redirect/save it to the file text.shar:

shar *.txt > text.shar

--help	Display help information and exit.
--version	Display version number and exit.
-q, --quiet	Run with fewer than normal messages.
-p, --intermix-type	Allow options on the command line to be entered via standard input on a line other than the standard input. (-M, -B, -T, -z and -Z only)
-S, --stdin-file-list	Get file list interactively rather than from the command line.
-o *PREFIX*, ***--output-prefix=****PREFIX*	Save the archive to files PREFIX.01 through PREFIX.NNN instead of standard output.
-l *KB*, ***--whole-size-limit=****KB*	Limit the size of output file to the specified number of kilobytes, but do not split input files.
-L *SIZE*, ***--split-size-limit=****SIZE*	Limit the size of output file to the specified number of kilobytes, splitting files as necessary.

***-n** NAME, **--archive-name=**NAME*	Specify the archive name which will be included in the header of the shar file.
***-s** ADDRESS, **--submitter=**ADDRESS*	Override the default email address for the submitter.
-a, --net-headers	Tell shar to automatically generate headers.
-c, --cut-mark	Start the shar with a cut line.
-T, --text-files	Treat all files as text.
-B, --uuencode	Treat all files as binary and use uuencode prior to packing.
-M, --mixed-uuencode	Tell shar to automatically determine if the files are text or binary and treat them accordingly.
-z, --gzip	Tell shar to use gzip and uuencode on all files prior to packing.
***-g** LEVEL, **--level-for-gzip=**LEVEL*	Use the specified level as a parameter to gzip when doing compression.
-Z, --compress	Tell shar to use compress and uuencode prior to packing.
***-b** BITS, **--bits-per-code=**BITS*	Use -bX as a parameter to compress.
-w, --no-character-count	Turn off wc -c checking.
-D, --no-md5-digest	Turn off md5sum checking.
-F, --force-prefix	Force shar to prepend the prefix character to every line even if not required.

***-d** STRING, **--here-delimiter=**STRING*	Delimit the files in the shar with the specified string rather than SHAREOF.
-V, --vanilla-operation	Produce a more widely usable shar.
-P, --no-piping	Specify a temporary file to be used instead of pipes.
-x, --no-check-existing	Tell shar to overwrite existing files without checking.
-X, --query-user	Do not overwrite files without first prompting the user.
-m, --no-timestamp	Do not "touch" the unpacked archive files (preserves original timestamp).
-Q, --quiet-unshar	Do not spray the user with comments when unpacking.
-f, --basename	Use only the filename (not the directory path) when building a shar.

tar [-] A -catenate -concatenate | c -create | d --diff --compare || r --append || t --list || u --update || x -extract --get [--atime-preserve] [-b, --block-size N] [-B, --read-full-blocks] [-C, --directory *DIR* **] [--checkpoint] [-f, --file [[***HOSTNAMEE***:]]***F* **] [--force- local] [-F, --info-script F --new-volume-script F] [-G, --incremental] [-g, --listed-incremental F] [-h, --dereference] [-i, --ignore-zeros] [--ignore-failed- read] [-k, --keep-old-files] [-K, --starting-file F] [-l, --one-file-system] [-LL, --tape-length N] [-m, --modification-time] [-MM, --multi-volume] [-N, --after-date DATE, --newer DATE] [-o, --old-archive, --portability] [-O, --to-stdout] [-p, --same-permis- sions, --preserve-permissions] [-PP, --**

absolute-paths] [--preserve] [-R, --record-number] [--remove-files] [-s, --same-order, --preserve-order] [--same-owner] [-S, --sparse] [-T, --files-from *FF*] [--null] [--totals] [-v, --verbose] [-VV, --label *NAME*] [--version] [-w, --interactive, --confirmation] [-WW, --verify] [--exclude *FILE*] [-XX, --exclude-from FILE] [-ZZ, --compress, --uncompress] [-z, --gzip, --ungzip] [--use-compress-program PROG] [--block-compress] [-[[0-7]][[lmh]]] *filename1* [*filename2*, ... *filenameN*] *directory1* [*directory2*, ...*directoryN*]

Tar is the **t**ape **ar**chive utility, though you don't necessarily need to use it with tapes. Its purpose in life is to pack a bunch of files all together into one file in such a way that they can later be unpacked and separated to their original state. Most Linux distributions rely on tar in one form or another.

TIP

By default, **tar** does not compress the files it is archiving. This means that your resultant archive file takes up more or less the same amount of disk space as the files that went into it. Generally you'll want to use one of the compression options (--**gzip**, --**compress**) when archiving.

Example: To create (**-c** option) a tar archive of all the files under your home directory and store them in the archive file mystuff.tar (**-f** option tells tar that the next argument will be the destination file, in this case, “mystuff.tar”):

tar -cvf mystuff.tar /home/myhomedir

The -v option tells tar to list the files as it's saving them, just so you have something to watch.

Example: To extract (**-x** option) all the files from the archive created in the previous example:

tar -xvf mystuff.tar

Example: To create a tar archive just like the one in the first example (above), but compress (**-gzip** option) at the same time:

tar -gzip -cvf mystuff.tar /home/myhomedir

The file would be uncompressed with:

tar -gunzip -xvf mystuff.tar

Tar requires that you specify at least one of the following options:

-A, --catenate, --concatenate	Append files to an archive.
-c, --create	Create a new archive.
-d, --diff, --compare	Display the differences between an archive and the unarchived files, if any.
--delete	Remove from the archive.
-r, --append	Append files at the end of an archive.
-t, --list	Display the contents of the specified archive.
-u, --update	Tell tar to append only files that are newer than copy in the archive.
-x, --extract, --get	Extract files from the specified archive

Other options

--atime-preserve	Retain access time on dumped files.
-b, --block-size N	Specify a block size of Nx512 bytes.
-B, --read-full-blocks	Reblock as read on 4.2 BSD pipes.
-C, --directory DIR	Change to the specified directory.
--checkpoint	Display directory names while reading the archive.
-f, --file [[HOSTNAME:]FILE]	Use the specified archive file or device.
--force-local	Force tar to consider the archive file to be local even if the filename contains a colon.
-F, --info-script F ***--new-volume-script F***	Tell tar to run the specified script at the end of each tape.

-G, --incremental	Tell tar to create, list, or extract old GNU-format incremental backup.
-g, --listed-incremental FF	Tells tar to create, list, or extract new GNU-format incremental backup
-h, --dereference	Tell tar to archive files which symbolic links point to rather than the links themselves.
-i, --ignore-all	Tell tar to ignore blocks of zeros in archive
--ignore-failed-read	Tell tar not to exit with non-zero status when files are unreadable.
-k, --keep-old-files	Do not overwrite existing files in the archive.
-K, --starting-file F	Begin at the specified file in the archive.
-l, --one-file-system	Remain in local file system when creating an archive.
-L, --tape-length N	Will generate a prompt to change tapes after the specified number of kilobytes.
-m, --modification-time	Suppress extraction of file modification time.
-M, --multi-volume	Creation, listing, or extraction of multi-volume archive.
-N, --after-date DATE, --newer DATE	Tell tar to store only files newer than DATE.
-o, --old-archive, --portability	Store archive in V7 format rather than ANSI format.
-O, --to-stdout	Send output to standard out.
-p, --same-permissions, --preserve-permissions	Retain all security information.

-P, --absolute-paths	Suppress stripping of leading "/"s from file names.
--preserve	Same as -p -s.
-R, --record-number	Include record number within archive with messages.
--remove-files	Delete daily files from filesystem after adding them to the archive.
-s, --same-order, --preserve-order	Tell tar to sort list of target names to match archive.
--same-owner	Retain ownership when extracting files.
-S, --sparse	Tweak performance to handle sparse files better.
-T, --files-from F	Specify that file F will contain name list.
--null	When used with -T, specifies that filenames will be null terminated.
--totals	Display total bytes written when creating archive.
-v, --verbose	Verbose output (list files).
-V, --label *NAME*	Create archive with the specified volume name.
--version	Output version information.
-w, --interactive, --confirmation	Prompt for confirmation before taking action.
-W, --verify	Verify archive after writing.
--exclude *FILE*	Exclude the specified file from processing.
-X, --exclude-from *FILE*	Exclude from processing all files specified in file.

-Z, --compress, --uncompress	Compress or uncompress the archive with compress.
-z, --gzip, --ungzip	Compress or uncompress the archive with gzip.
***--use-compress-program** PROG*	Filter the archive through the specified program. (PROG must accept the -d option.)
--block-compress	Block the output of any compression program for tapes.
-[0-7][lmh]	Allows the user to specify drive and density.

unshar [OPTION] ... [FILE ...]

Unpack a shar file. Shar files are "shell archive" files, created with the shar command (see above).

Example: To unpack the shar file text.shar:

unshar text.shar

--version	Display version information and exit.
--help	Display help information and exit.
-d DIRECTORY, --directory=DIRECTORY	Relocate to the specified DIRECTORY before unpacking files.
-c, --overwrite, -f, --force	Tell shar to overwrite existing files.
-e, --exit-0	In the case where unpacking from an single mail folder containing many shar archives, split them up when unpacking. (Assumes the various shars are delimited by an exit 0).
-E STRING, --split-at=STRING	Similar to -e, but allows you to specify the delimiter string.

uuencode [-m] [*file*] *name*

uudecode [-o *outfile*] [*file*]...

The **uuencode/uudecode** programs are used to encode binary files for transmission over media which support only transmission of ASCII data.

Example: To encode the binary file program and mail to user someguy@wherever.com:

uuencode program | mail someguy@wherever.com

-m	Use base64 encoding format.
-o	Write output to the specified file.

zcmp [cmpoptions] *file1* [*file2*]

zdiff [diffoptions] *file1* [*file2*]

Compare files which are currently compressed. The options for these commands are exactly the same as the options for cmp and diff, respectively.

Example: To compare the contents of the compressed file a.gz with the compressed file b.gz:

zcmp a.gz b.gz

zgrep [grepoptions] [-e] *pattern filename*...

This command is used to **grep** through compressed or zipped files. The options for this command are the same as for **grep**.

Example: To look for the string "important clue" in all the compressed files in your current directory (assuming they have a .gz file extension):

zgrep "important clue" *.gz

zmore [name ...]

View compressed files. The zmore command is interactive, the following keys apply:

Example: To display the contents of the zipped file a.txt.gz:

zmore a.txt.gz

#<space>	Display # more lines, or another screenful if no # specified.
^D,d	Scroll forward.
#z	Same as a space, but may be used to specify a new window size.
#s	Skip # lines and print a screenful starting at that point.
#f	Skip # screenfuls and print a screenful starting at that point.
q, Q	Quit reading the current file and go on to the next one.
e	Exit
s	Skip the next file and continue.
=	Display the current line number.
#/expr	Search for the #th occurrence of the specified regular expression.
#n	Where # is some number, search for the #th occurrence of the last regular expression entered.
!command	Run the specified shell command.
:q or :Q	Stop displaying the current file.
.	Repeat the previous command.

znew [-ftv9PK] [*name*.Z ...]

Recompress the specified files from compress (.Z) format to gzip (.gz) format.

Example: To convert the file program.Z from compress format to gzip format:

znew program.Z

-f	Force recompression even if the .gz file already exists.
-t	Test any new zip files before deleting originals.

-v	Verbose output.
-9	Optimal compression, slowest execution.
-P	Reduce disk space usage by using pipes in the conversion.
-K	If the .Z file is smaller than the .gz file, keep it.

PART

3

COMMON TASKS

CHAPTER 22

STARTUP & SHUTDOWN

Introduction

Starting and stopping a Linux machine is a fairly intricate process.

Startup

When the machine is turned on, it searches its own hardware for a bootable file. The exact search order is system dependent, but these days you typically see the machine looking at its floppy drive, then the CD-ROM, then the master hard disk. Check your BIOS configuration for information about your particular machine.

Usually, Linux systems are started by **LILO** (the LInux LOader), a program which can boot multiple operating systems. LILO works well when placed in the Master Boot Record of your hard drive and can be configured to invoke Windows or other operating systems in addition to Linux. However, if you are using Windows NT or OS/2, you may be forced to install LILO somewhere other than the master boot record as these operating systems demand total control of the MBR. In addition, Linux may be started from a boot floppy or CD-ROM.

Regardless of your boot method, the first thing that happens is your kernel is loaded. The kernel initializes its own internal data structures and loads its device drivers. If all goes well, the kernel then starts the **init** program which, in turn, forks off clones to create the various user processes.

Linux uses the concept of **runlevel**s to define which processes the system allows to run at a given time. A **runlevel** is a numeric system variable between 0 and 6 which has a set of allowable processes associated with it. When the system transitions between runlevels, it consults the ***/etc/inittab*** file to see what processes to start or stop.

Runlevel	Meaning
0	system halted
1	administrative runlevel
2, 3, 4, 5	user definable run levels
6	reboot runlevel

A great deal of boot- time system configuration is accomplished via script. The ***/etc/rc.d/rc{runlevel}.d*** directories contain scripts associated with the various runlevels. These scripts are executed by **init** in order of their appearance in the output of the **ls** command upon entering that runlevel.

Shutdown

When the **shutdown** command is invoked, the system sends messages notifying users of the impending shutdown. Usually you like to give them a bit of warning lest they come back from the cafeteria and find a day's work destroyed.

Next, the executing processes are sent a signal and they terminate with varying degrees of grace. The subsystems are shut down, any users who didn't take the hint are kicked off by force, and any processes which didn't respond to the signal are killed. Any filesystem updates are written out to disk via sync and, finally, init takes the system to its new runlevel.

TIP A **shutdown** can be aborted by getting the process id of the shutdown process and killing it manually. However, this may interrupt things which are best left alone, so it is almost always safer just to let the shutdown finish and then start things back up again.

The following commands are utilized in the startup/shutdown sequence:

dmesg	display bootup messages
halt	halt the system
reboot	reboot the system
poweroff	power the system off
lilo	install the LILO boot loader
rdev	display system startup configuration info
runlevel	show the current system runlevel
shutdown	bring the system down
swapon	enable the paging hardware
swapoff	disable the paging hardware
sync	write buffered memory out to disk
init	start system processes
telinit	move the system to a new runlevel

Related Files

/var/log/wtmp	Login records file
/fastboot	This file's existence constitutes a request by the system to skip fsck at reboot time.
/etc/inittab	Defines what processes are to be started at what runlevel.
/etc/shutdown.allow	Users specified in this file are permitted to invoke the shutdown command.
/etc/rc	Multiuser initialization file.
/etc/fstab	Contains mount information for filesystems
/etc/hd??	Disk device
/etc/sd??	SCSI disk device
/etc/initscript	If exists, used by init to start new processes.
/dev/console	Console device driver.
/etc/ioctl.save	Specifies console's ioctl states.
/etc/lilo.conf	Specify LILO configuration options.

Commands

dmesg [-c] [-n *level*] [-s *bufsize*]

This command is used to display or control the contents of the kernel ring buffer, which contains the bootup messages.

Example: To get the boot messages from your last system startup:

dmesg | less

Example: To set your console to display messages with annoying frequency:

dmesg -n 3

-c	Clear the contents of the ring buffer after printing.
***-s**bufsize*	Specify the size of the buffer used to query the kernel ring buffer. Default is 8196.
***-n**level*	Specify the level at which log messages are displayed to the console. Note that messages are sent to /proc/kmsg regardless of level. Typically, this is set to 1, which filters all but panic messages.

halt [-n] [-w] [-d] [-f] [-i] [-p]

reboot [-n] [-w] [-d] [-f] [-i]

poweroff [-n] [-w] [-d] [-f] [-i]

Halt and its synonyms tell the kernel to do one of three things: reboot, halt, or power the system off. When called, they make an entry in the ***/var/log/wtmp*** file. You must be logged in as the superuser to use this command.

Example: To force a halt of the system:

halt -f

ROOT

-n	Do not sync.
-w	Write the wtmp entry but do not actually reboot or halt.
-d	Do not write the wtmp entry.
-f	Force the halt or reboot.
-i	Shutdown all network interfaces before halting/rebooting.
-p	After halting, perform a poweroff.

lilo options

This program installs the lilo boot loader. It depends heavily on the information stored in its configuration file, ***/etc/lilo.conf*** by default.

Example: Lilo is usually run without options:

ROOT

/sbin/lilo

-v	Run verbosely.
-q	Display the currently mapped kernel files as specified in */boot/map.*
-m *map-file*	Use the specified boot map file rather than /boot/map.
-C *config-file*	Use the specified config file, /etc/lilo.conf by default.
-d *delay*	Specify the delay time before lilo boots the default kernel.
-D *label*	Specify that the kernel with the label will be the default.
-r *root-directory*	Force LILO to perform a chroot on the indicated directory. Used for repairing a setup from a boot floppy.
-t	Test only, do not actually write a new boot sector.
-c	Map compaction.
-f *disk-tab*	Use the specified disk geometry source file (default is /*etc/disktab*).
-i *boot-sector*	Use the specified file as the new boot sector.
-l	Use linear sector addresses rather than sector/head/cylinder addressing.
-P {fix|ignore}	Specify whether to fix or ignore faulty partition tables.
-s *save-file*	Use the specified file to save data from the overwritten boot sector.
-S *save-file*	Allow overwriting of save files.
-u *device-name*	Uninstall LILO. (Copy the specified boot sector save file back to the MBR.)
-U *device-name*	Uninstall LILO without checking time stamps.

***-R** command line*	Set the default command for the next execution of the boot loader.
***-l** label*	Display the path name of the running kernel after startup.
-V	Display version number.

rdev [-rsvh] [-o *offset* **] [** *image* **[** *value* **[** *offset* **]]]**

rdev [-o *offset* **] [** *image* **[** *root_device* **[** *offset* **]]]**

swapdev [-o *offset* **] [** *image* **[** *swap_device* **[** *offset* **]]]**

ramsize [-o *offset* **] [** *image* **[** *size* **[** *offset* **]]]**

vidmode [-o *offset* **] [** *image* **[** *mode* **[** *offset* **]]]**

rootflags [-o *offset* **] [** *image* **[** *flags* **[** *offset* **]]]**

If called with no arguments, **rdev** displays an ***/etc/mtab*** line for the current root file system.

This command is generally used to display the pairs of bytes found in the bootable image which specify the root device, the video mode, the size of the RAM disk, and the swap device. By default the information begins at offset 504 in the kernel image.

Example: To get mount information for your current root filesystem:

rdev ROOT

Typically, the offsets are among the following:

498 Root Flags
(500 and 502 Reserved)
504 RAM Disk Size
506 VGA Mode
508 Root Device
(510 Boot Signature)

The image parameter is typically one of the following:

/vmlinux

/vmlinux.test

/vmunix

/vmunix.test

/dev/fd0

/dev/fd1

The root device or swap device parameters are one of the following:

/dev/hda[1-8]

/dev/hdb[1-8]

/dev/sda[1-8]

/dev/sdb[1-8]

size	Specify the size of the RAM disk in kilobytes.
flags	Contain extra information used when mounting root.
mode	Specify video mode as one of the following: -3 = Prompt -2 = Extended VGA -1 = Normal VGA 0 = as if "0" was pressed at the prompt 1 = as if "1" was pressed at the prompt 2 = as if "2" was pressed at the prompt n = as if "n" was pressed at the prompt
-s	Cause rdev to act like swapdev.
-r	Cause rdev to act like ramsize.
-R	Cause rdev to act like rootflags.
-v	Cause rdev to act like vidmode.
-h	Provide help.

runlevel [utmp]

Display the previous and current runlevel.

Example: To display the current runlevel as specified by the (non-standard) utmp database file **/usr/bin/utmp.old**:

runlevel /usr/bin/utmp.old

shutdown [-t sec] [-rkhncfF] time [warning-message]

Bring the system down gracefully and securely. Shutdown automatically prints out a notification to any logged-in user, and prevents any further logins. Processes are passed a SIGTERM signal to warn them that the system will be halting shortly.

Example: To shutdown and reboot the system immediately:

shutdown -r now

ROOT

Example: To shut down and halt the system in ten minutes with the warning message "Important repairs going on":

shutdown -h +10 "Important repairs going on"

TIP

Shutdowns *can* be cancelled with the <Ctrl>-C character combination, but it's usually best to just let them run.

-t sec	Specify a delay in seconds between the warning and the process actually getting killed.
-k	Send the warning message but do not actually shut down.
-r	Reboot after shutdown.
-h	Halt after shutdown.
-n	Perform the actual shutdown rather than allowing init to do it. Use is discouraged.
-f	Do not do an fsck after reboot. (Fast reboot.) This option may be ignored at reboot time.
-F	Force an fsck after the reboot.
-c	Cancel a shutdown in progress.
time	Specify a time to shutdown (hh:mm, the word 'now', +minutes).
warning-message	Optional message to be written to active users.

---

swapon [-h -V]

---

swapon -a [-v]

---

swapon [-v] [-p priority] specialfile ...

---

swapon [-s]

---

swapoff [-h -V]

---

swapoff -a

---

swapoff specialfile ...

Swapon and swapoff enable/disable devices on which paging is to take place. They are normally invoked by ***/etc/rc***.

Example: To disable swapping:

ROOT

swapoff

-h	Display help and exit.
-V	Display version number and exit.
-s	Provide usage summary of swap device(s).
-a	Make any swap device (as specified by sw mark in /etc/fstab) available.
-p *priority*	Specify priority for swapon.

---

sync

Write data buffered in memory out to disk. Generally called automatically at shutdown time to prevent data loss when power is cut.

Example: To force a write of buffered data out to disk:

sync

init [0123456Ss]

telinit [-t sec] [0123456sSQqabcUu]

Init is the ultimate ancestor of all processes on the system. It is invoked at boot time to spawn processes as specified in the file ***/etc/inittab***.

Telinit is used after system boot to get init to do various things. It is a privileged command.

Example: To switch to runlevel 4:

init 4

0,1,2,3,4,5 or 6	Switch to the specified run level.
a,b,c	Process only those /etc/inittab file entries having runlevel a,b or c.
Q or q	Re-examine the /etc/inittab file.
S, s	Change to single user mode.
U, u	Re-execute init, returning ultimately to the current state.

CHAPTER

23

X WINDOW SYSTEM

Introduction

The X Window system is Linux's Graphical User Interface (GUI).

These days most of the commercial Linux distributions will do a good bit of the work of configuring the X system for you. However, in order for things to run smoothly, you will need the following information:

- Horizontal Synchronization Rate of your monitor
- Vertical Refresh Rate of your monitor
- Chipset and Memory size of your video card

The **SuperProbe** program may or may not be able to automatically detect some of this information for you. There was a time when you could count on that information being included in the documentation that came with your machine. These days you're probably going to have to go to your manufacturer's Web site. Encouragingly, however, I have noted that many manufacturers are starting to provide Linux-specific documentation.

Having installed X successfully, you may wish to run **xvidtune** to tweak your video settings.

X purists will probably want to configure **xdm**, the X Display Manager. This program can be used in place of the ***init-getty-login*** triptych familiar to the text-based Linux world to control access to your machine.

The X Window system allows you to specify a **window manager** (e.g., **fvwm, WindowMaker**) which will be your gateway to the system.

TIP To decorate your desktop, get a new theme. Themes are wallpaper+window graphics files which are designed to be easy on the eyes (e.g., movies, celebrities, neat graphical hacks...). A vast assortment of cool themes are freely available from:

www.themes.org

Please note that most of the commands in this section are GUI and interactive, so the examples provided may not be very informative. Fortunately, the programs, once invoked, are more or less self-explanatory.

TIP The way to shut down an X session gracefully is with the key combination:

<Ctrl><Alt><Backspace>

TIP To copy text from one X Window to another:

1. Open an edit session (vi, emacs) in the target window.
2. Highlight the text you want to copy.
3. Left click, then right click, in the target window.

The commands in this section include:

XF86Setup	Configure X Window system
X	X Window display server
startx	Front-end script for xinit
xdm	X Display Manager; can handle login
xf86config	Configure X Window system
xinit	Start X Window system
xmseconfig	Configure mouse
xterm	Start an X-Window
xvidtune	Tweak video display parameters

Related Files

<XRoot>/lib/X11/xdm/xdm-config	The default configuration file
$HOME/.Xauthority	User authorization file where xdm stores keys for clients to read
$HOME/.xresources	Startup script executed by Xsession
<XRoot>/lib/X11/xdm/chooser	The default chooser
<XRoot>/bin/xrdb	The default resource database loader
<XRoot>/bin/X	The default server
<XRoot>/bin/xterm	The default session program and failsafe client
<XRoot>/lib/X11/xdm/A<display>-<suffix>	The default place for authorization files
/tmp/K5C<display>	Kerberos credentials
<xroot>/lib/X11/Cards	Video cards database
xinitrc	Default client script
xterm	Client to run if .xinitrc does not exist
.xserverrc	Default server script
X	Server to run if .xserverrc does not exist

Commands

XF86Setup [-sync] [-name *appname*] [-nodialog] [-- arg ...]

XF86Setup [-sync] [-name *appname*] [-script] [-display *display*] [-geometry *geometry*] filename [[--] arg ...]

This command is used to manipulate the configuration of the X servers. It can be used either to do the initial setup or to make adjustments later. If you're using it to set up XF86 for the first time, your initial data will be entered via the VGA 16 server (the resolution is lousy but it will work on almost any machine).

Example: To invoke XF86Setup, an interactive GUI program:

XF86Setup

-sync	Synchronize all communication with the X server.
-name *appname*	Use the specified name as the window name.
-display *display*	Specify the display to work with.
-nodialog	Do not use the Dialog program to interact with the user.
-geometry *geomspec*	Specify the initial geometry for the window.
filename	If used, this argument should be the name of a file containing Tcl/Tk commands to be run at startup.
-script	Look for the specified filename in the scripts directory rather than searching the user's PATH.

X [option ...]

X is the X-window display server, sort of. Usually it's a link to whichever server is appropriate for the particular hardware on which it is running. Let me restate that: There is no single X program. Instead, X is a link to or copy of whatever server (vga, svga...) is doing the actual work. The fact that this command is not a program but rather a committee complicates the discussion of options somewhat. Also, typically, this program is invoked by the X display manager (**xdm**) or as a result of the **startx** script.

Example: In a correctly configured system, you will not need to invoke X by hand.

:displaynumber	Specify a display number for the X server to run as. The default is, of course, 0. Typically, this option is used when you have multiple servers running on the same host.
-a *number*	Specify the pointer acceleration. Pointer acceleration is the ratio of how much is displayed to how much the user actually moved the pointer.
-ac *d*	Disable any host based access control mechanisms.
-audit *level*	Specify audit trail level.
-auth *authorization-file*	Authorization-file contains a set of authorization records used to authenticate access.
-bc	Bug compatibility. Disables some error checking.
-bs	Disable backing store support on all screens.
-c	Key-click off.
c *volume*	Specify a key-click volume (0-100).
-cc *class*	Specify a visual class for the root window of color screens.
-co *filename*	Set name of RGB color database.
-core	Enable generation of core dump on fatal errors.
-dpi	Specify the dpi resolution of the screen.

resolution	Specify resolution in dots per inch. Use when server cannot determine screen size from hardware.
dpms	Enable DPMS (when supported).
-dpms	Disable DPMS.
-deferglyphs *whichfonts*	Specify which type of font on which server should attempt deferred glyph loading.
-f *volume*	Set bell volume. Range = 0-100.
-fc *cursorFont*	Specify default cursor font.
-fn *font*	Specify default font.
-fp *fontPath*	Specify search path for fonts, where fontPath is a comma-separated list of directories.
-help	Display help information.
-I	Ignore all remaining command line arguments.
***-k**b*	Disable XKEYBOARD extension.
-nolisten *trans-type*	Disable a transport type (e.g., TCP/IP).
-nolock	Disable use of an X server lock file.
-p *minutes*	Set screen saver pattern cycle time in minutes.
-pn	Allow server to continue operation if some (not all) sockets fail to connect.
-r	Turn off auto-repeat.
r	Turn on auto-repeat.
-s *minutes*	Specify screen-saver timeout in minutes.
-su	Disable save under support on all screens.

***-t** number*	Specify number of pixels after which pointer acceleration should take effect.
-terminate	Terminate server at server reset rather than continuing to run.
-to seconds	Specify default connection timeout in seconds.
-tst	Disable all testing extensions.
ttyxx	Ignored, for servers started the ancient way (from init).
v	Set video-off screen-saver preference.
-v	Set video-on screen-saver preference.
-wm	Force the default backing-store of all windows to be WhenMapped.
***-x** extension*	Load the specified extension at init.

SOME X SERVERS ACCEPT THE FOLLOWING OPTIONS:

***-ld** kilobytes*	Specify the server's data space limit in kilobytes.
***-lf** files*	Specify a limit on the number of open files (0=as large as possible, -1=unchanged).
***-ls** kilobytes*	Specify stack space limit of the server.
-logo	Turn X Window System logo on.
nologo	Turn X Window System logo off.

XDMCP OPTIONS

***-query** host-name*	Enable XDMCP and send Query packets to the specified host.
-broadcast	Enable XDMCP and broadcast BroadcastQuery packets to the network.

-indirect *host-name*	Enable XDMCP and send IndirectQuery packets to the specified host.
-port *port-num*	Specify an alternate port number for XDMCP packets.
-displayID *display-id*	Allow the XDMCP display manager to identify each display so it can locate the shared key.

XKEYBOARD OPTIONS

X servers that support the XKEYBOARD extension accept the following options:

-xkbmap *filename*	Keyboard description to load on startup.
[+-]accessx	Enable(+) or disable(-) AccessX key sequences.
-ar1 *milliseconds*	Specify the length of time in milliseconds before autorepeat starts.
-ar2 *milliseconds*	Specify the length of time in milliseconds between autorepeat-generated keystrokes.

startx [[*client*] options ...] [-- [*server*] options ...]

startx is a site-configurable script used to start an X Window session. It is a front end to the xinit command. Generally, **startx** is run without arguments as any necessary configuration is done within the script.

Example: To invoke the X Window system, type:

startx

SuperProbe [-verbose] [-no16] [-excl *list*] [-mask10] [-order *list*] [-noprobe *list*] [-bios *base*] [-no_bios] [-no_dac] [-no_mem] [-info]

SuperProbe is handy when attempting to install and configure X Windows. It can determine the type of video hardware installed in an EISA/ISA/VLB-bus system. SuperProbe is not perfect and does not guarantee results.

Example: To probe your video hardware type:

SuperProbe

If using a MicroChannel or PCI machine, use the -no_bios option. TIP

-verbose	Display tons of information while running.
-no16	Do not attempt to use any ports which require 16-bit I/O address decoding.
***-excl** list*	Do not attempt to access any of the I/O ports specified in list. List is a comma separated list of ports or port ranges.
-mask10	When comparing an I/O port against the exclusion list, mask the port to 10 bits.
***-order** list*	Test only those chipsets in list in the specified order.
***-noprobe** list*	Do not test chipsets in the specified list.
***-bios** base*	Specify the base address for graphic-hardware BIOS.
-no_bios	Do not read the video BIOS and assume that an EGA or later (VGA, SVGA) board is the primary video hardware.
-no_dac	Do not probe for RAMDAC type when an (S)VGA is identified.
-no_mem	Do not probe for the amount of installed video memory.
-info	Display a list of all hardware which SuperProbe knows how to identify.

xdm [-config configuration_file] [-nodaemon] [-debug debug_level] [-error error_log_file] [-resources resource_file] [-server server_entry] [-session session_program]

X Display Manager. Supports XDMCP. The host may be local or remote. Xdm provides login and authentication services similar to those provided by getty and login on character terminals.

Example: To start xdm, type:

xdm

TIP When configuring xdm, try to have at least one other mechanism for accessing your machine (e.g., network access, ASCII terminal), as it is possible to mess up the configuration so badly that you can't log in.

-config *configuration_file*	Specify a configuration file for xdm. Default is <XRoot>/lib/X11/xdm/xdm-config.
-nodaemon	Do not run xdm as a daemon. (DisplayManager.daemonMode=false).
-debug *debug_level*	Specify a debug level.
-error *error_log_file*	Specify a log file into which error messages are written.
-resources *resource_file*	Specify the file used to specify configuration parameters for the authentication widget.
-server *server_entry*	Specify a value for the DisplayManager.servers resource.
-udpPort *port_number*	Specify the port number which will be monitored for XDMCP requests.
-session *session_program*	Specify the program to be run after the user has logged in.
-xrm *resource_specification*	Permit specification of an arbitrary resource as in most X Toolkit applications.

xf86config

xf86config generates an XF86Config file to be used with XFree86 servers. It is interactive.

Example: To interactively generate an XF86Config file, type:

xf86Config

xinit [[*client*] options] [-- [server] [*display*] options]

The **xinit** program can be used to start the X Window server. (Typically, it is invoked via the startx script.) In the absence of any specified client, xinit looks for an .xinitrc file in the user's home directory for most of its configuration information. Lacking a specified server, xinit looks in the user's home directory for a file .serverrc to be run as a shell script to start the server.

Example: To start the X Window server:

xinit

xmseconfig [-sync] [-display *display*] [-geometry *geometry*]

This program is used to change the server's mouse configuration. Changes are not saved for the next session.

Example: To configure your mouse:

xmseconfig

-sync	Synchronize all communication with the server.
-display *display*	Specify a display.
-geometry *geomspec*	Specify the window's initial geometry.

xterm [-toolkitoption ...] [-option ...]

This program is the terminal emulator for the X Window System. It can also be configured as a DEC VT102/VT220 compatible or Tektronix 4014 compatible terminal for programs which can't use the window system directly.

The following termcap entries work with xterm: xterm, vt102, vt100, ansi.

Example: To invoke an xterm with a large scrollback buffer (**-sl** option):

xterm -sl 2000 &

Options

The following options are accepted in addition to the standard X Toolkit options. If you invoke the option with a plus sign ("+") rather than the standard dash("-"), the option will be reset to its default value.

-version	Display version information.
-help	Display help information to standard error.

Appearance & Behavior Options

-132	Do not ignore the VT102 DECCOLM escape sequence that switches between 80 & 132 columns.
-ah	Always highlight the text cursor.
+ah	Do text cursor highlighting based on focus.
-ai	Disable active icon support (if compiled into xterm).
+ai	Enable active icon support (if compiled into xterm).
-aw	Allow auto-wraparound to next line.
+aw	Do not allow auto-wraparound.
-b number	Specify the distance between the window border and the outer edge of the characters.
-bdc	Do not display characters with the bold attribute as color rather than bold.
+bdc	Display characters with the bold attribute as color rather than bold.
-cb	Set the vt100 resource cutToBeginningOfLine to FALSE.
+cb	Set the vt100 resource cutToBeginningOfLine to TRUE.
-cc characterclassrange:value[,...]	Set classes indicated by the given ranges for using in selecting by words. (See the section on specifying character classes.)

-cm	Disable recognition of ANSI color-change escape sequences.
+cm	Enable recognition of ANSI color-change escape sequences.
-cn	Do not cut newlines in line-mode selections.
+cn	Cut newlines in line mode selection.
-cr color	Specify the color to use as the text cursor.
-cu	This option is a workaround for a bug in the more program. The bug causes it to incorrectly display lines which are exactly the width of the window and are followed by a line beginning with a <tab> (the leading tabs are not displayed).
+cu	Do not work around the more bug described above.
-dc	Disable the escape sequence to change dynamic colors.
+dc	Enable the escape sequence to change dynamic colors.
-e *program [arguments ...]*	Specify the program (and, optionally, that program's command line arguments) to be run in the xterm window.
-fb *font*	Specify a font to be used when displaying bold text.
-fi	Set the font for active icons, if that feature was compiled into xterm.
-hc *color*	Specify the color to use for the background of selected or otherwise highlighted text. If not specified, reverse video is used.

-im	Turn on the useInsertMode resource.
+im	Turn off the useInsertMode resource.
-j	Enable jump scrolling (scrolling multiple lines) so that xterm doesn't fall too far behind.
+j	Do not do jump scrolling.
-leftbar	Put the scroll bar on the left side of the VT100 screen.
-ls	This option tells xterm that the shell started in the xterm window will be a login shell. This means that the first character of argv[0] will be a dash, which tells the shell to read the user's *.login* or *.profile*.
+ls	Tell xterm not to start the shell as a login shell.
-mb	Ring a margin bell when the user types near the right end of the line.
+mb	Do not ring a margin bell when the user types near the right end of the line.

TIP If you're working in a room with more than just one person, turn your margin bell off. In fact, turn off all your bells. Use wire cutters, if necessary. It's good manners, and a cost-effective way of preventing workplace violence. (See also **-vb** option.)

-mc milliseconds	Allow the user to specify the maximum time between multi-click selections.
-ms *color*	Specify the color to be used for the pointer cursor.
-nb *number*	Specify the number of character from the right end of a line at which the margin bell, if enabled, will ring (default = 10).

-nul	Enable display of underlining.
+nul	Disable display of underlining.
-pc	Enable PC-style use of bold colors.
+pc	Disable PC-style use of bold colors.
-rightbar	Force scrollbar to the right side of VT100 screen.
-rw	Enable reverse wraparound. This allows the cursor to wrap from the leftmost column of the current line to the rightmost column of the previous line.

Enable reverse wraparound.

+rw	Do not allow.
-s	Allow xterm to scroll asynchronously. That is, do not force xterm to keep the screen completely up-to-date when scrolling.
+s	Force xterm to scroll synchronously.
-sb	Turn on scrollback. This means that the lines you've looked at most recently will be saved in a buffer and may be accessed via the scroll bar on the screen.
+sb	Do not display the scrollbar.
-sf	Generate Sun Function Key escape codes for escape keys.
+sf	Generate standard escape codes for escape keys.
-si	Do not automatically reposition the screen to the bottom of the scrolling region following output to a window.
+si	Automatically reposition the screen to the bottom of the scrolling region following output to a window.
-sk	Automatically reposition a window in the normal position at the bottom of the scroll region when you press a key and use a scrollbar at the same time.

+sk	Do not reposition a window when pressing a key and using a scrollbar at the same time.
***-sl** number*	Specify the number of lines which have scrolled off the top of the screen to save (default = 64 lines).
-sp	Assume the Sun/PC keyboard.
+sp	Generate standard escape codes for the keypad and function keys.
-t	Start xterm in Tektronix mode rather than VT102 mode.
+t	Start xterm in VT102 mode.
***-tm** string*	Specify a series of terminal setting keywords followed by the characters which should be bound to those functions. Allowable keywords include: intr, quit, erase, kill, eof, eol, swtch, start, stop, brk, susp, dsusp, rprnt, flush, weras, and lnext. Control characters may be specified as ^char (e.g., ^c or ^u) and ^? may be used to indicate delete.
***-tn** name*	Specify the name of the terminal type to be set in the TERM environment variable.
-ulc	Disable the display of characters with underline attribute as color rather than underlined.
+ulc	Enable the display of characters with underline attribute as color rather than with underlining.
-ut	Do not write a record into the system log file /etc/utmp.
+ut	Write record into the system log file /etc/utmp.
-vb	Use a visual bell rather than an audible one.
+vb	Do not use a visual bell.
-wf	Wait for the window to be mapped the first time before starting the subprocess. This ensures that initial terminal size settings and environment variables are correct.
+wf	Don't wait before starting the application.

-C	Indicate the xterm should receive consold output.
-Sccn	Specify the last two letters of the name of a pseudo-terminal to use in slave mode.

The following standard X Toolkit command line arguments are commonly used with xterm:

-bd *color*	Specify a border color. Default=black.
-bg *color*	Specify a background color. Default=white.
-bw *pixels*	Specify in pixels the width of the window border.
-display *display*	Specify the X server to contact.
-fg *color*	Specify a foreground (text) color. Default = black.
-fn *font*	Specify normal text font. Default = fixed.
-geometry *geometry*	Specify size & position of VT102 window.
-iconic	Tell xterm to ask the window manager to start the specified term as an icon rather than a window.
-name *name*	Specify an application name under which resources are to be obtained rather than the default executable file name.
-rv	Simulate reverse video by swapping the foreground & background colors.
-title *string*	Specify the window title string.
-xrm *resourcestring*	Specify a resource string to be used.

RESOURCES

The program understands all of the core X Toolkit resource names and classes as well as:

iconGeometry *(class IconGeometry)*	Specify the preferred size and position of the application when iconified.
iconName *(class IconName)*	Specify the icon name.
sunFunctionKeys *(class SunFunctionKeys)*	Generate Sun Function Key escap codes rather than standard escape sequences.
sunKeyboard *(class SunKeyboard)*	Specify whether or not to assume Sun/PC keyboard layout rather than DEC VT220.
termName *(class TermName)*	Specify the terminal type name to be set in the TERM environment variable.
title *(class Title)*	Tell the window manager to use the specified string when displaying this application.
ttyModes *(class TtyModes)*	Specify a string containing terminal setting keywords and the characters to which they may be bound.
useInsertMode *(class UseInsertMode)*	Force use of insert mode by adding appropriate entries to the TERMCAP environment variable.
utmpInhibit *(class UtmpInhibit)*	Specify whether or not xterm should try to record the user's terminal in */etc/utmp*.
waitForMap *(class WaitForMap)*	Specify whether or not xterm should wait for the initial window map before starting the subprocess.

xvidtune [-prev | -next | -unlock |]] [-toolkitoption...]

Xvidtune is a neat program used to twiddle the video mode settings of the X display. The following buttons are active.

Example: To interactively tune your video display system:

xvidtune

<Left>, <Right>, <Up>, <Down>	Move the displayed image around on the screen.
<Wider>, <Narrower>, <Shorter>, <Taller>	Adjust the displayed image as specified.
Quit	Exit the program.
Apply	Apply any changes made to the server.
Auto	Toggle whether or not any changes made will be applied immediately.
Test	Temporarily switch to the selected settings.
Restore	Return the settings to their original values.
Fetch	Retrieve current settings from the server.
Show	Display the current settings to stdout.
Next	Switch the Xserver to the next video mode.
Prev	Switch the Xserver to the previous video mode.
InvertVCLK	Change the VCLK invert/non-invert state.
EarlySC	Change the Early SC state. This affects screen wrapping.
BlankDelay1, BlankDelay2	Set the blank delay values. These affect screen wrapping.

Options

-prev	Switch the Xserver to the previous video mode.
-next	Switch the Xserver to the next video mode.
-unlock	Allow switching of video modes via hot-keys as xvidtune is running.

CHAPTER

24

SCHEDULING

Introduction

The commands in this section are all used to tell the system to do something at (or until) a later time.

Proper use of these commands is the key to an efficiently run system. Throughout this book I have made suggestions about tasks which should be automated and run on a regular basis. These include, but are not limited to:

- system security checks (passwords, file access...)
- cleanup of temporary files (rm /tmp/*)
- updating system databases (updatedb)
- backups and archiving (tar, shar)

The following commands are included in this section:

at	Add a job to the scheduling queue
atq	Display the contents of the scheduling queue
atrm	Remove a job from the scheduling queue
batch	Execute queue only when system resources permit
crontab	Maintain schedule of jobs to be executed

 ***sleep***	Wait some number of seconds
usleep	Wait some number of microseconds

Related Files

/var/spool/at	List of at commands to be spooled
/var/spool/at/spool	Spooled at commands
/proc/loadavg	Contains system load average
/var/run/utmp	Database of users currently logged in
/etc/at.allow	Users permitted to use at
/etc/at.deny	Users prohibited from using at
/etc/cron.allow	Users permitted to use cron
/etc/cron.deny	Users prohibited from using cron

Commands

at [-V] [-q *queue*] [-f file] [-mldbv] TIME

at -c job [*job*...]

atq [-V] [-q *queue*] [-v]

atrm [-V] *job* [*job*...]

batch [-V] [-q *queue*] [-f *file*] [-mv] [TIME]

The **at** command suite (**at, atq, atrm, batch**) is a utility for executing commands at a later time. More than one command may be scheduled for execution at a time. A set of scheduled commands is called a **queue**.

at	Execute commands at a specified time.
atq	List the current user's queued jobs. (If superuser, list all jobs.)
atrm	Delete jobs from the queue.
batch	Run only the commands when the system load levels permit.

SPECIFYING A TIME:

There are three ways to specify a time: Absolute, Relative, or Verbal.

Absolute:	MM/DD/YY or DD.MM.YY or MMDDYY (with or without HH:MM)
Relative:	<some absolute time> + <delay>
	where
Delay is:	<some number> [minutes|hours|days|weeks]
Verbal:	noon, midnight, teatime, AM, PM, tomorrow, +

Example: To run the script "backup.sh" at midnight:

at midnight -f backup.sh

Example: To find out what job number the job submitted in the example above is:

atq

which would produce results like

```
3       1999-07-25 00:00 a
```

Example: To cancel execution of the script "backup.sh" as implemented in the examples above:

atrm 3

-V	Display version information.
-q *queue*	Specify a queue. Valid values for queue are [a-z][A-Z], and = for currently running jobs. Default values are a for at and b for batch. Queues with higher letters run with increased nice values.
-m	Send mail to the user when the job finishes running.
-f *file*	Commands to be run will be taken from the specified file rather than standard input.
-l	List queued jobs.
-d	Remove previously queued job.
-v	For atq, shows completed but not yet deleted jobs in the queue. For all others, it shows the time the job will be executed.
-c	Display the jobs listed on the command line to standard output.

crontab [-u *user*] *file*

crontab [-u *user*] { -l | -r | -e }

Crontab is the command used to maintain your list of cron jobs. A cron job is a job scheduled to be executed automatically by the system at some specified time or interval. In order for this to work, the **cron daemon** must be running.

Confusingly, cron jobs are stored in files which are also called **crontabs**. On most systems, each user can set up his or her own **crontab**. (It is possible to configure cron such than no one but the superuser can use cron). If your user name is listed in a file ***/etc/cron.deny***, you cannot use cron. Similarly, if the file ***/etc/cron.allow*** exists, you must be listed in it or you cannot use cron.

When you use crontab for the first time, your default editor (usually vi) is invoked and you're looking at a blank file. You use crontab by adding and deleting entries from this file. Entries are in the following format:

Variable:	minutes	hours	day-of-month	month	weekday	command
Range:	0-59	0-23	1-31	1-12	0-6	

When you're done editing, quit out of the editor the normal way. Cron will look at what you've done and tell you if you made formatting errors. Otherwise, the jobs will be executed as specified. Note that for the weekdays field, 0=sunday.

Note: Depending on what you're trying to do with cron, some of the fields will always be blank. **Always mark the unused fields with asterisks, "*".**

Example: To edit your crontab:

crontab -e

To run the shell script "cleanup.sh" at midnight on Fridays, add the following line to the crontab file:

```
0 0 * * 5 crontab.sh
```

TIP

You can, technically, edit your cron files without using crontab. But it isn't a good idea.

-u user	Specify a crontab other than the default.
-l	List the crontab to standard output.
-r	Remove the entire crontab.
-e	Edit the crontab. Note that when you exit the editor, any changes you make will be automatically submitted to the cron daemon.

sleep [NUMBER[smhd]]...

Sleep for the specified length of time. Time is specified in one of the following units:

s	**seconds**
m	**minutes**
h	**hours**
d	**days**

Example: To run the command **wall < message** (which displays the contents of the file "message" to the screens of all users currently logged in) after a two-minute delay:

sleep 120; wall < message

--help	Display help information.
--version	Display version information.

usleep [number]

Sleep some number of microseconds.

Example: To run the command synctest twice with a delay of fifteen microseconds between executions:

synctest; usleep 15; synctest

--help	Print help information.
-v	Print version information.

CHAPTER

25

FINDING STUFF

Introduction

This section is an amalgamation of some very different programs which are united under the eponymous purpose of "finding stuff," but work in quite different ways.

Generally speaking, **find** (the biggie), searches the directory tree for a file or files specified by the command line. This happens to present a golden opportunity for hard-core programming in that it is a real world example of a classic computer science problem. As such, the **find** command has quite a few options and is perhaps more complex than necessary. For those of you simply wishing to learn the location of a particular file in a timely and painless manner, I recommend **locate**.

REGULAR EXPRESSIONS

Most of the search mechanisms listed below use regular expressions in one form or another. A **regular expression** is a mathematical mechanism for specifying the ordering of symbols. Historically, regular expressions originated from discussions of the Theory of Computation, a seriously hard-core branch of mathematics which is far removed from the day-to-day rigors of, say, locating the smutty email to your girlfriend you misplaced in some gargantuan file system at work.

However, the same principles govern both tasks. In order to get full value for your Linux dollar, you will need some understanding of regular expressions and how they are used to specify search patterns.

Regular expressions exist to give you a mechanism to specify patterns of characters. The implementation of a regular expression includes three classes of characters:

literals	The literal character you typed in (a, b, c..., 1,2,3... etc.).
wildcards	Special characters used to represent one or more characters other than themselves. For example, the * character will match any number of any other characters ("d*" matches "date", "day", "dally" and anything else starting with the letter d.) The . character will match one instance of any other character ("d.te" matches with "date" and "dote").
metacharacters	Metacharacters are characters which have a special meaning. For example, the caret character "^" usually matches the beginning of a line. The "$" character matches the end of a line.

In addition, it is possible to specify groups of characters. For example, the regular expression "[aAbB]*"would match any string of any length which started with the letter a or b, either uppercase or lowercase. (This group is delimited by square braces.) See the **grep** entry for more information about the implementation of **regular expressions**.

The commands covered in this section include:

egrep	Grep with extended regular expressions
find	Search the directory tree
finger	Display information about a user
fgrep	Grep variation for matching fixed strings
grep	Search for a pattern in a file
locate	Search the locate database for a file
updatedb	Update the locate database
which	Search the directories of your $PATH for a file

Related Files

/var/lib/locatedb	**Default locate database.**

Commands

find [path...][expression]

The **find** command searches the directory tree specified by the path argument for the pattern(s) indicated in the expression argument.

The expression consists of options, tests, and actions. Options affect overall operation rather than the processing of a specific file. Tests return a true or false value based on evaluation of some condition. Actions have side effects and return a true or false value.

Example: To search the entire system for a file named “abcd.txt”:

find / -name abcd.txt -print

Example: To search all the files in the directory tree of user “someguy” for the string “blah”:

find /home/someguy -type f -print |xargs grep -n "blah"

TIP

A common mistake with the **find** command is assuming that it displays output by default. It doesn't. If you want to see what **find** found, you must specify one of the various print options (e.g., -print).

-daystart	Tell find to measure times relative to the start of the current calendar day rather than 24 hours ago.
-depth	Perform a depth first search rather than a breadth first search. That is, search the contents of each directory before the directory itself.
-follow	Follow any symbolic links encountered in the search.
-help, --help	Display a help summary and exit.
-maxdepth levels	Descend at most the specific number of levels below the starting point.

-mindepth levels	Do not act on directories above the specified depth.
-mount	Do not traverse directories on other filesystems.
-noleaf	Do not increase search speed by discounting the "." and ".." directories in calculations. Used in searching CD-ROM and MS-DOS filesystems.
-version, --version	Display the version number and exit.
-xdev	Do not traverse directories on other filesystems.

TESTS

Numeric arguments can be specified as:

+n	greater than n
-n	less than n
n	exactly n

***-amin** n*	Specify that the file was last accessed n minutes ago.
***-anewer** file*	Look for files last accessed more recently than the specified file was modified.
***-atime** n*	File was last accessed n*24 hours ago.
***-cmin** n*	File's status was last changed n minutes ago.
***-cnewer** file*	File's status was last changed more recently than file was modified. -cnewer is affected by -follow only if -follow comes before -cnewer on the command line.
***-ctime** n*	File's status was last changed n*24 hours ago.
-empty	File is empty and is either a regular file or a directory.
-false	Always false.
***-fstype** type*	Search for the file on filesystems of the specific type.

-gid *n*	Specify the file's numeric group id.
-group *gname*	Specify the file group name (or, allowably, numeric group ID).
-ilname *pattern*	Like -lname, but the match is case insensitive.
-iname *pattern*	Case insensitive lname match.
-inum *n*	File has inode number n.
-ipath *pattern*	Like -path, but the match is case insensitive.
-iregex *pattern*	Case insensitive regex search.
-links *n*	Specifies that file has n links.
-lname *pattern*	File is a symbolic link whose contents match the specified pattern.
-mmin *n*	File's data was last modified n minutes ago.
-mtime *n*	File's data was last modified n*24 hours ago.
-name *pattern*	Tell find to look for a file whose basename matches the specified shell pattern.
-newer *file*	Tell find to look for files modified more recently than the specified file.
-nouser	No user corresponds to file's numeric user ID.
-nogroup	No group corresponds to file's numeric group ID.
-path *pattern*	Match file name to the specified shell pattern.
-perm *mode*	Exactly match the file permissions to the specified mode.
-perm -mode	All of the permission bits mode are set for the file.
-perm +mode	Any of the permission bits mode are set for the file.
-regex *pattern*	Match filename to the specified regular expression.

-size n[bckw]	Match file size to the specified unit of space (b=512 byte blocks, c==bytes, k=kilobytes, w=2 byte words).
-true	Always true.
-type c	Specify file type (one of the following): **b** block (buffered) special **c** character (unbuffered) special **d** directory **p** named pipe (FIFO) **f** regular file **l** symbolic link **s** socket
-uid *n*	Match file's user id to n.
-used *n*	File was last accessed n days after its status was last changed.
-user *uname*	Uname is the file's owner.
-xtype *c*	The same as -type unless the file is a symbolic link. If the file is a symbolic link and the -follow option is not set, then true if the file is a link to file of type c. If the -follow option is not set, then true if the specified type is l.

ACTIONS

-exec command ;	Execute the specified command. The semicolon ";" indicates termination of command's argument set.
-fls *file*	True; like -ls but write to file like -fprint.
-fprint *file*	True; redirect file name output into the specified file.
-fprint0 *file*	True; like -print0 but write to file like -fprint.
-fprintf *file format*	True; like -printf but write to file like -fprint.
-ok *command ;*	Like -exec option, but prompt before running.
-print	Send filenames to standard output.

-print0	Send filenames to standard output teminated with a null character.
-printf *format*	Use the specified format when printing to standard output. Recognizes the following "\" escapes and "%" directives: **\a** Alarm bell. **\b** Backspace. **\c** Stop printing and flush output immediately. **\f** Form feed. **\n** Newline. **\r** Carriage return. **\t** Horizontal tab. **\v** Vertical tab. \\ A literal backslash ("\"). %% A literal percent sign. **%a** File's last access time. **%Ak** File's last access time in the format specified by k, which is either "@" or a directive for the C "strftime" function (specified below). @ seconds since Jan. 1, 1970, 00:00 GMT.

TIME FIELDS:

H	hour (00..23)
I	hour (01..12)
k	hour (0..23)
l	hour (1..12)
M	minute (00..59)
p	locale's AM or PM
r	time, 12-hour (hh:mm:ss [AP]M)
S	second (00..61)
T	time, 24-hour (hh:mm:ss)

X	locale's time representation (H:M:S)
Z	time zone (e.g., EDT)

DATE FIELDS:

a	weekday name abbreviations (Sun., Mon....)
A	weekday name (Sunday, Monday...)
b	month name abbreviations (Jan., Feb....)
B	full month name (January, February...)
c	date and time (Sat Nov 04 12:02:33 EST 1989)
d	day of month (01..31)
D	date (mm/dd/yy)
h	same as b
j	day of year (001..366)
m	month (01..12)
U	week number of year with Sunday as first day of week (00..53)
w	day of week (0..6)
W	week number of year with Monday as first day of week (00..53)
x	locale's date representation (mm/dd/yy)
y	last two digits of year (00..99)
Y	year (1970...)

%b	File size in blocks.
%c	Last file status change time.
%Ck	File's last status change time in the format specified by k.
%d	File's depth in the directory tree.
%f	File name with leading directories removed.
%F	Type of the filesystem where the file is located.
%g	File's group name.
%G	File's numeric group ID.
%h	Leading directories of file's name.
%H	Command line argument under which the file was found.
%i	File's inode number (in decimal).
%k	File's size in 1K blocks.
%l	Object of symbolic link (empty if file is not symbolic link).
%m	File's permission bits (in octal).
%n	Number of hard links to file.
%p	File's name.
%P	File's name minus the command line argument under which it was found.
%s	File's size in bytes.
%t	File's last modification time.
%Tk	File's last modification time in the format specified by k (see %A above, for format details).
%u	File's user name.
%U	File's numeric user ID.

-prune	If -depth is not given, true; do not descend the current directory. If -depth is given, false; no effect.
-ls	True; list current file n ls -dils' format on standard output.

OPERATORS

Listed in order of decreasing precedence:

(expr)	Force precedence.
!, -not	Logical negation; expr True if expr is false.
expr1 expr2, *expr1 -a expr2,* *expr1 -and expr2*	Logical and. expr2 not evaluated if expr1 is false.
expr1 -o expr2, *expr1 -or expr2*	Logical or. expr2 not evaluated if expr1 is true.
expr1 , expr2	List; both expr1 and expr2 are always evaluated. The value of expr1 is discarded; the value of the list is the value of expr2.

finger [-lmsp] [user ...] [user@host ...]

The **finger** command displays information about system users. If no argument is specified, finger will print out information on all users currently logged in. User may be a remote user; if so, use the "user@host" style of specification.

Example: To get information about the login status of user "jlevy":

finger jlevy@diana.gov

TIP Information stored in the file **.plan** in your home directory is printed to the screen whenever anyone **finger**s you. This was originally included so that you could keep fellow users up to the minute on your current doings (e.g., "In important meeting", "At lunch, back in an hour."). In actual practice, no one bothers to keep his or her .**plan**s up to date and the file is almost universally used as a repository for obscure quotations.

-s	Display user's login name, real name, terminal name, write status, idle time, login time, office location, and office phone number.
-l	Long list. Display home directory, phone number, login shell, mail status, and .plan, .project, and .forward files.
-p	Do not display .plan and .project files.
-m	Do not match user names.

grep [-[AB] NUM] [-CEFGVbchiLlnqsvwxyUu] [-e PATTERN | -f FILE] [--extended-regexp] [--fixed-strings] [--basic-reg-exp] [--regexp=*PATTERN*] [--file=FILE] [--ignore-case][--word-regexp] [--line-regexp] [--line-regexp] [--no-messages] [--revert-match] [--version] [--help] [--byte-off-set] [--line-number] [--with-filename] [--no-filename][--quiet] [--silent] [--files-without-match] [--files-with-matcces] [--count] [--before-context=NUM] [--after-context=NUM] [--context] [--binary] [--unix-byte-offsets] *files...*

grep (Global Regular Expression Parser) searches through the input set for any matches to the specified pattern and (by default) outputs any matching lines. The command may also be invoked as **egrep** (a.k.a. grep -e) or **fgrep** (a.k.a. grep -f).

Example: To output the lines and numbers of any variable starting with "cha" in the c files in the current directory:

grep -n cha *.c

Grep has three modes of use, as specified by the following options:

-G, --basic-regexp	Interpret the specified pattern as a basic regular expression.

-E, --extended-regexp	Interpret the specified pattern as an extended regular expression.
-F, --fixed-strings	Interpret the specified pattern as a list of fixed strings to be matched.

The **grep** family accepts the following options:

-NUM	Include the specified number of lines of leading and trailing context.
-A *NUM*	Include the specified number of lines of trailing context.
-B *NUM*	Include the specified number of lines of leading context.
-b, --byte-offset	Include byte offset in any output.
-c, --count	Instead of matching lines, output a count of matching lines.
-e PATTERN, --regexp=PATTERN	Use the specified pattern (including those beginning with "-").
-f FILE, --file=*FILE*	Use the specified FILE as the pattern source.
-h, --no-filename	Do not include filenames in output.
-i, --ignore-case	Treat uppercase and lowercase letters as equivalent.
-L, --files-without-match	Output only the names of files which contain no matches to PATTERN.
-l, --files-with-matches	Output only the names of files which contain matches to PATTERN.
-n, --line-number	Include line numbers in any output.
-q, --quiet	Output nothing, halt if match found.

-s, --silent	Do not output error messages about bad files.
-v, --revert-match	Output only those lines which do NOT match the specified pattern.
-w, --word-regexp	Output only those lines which match whole words.
-x, --line-regexp	Output only full line matches.
-y	Synonym for -i.
-U, --binary	Treat all files as binary.
-u, --unix-byte-offsets	Output Unix-style byte offsets.

Grep recognizes the following in pattern specification:

SPECIFYING CHARACTER CLASSES

[:alnum:]	Alphanumeric characters [0-9A-Za-z]
[:alpha:]	Alphabetic characters [A-Za-z]
[:cntrl:]	Control characters
[:digit:]	Digits
[:graph:]	Graphic characters
[:lower:]	Lowercase characters
[:print:]	Printable characters
[:punct:]	Punctuation characters
[:space:]	Whitespace (space, tab...)
[:upper:]	Uppercase characters
[:xdigit:]	Hexadecimal digits

Specifying Position

.	Matches any single character
^	The beginning of a line
$	The end of a line
\<	Beginning of a word
\>	End of a word
\b	Empty string at edge of a word
\B	Empty string not at edge of a word

Specifying Pattern Repetition

?	Match the preceding item at most once.
*	Match the preceding any number of times (including none).
+	Match the preceding one or more times.
{n}	Match the preceding exactly n times.
{n,}	Match the preceding n or more times.
{,m}	Match the preceding 0-m times.
{n,m}	Match the preceding at least n but no more than m times.

locate [-d path][--database=path][--version][--help] pattern...

Locate searches a database of system files and locations for the specified pattern. The pattern specification can include shell metacharacters (*, ?, . , etc.)

Example: To find the file abcd.txt on any directory indexed by the **updatedb** command:

locate abcd.txt

TIP

Locate is a quick and simple alternative to the **find** command, but you need to update the database regularly with **updatedb**.

-d path, --database=path	Tell locate to search the specified database for the pattern rather than the default database.
--help	Print a summary of the options to locate and exit.
--version	Print the version number of locate and exit.

updatedb [options]

This command updates the database of file names and locations used by the **locate** command.

Example: To update the default database file:

updatedb

ROOT

TIP

Set your **cron** to run **updatedb** every so often.

--localpaths='path1 path2...'	Specify the (non-network) directories to be included in the database.
--netpaths=*'path1 path2...'*	Specify the network directories to be included in the database.
--prunepaths=*'path1 path2...'*	Specify directories to be excluded from the database.
--output=*dbfile*	Specify the database file to be built (typically */usr/local/var/locatedb*).
--netuser=*user*	Specify the user identity to be used when searching network directories.
--old-format	Specify the database will be created in the old format.
--version	Display version information and exit.
--help	Display help information and exit.

which progname ...

Searches the user's path for the specified program and prints its full pathname, if found.

Example: To find the location in the directory tree of the ls command:

which ls

CHAPTER

26

DIAGNOSTICS & SYSTEM PERFORMANCE

Introduction

The commands in this section are your tools for monitoring the physical resources (disk space, swap space, memory) and performance of your system.

Frequently, an executing program is too large for the entire program to be contained in your system RAM. In such a case, the system writes a portion of the program which is not currently executing out to disk temporarily. This process is known as **paging**, because the programs are broken up into units called **pages**. When an executing process needs a page not currently stored in the RAM, that is a **page fault**. Lots of page faults are bad; they can slow the system to a crawl. The portion of disk space used for paging is called the **swap partition**.

TIP Disk space is cheap. Don't skimp on the size of your swap partition. It should be at least as large as your physical memory, and potentially much larger.

The most complete picture of your system's memory use is obtained via the **vmstat** command. Learn how to read it and use it regularly; it will give you a clear picture of how well your system resources are being utilized.

If you have an immediate and acute problem, the **top** command will give you a quick highlight of what your system is doing.

Shared memory is allocated memory which is accessible by more than one process.

A **semaphore** is anything (e.g., system file, program variable) used to indicate that a resource is in use.

df	Display filesystem information
dmesg	Display bootup messages
free	Snapshot of system memory
ipcs	Shared memory, semaphores, message queues
ps	Get process information. See Chapter 3.
pstree	Display process family tree
runlevel	System runlevel information
tload	Graph CPU usage information
top	System usage information
vmstat	Memory information
who	User information

Related Files

/proc/loadavg	**load average information**
/etc/utmp	**information about who is currently logged on**
/proc	**"filesystem" which contains process information**
/proc/meminfo	**memory information**

Commands

df [option, ...] [file,...]

Report the amount of space used and available on filesystem(s).

Example: To print out the current state of the filesystems with size in megabytes:

df -h

```
Filesystem     Size  Used  Avail  Capacity Mounted on
/dev/hda5      167M   45M   114M     28%    /
/dev/hda7      402M  2.9M   379M      1%    /home
/dev/hda6      1.6G  815M   703M     54%    /usr
```

where **Filesystem** is the disk partition corresponding to the mounted filesystem. **Mounted on** gives the entry in ***/etc/fstab*** corresponding to the disk partition. **Size, Used**, and **Avail** are the obvious (though normally displayed by block count rather than megabytes).

TIP

Filesystems do fill up. The following commands may be used to present some good candidates for archiving or deletion. To list the files in **descending order by size**:

du -a / | sort -rn | less

To list files that **haven't been accessed in the last 90 days:**

find / -atime +90 -print | less

-a, --all	Also list filesystems of size 0, which are omitted by default.
-h, -human-readable	Append letters to specify units of measurement (e.g., M=megabyte, K=kilobyte).
--inodes	List inode usage infomation instead of block usage.
-k, --kilobytes	Print size in 1024 byte blocks.
-m, --megabytes	Print size in megabyte blocks.
--no-sync	Do not run the sync system call before getting usage data.
-P, --portability	Use the POSIX output format.
--sync	Invoke the sync system call before getting usage data.
***-t** FSTYPE,**--type=**FSTYPE*	List only filesystems of type FSTYPE.
-T,--print-type	Include the filesystem type (nfs, 4.2, ufs, efs, hsfs, cdfs, pcfs) in the listing.
***-x** FSTYPE, **--exclude-type=**FSTYPE*	Exclude from the listing filesystems of type FSTYPE.
-v	Ignored; for compatibility with System V versions of "df".

dmesg [-c] [-n *level*] [-s *bufsize*]

This command is used to display or control the contents of the kernel ring buffer, which contains the bootup messages.

Example: To get the boot messages from your last system startup:

dmesg | less

Example: To set your console to display messages with annoying frequency:

dmesg -n 3

-c	Clear the contents of the ring buffer after printing.
-sbufsize	Specify the size of the buffer used to query the kernel ring buffer. Default is 8196.
-nlevel	Specify the level at which log messages are displayed to the console. Note that messages are sent to /proc/kmsg regardless of level. Typically, this is set to 1, which filters all but panic messages.

free [-b | -k | -m] [-o] [-s *delay*] [-t] [-V]

Free gives a snapshot of the system memory. It displays information on physical memory, swap memory, shared memory, and buffers.

Example: To get the default information (see display below):

free

	total	used	free	shared	buffers	cached
Mem:	95460	88832	6628	24208	33912	34968
-/+ buffers/cache:	19952	75508				
Swap:	104384	0	104384			

-b	Displays given in bytes.
-k	Displays given in kilobytes.
-m	Displays given in megabytes.
-o	Do not display "buffer adjusted" line.
***-s** seconds*	Use of this option will run free continuously with a delay of the specified number of seconds.
-t	Totals included in display.
-V	Display version information.

ipcs [-asmq] [-tclup]

ipcs [-smq] -i id

ipcs -h

Display information on shared memory segments, semaphore arrays, and message queues.

Example: To get full information from ipcs (see example below):

ipcs

```
------ Shared Memory Segments --------
key        shmid      owner      perms      bytes      nattch     status

------ Semaphore Arrays --------
key        semid      owner      perms      nsems      status

------ Message Queues --------
key        msqid      owner      perms      used-bytes   messages
0x00000000 0          root       700        0            0
```

-m	Display information on shared memory segments.
-q	Display information on message queues.
-s	Display information on semaphore arrays.
-a	Display information on everything.
-t	Output time information.
-p	Output pid information.
-c	Output creator information.
-l	Output limit information.
-u	Output summary information.

pstree [-a] [-c] [-h] [-l] [-n] [-p] [-u] [-G|-U] [pid|user]

pstree -V

Output the family tree of running processes. If no process id or user name is specified, the tree is rooted at init. Identical branches are merged in the display by prefixing the process name with a count.

Example: Say your xinit process has a PID of 430. To display it and all its descendants in tree form with their PIDs (see output, below):

pstree 430 -p

```
xinit(431)-+-X(432)
           `-wmaker(434)-+-wmclock(443)
                         |-xterm(637)---bash(638)
                         |-xterm(715)---bash(716)---pstree(2118)
                         |-xterm(718)---bash(719)---top(720)
                         |-xterm(721)---bash(722)---
  vi(2051)
                         `-xterm(724)---bash(725)
```

-a Include command line arguments in the display.

-c Do not compact the identical subtrees.

-G Graphical display. (Use vt100 line drawing characters.) Very cool.

-h Highlight family tree of current process.

-l Do not truncate long lines.

-n Numeric sort by PID.

-p Include PIDs in display.

-u Include uid transitions in display.

-U Graphical display. Uses UTF-8 (Unicode) graphical characters in display.

-V Display version information.

runlevel [utmp]

Runlevel consults the system utmp file and displays the current and previous system runlevel. A value of "N" indicates that there was no previous runlevel.

Example: To display the current and previous runlevel:

ROOT

runlevel

utmp	Specifies a utmp file to be read.

tload [-V] [-s *scale*] [-d *delay*] [tty]

Displays a graph of the current system load average.

Example: To set up a window to monitor system performance with a delay of 5 seconds between updates:

tload -d 5

-s	Specify a vertical scale for the output. A smaller value represents a larger scale.
-d	Specify a delay (in seconds) between graph updates.

top [-] [d *delay*] [q] [c] [S] [s] [i]

Top displays a listing of the processes utilizing the CPU. Output may be ordered by CPU usage, memory usage or runtime. Note that **top** is itself a CPU-intensive task, so you might want to use it sparingly. To change options while **top** is running, use the **s** command at the prompt and specify the new options.

Example: In my experience, **top** is generally run without arguments.

top

It produces output like the following:

```
8:59am  up 3 days, 16:42,  3 users,  load average: 0.00, 0.00, 0.00
39 processes: 38 sleeping, 1 running, 0 zombie, 0 stopped
CPU states:  0.9% user,  0.0% system,  0.0% nice, 99.1% idle
Mem:   95460K av,  87380K used,   8080K free,  17648K shrd,  33748K buff
Swap: 104384K av,      0K used, 104384K free                 37184K cached

  PID USER      PRI  NI  SIZE  RSS SHARE STAT  LIB %CPU %MEM   TIME COMMAND
 6543 root       19   0   716  716   556 R       0  0.9  0.7   0:00 top
    1 root        0   0   388  388   328 S       0  0.0  0.4   0:03 init
    2 root        0   0     0    0     0 SW      0  0.0  0.0   0:00 kflushd
```

```
   3 root     -12 -12    0    0    0 SW<     0  0.0  0.0   0:00 kswapd
   4 root       0   0    0    0    0 SW      0  0.0  0.0   0:00 md_thread
   5 root       0   0    0    0    0 SW      0  0.0  0.0   0:00 md_thread
 402 news      19   0  708  708  576 S       0  0.0  0.7   0:00 innwatch
1287 root       0   0  796  796  656 S       0  0.0  0.8   0:00 bash
 395 root       0   0  296  296  248 S       0  0.0  0.3   0:00 mingetty
  36 root       0   0  364  364  312 S       0  0.0  0.3   0:00 kerneld
 210 bin        0   0  332  332  264 S       0  0.0  0.3   0:00 portmap
 224 root       0   0  472  472  396 S       0  0.0  0.4   0:00 syslogd
 233 root       0   0  536  536  324 S       0  0.0  0.5   0:00 klogd
 244 daemon     0   0  404  404  328 S       0  0.0  0.4   0:00 atd
 255 root       0   0  472  472  392 S       0  0.0  0.4   0:00 crond
 267 root       0   0  396  396  328 S       0  0.0  0.4   0:00 inetd
 278 root       0   0 1168 1168  580 S       0  0.0  1.2   0:00 named
```


-d	Use the specified delay (in seconds) between updates.
-q	Refresh constantly with no delay.
-S	Include in usage calculations the usage of the process' children.
-s	Run in secure mode.
-i	Tell top to ignore idle or zombie processes.
-c	Include the process' entire command line in the output

Summary of Display Options

uptime	How long the system has been running, plus the average number of processes ready to run in the last 1, 5, and 15 minutes.
processes	Count of the number of processes running at the last update.
CPU states	Percentage of CPU time in user mode, system mode, niced tasks and idle.
Mem	Memory statistics (total K, free K, used K, shared K, buffer K).
Swap	Swap statistics (total K, available K, used K, cached).

PID	PID of the process
PPID	PID of the process' parent
UID	UID of the process' owner

USER	User name of the process' owner
PRI	Priority of the task
NI	Nice value of the task
SIZE	Size of code + data + stack space, in kilobytes
TSIZE	Code size of the task
DSIZE	Size of data + stack space
TRS	Text Resident Size
SWAP	Size of part of task currently swapped out
D	Size of dirty memory pages
LIB	Size of library pages
RSS	Total amount of physical memory used by the task
SHARE	Amount of shared memory used by the task
STAT	State of the task (Z=zombie, S=sleeping, T=stopped)
WCHAN	Show the address or name of the kernel function task is sleeping in
TIME	Total CPU time used by task since invoked
%CPU	Percentage of CPU time used by task since last update
%MEM	Percentage of physical memory used by task
COMMAND	Name of command which started task

Once invoked, **top** may be used interactively. The following are supported:

<space>	Update display information immediately.
^L	Repaint the screen.
h, ?	Display help information.

k	Kill a process--top will prompt for pid.
i	Ignore zombie processes and idle processes.
n, #	Show the specified number of processes.
q	Quit.
r	Renice a process.
S	Toggle cumulative mode on/off.
s	Specify new delay (in seconds) between updates.
f, F	Add specified fields to display.
o, O	Change order of displayed fields.
l	Toggle display of load average and uptime information.
m	Toggle display of memory information.
t	Toggle display of CPU state and process information.
c	Toggle display between command name/full command line.
M	Order display by memory usage.
P	Order display by CPU usage.
T	Order display by time/cumulative time.
W	Write current setup to ~/.toprc.

vmstat [-n] [*delay* [*count*]]

vmstat[-V]

Display information about current processes, memory, paging, block IO, traps and CPU activity. Output is either one-time or periodic. The first line of the display shows averages since last reboot.

Example: To get vmstat information for five seconds at one-second intervals (see output below):

vmstat 1 5

```
procs                     memory     swap         io    system          cpu
r b w   swpd   free  buff  cache   si   so   bi   bo   in   cs  us  sy  id
0 0 0      0 12396 33976 29300    0    0    1    0  101   77   0   0  99
0 0 0      0 12396 33976 29300    0    0    0    0  103   50   0   1  99
0 0 0      0 12396 33976 29300    0    0    0    0  102   54   0   1  99
0 0 0      0 12396 33976 29300    0    0    0    0  102   43   0   1  99
0 0 0      0 12396 33976 29300    0    0    0    0  102  151   2   2  96
```

-n	Display the header only once (default is regular display).
delay	Specify a delay between updates (in seconds).
count	Specify the number of updates.
-V	Display version information.

The Output Explained

PROCS

r:	Processes waiting for runtime.
b:	Processes in uninterruptable sleep.
w:	Processes swapped out but otherwise runnable.

MEMORY

swpd:	Virtual memory used (kB).
free:	Idle memory (kB).
buff:	Memory used as buffers (kB).

SWAP

si:	Memory swapped in from disk (kB/s).
so:	Memory swapped to disk (kB/s).

IO

bi:	Blocks sent to a block device (blocks/s).
bo:	Blocks received from a block device (blocks/s).

SYSTEM

in:	Interrupts per second, including the clock.
cs:	The number of context switches per second.

CPU

us:	Percentage user time.
sy:	Percentage system time.
id:	Percentage idle time.

who [OPTION] [FILE] [am i]

Display information about the users currently logged in. With no options, the display includes: login name, terminal line, login time, remote hostname or X display.

Example: To find out who's logged in to the system:

who

FILE	If present, who will use this as the source for users logged on rather than /etc/wtmp.
-m	Same as "who am I".
-q, -count	Display only the count of users logged on and their login names.
-s	No effect; included for compatibility.

-i, -u, -idle	Include idle time in display. "." in the idle time field means the user has been active in the last minute; "old" means they have been idle for more than 24 hours.
-H, -heading	Print a line of column headings.
-w, -T, -mesg, -message, -writable	After each login name, print a character indicating the user's message status: + allowing "write" messages - disallowing "write" messages ? cannot find terminal device

CHAPTER

27

SECURITY

Introduction

Cryptography, which literally means "secret writing," is the process of turning a string of plain text into something that looks like chicken scratches and is more or less thoroughly unreadable (**encrypting**) and, optionally, turning it back into legible text again (**decrypting**).

Until the early nineties there was virtually no information publicly available on cryptography. I know, because I looked. With the advent of the Internet and the obvious need for good data security that is no longer true, and there are some excellent books and software easily available. The U.S. government is still somewhat grumpy about this, however. The PGP software discussed in this section is not part of a common Linux release. It is, in fact, illegal to export it beyond the boundaries of the United States. The source code, however, is covered under the freedom of the press laws, and is promptly disseminated across the borders to any interested terrorists, conveniently formatted for electronic scanning and later compilation.

PGP is an implementation of a concept called **Public Key Cryptography**. In public key cryptography, there are two **keys** (sequences of bits referred to in the encoding and decoding processes). One of them, the **public key**, is, as the name implies, publicly available. You give it out to anyone from whom you might want to receive a private message. The other, **private key** is used to decrypt messages encrypted with the public key. The private key is not derivable from the public key. In this way secret communication is possible.

PGP stands for Pretty Good Privacy. It is the brainchild of Phillip Zimmerman. It is a suite of programs which implement Public Key cryptography, and comprises a large portion of this chapter.

A **firewall** is a specially configured computer through which all the traffic on your network passes.

The commands covered in this section include:

ipfwadm	IP firewall administration
pgpe	Encrypt file
pgpk	Generate PGP key
pgps	Sign file with PGP
pgpv	Decrypt encrypted file

Related Files

~/.pgp/pgp.cfg	**PGP configuration file**

Commands

ipfwadm -A command parameters [options]

ipfwadm -I command parameters [options]

ipfwadm -O command parameters [options]

ipfwadm -F command parameters [options]

ipfwadm -M [-l | -s] [options]

This command is used to set up and maintain IP firewall (both input -I and output -O) and accounting (-A option).

Example: To display your current rule set:

ipfwadm -l

-A [direction]	IP accounting rules. Direction specifies which direction of packet travel the accounting refers to (in, out, or both).
-I	IP input firewall rules.
-O	IP output firewall rules.
-F	IP forwarding firewall rules.
-M	IP masquerading administration. Use with -l and -s options.
-a [policy]	Append rules to the end of the list of rules.
-i [policy]	Insert one or more rules at the beginning of the list of rules.
-d [policy]	Delete one or more entries from the selected list of rules.
-l	Display all the rules in the selected list.
-z	Reset counter to zero.
-f	Flush the selected list of rules.
-p policy	Change the default policy for the selected type of firewall.
-s tcp tcpfin udp	Change the timeout values used for masquerading. This command always takes 3 parameters, representing the timeout values (in seconds) for TCP sessions, TCP sessions after receiving a FIN packet, and UDP packets, respectively.

-c	Check whether this IP packet would be accepted, denied, or rejected by the selected type of firewall.
-h	Help.

Use with the append, insert, delete, or check options.

-P protocol	The protocol of the rule or of the packet to check (tcp, udp, icmp, all).
-S address[/mask] [port ...]	Source specification (optional).
-D address[/mask] [port ...]	Destination specification (optional).
-V address	Address of an interface via which a packet is received or sent.
-W name	Name of interface via which a packet is received or sent.
-b	Bidirectional mode.
-e	Extended output.
-k	Match only TCP packets with the ACK bit set (this option will be ignored for packets of other protocols).
-m	Masquerade packets accepted for forwarding.
-n	Numeric output. IP addresses and port numbers will be printed in numeric format.
-o	Turn on kernel logging of matching packets.
-r [port]	Redirect packets to a local socket.
-t andmask xormask	Masks used for modifying the TOS field in the IP header.
-v	Verbose output.

-x	Expand numbers.
-y	Match only TCP packets with the SYN bit set and the ACK bit cleared (this option will be ignored for packets of other protocols).

pgpe -r <recipient> [-s [-u <myid>]] [-aftz] [-o <outfile>] file ...

pgpe -c [-aftz] [-o outfile] file ...

Encrypt and sign files using public key cryptography, or encrypt files using conventional cryptography.

Example: To encrypt the file "noonesbusiness.txt" using public key cryptography for mailing (-a option and -t options) to recipient testguy@yahoo.com:

pgpe -r testguy@yahoo.com -at noonesbusiness.txt

-a, --armor	Output a text-only version of the encrypted text, thereby rendering the resultant file safe for mailing.
-c	Conventional encrypting mode. (Encrypt via IDEA.)
-f	Stream mode. Accept input on stdin and place output on stdout.
-o outfile	Send output to the specified outfile.
-s	Tells pgpe to sign the document as well as encrypting it.
-t	Text mode. Useful when moving files from one operating system to another.
-u	Sets the ID of the key used for signing. Use with -s option.
-z	Batch mode.

pgpk [-a keyfile ... | -c [userid]] | -d <userid> | -e <userid> | -g | -l[l] userid] | --revoke[s] <userid> | -r[u|s] <userid> | -s <userid> [-u <yourid>] |-x <userid>] [-o <outfile>] [-z]

This program is used to manage public and private keys for PGP. Note that this program is stream-based rather than file-based.

Example: To generate a key:

pgpk -g

-a [keyfile] Add the contents of the specified keyfile to the keyring. If no file is specified, input is taken from stdin.

-c [userid] Check the signatures of all keys on the public keyring, or the key associated with the specified userid.

-d <userid> Toggle the disablement of <userid>'s key on your public keyring.

-e <userid> Edit the specified <userid>'s key.

-g Generate a public/private key pair.

-l[l] [userid] List information about a key.

-o outfile Send output to the specified file.

--revoke <userid> Permanently revoke the specified key.

--revokes <userid> Permanently revoke your signature on the specified key.

-r <userid> Remove the key associated with the specified userid from your keyring.

-ru <userid> Remove the specified userid from your public and private keyrings.

-rs <userid> Remove the specified signature from your public keyring.

-s <userid> [-u <yourid>] Sign the specified <userid>'s key with the default signing key.

-x <userid>	Extract the specified key in ASCII-armored format.
-z	Batch mode.
pgpk -g	Generate a key.

pgps [-u <userid>] [-abftv] [-z|-zs] [-o <outfile>] file ...

Sign files using public key cryptography.

Example: To sign and encrypt the file outmail for mailing (-a option) using secretguy@domain.com's key:

pgps -u secretguy@domain.com -a outmail

-a, --armor	Turn on ASCII armoring.
-b	Create a detached signature file rather than combining the signature with the message in the same file.
-f	Stream mode. Accept input from stdin and place results on stdout.
-o outfile	Send output to the specified file.
-t	Text mode. Used to convert input messages to a platform independent form. Useful when transferring messages between operating systems.
-u	Set the ID of the key used for signing.
-z	Batch mode.

pgpv [-dfKmqv] [-z|-zs] [-o <outfile>] file ...

Decrypt and verify messages encrypted and/or signed with PGP.

Example: To decrypt the mail someone just sent you which was encrypted with your public key:

pgpv mail.txt

-d	Leave signature intact; just verify.
-f	Stream mode. Accepts input from stdin and place output on stdout.
-o outfile	Send output to the specified file.
-K	Do not process any keys found in the message. (The default is to add any keys found to your keyring.)
-m	Display message output with PGP's internal pager or the pager specified in your pgp.cfg file.
-z	Batch mode.

CHAPTER

28

MISCELLANEOUS

Introduction

This chapter is exactly what it sounds like. The commands contained herein are important enough that I didn't want to leave them out, but they didn't really fit in any of the other chapters.

The commands covered in this chapter are:

cal	Display calendar information
date	Display or set time and date
fortune	Random display of quotations
ispell	Spell checker
rpm	Red Hat Package manager
strfile	Maintain fortune database

Related Files

/usr/share/games/fortunes	Typical location of the fortune database.
/usr/lib/ispell/*	Dictionaries for ispell.

Commands

cal [-jy] [*month* [*year*]]

Display a calendar, by default the current month.

Example: To display a calendar of the current month, type:

cal

Example: To display a calendar for the current year (this example valid until 1/1/2000):

cal 1999

Example: To display a calendar for the month of August in the year 3053:

cal 8 3053

TIP When first using **cal**, everyone makes the same mistake: 98, 99, 00 refer to years in the first century a.d., not recent times. For information on more recent years, be sure to include the 2-digit century.

The options are as follows:

-j	Display Julian calendar dates (days one-based, numbered from January 1).
-y	Display a calendar for the specified year.

date [OPTION]... [+FORMAT]

date [-u|--utc|--universal] [MDDHHMM[[CC]YY][.SS]]

Either display or set the time and date. This command sports a dizzying array of options which allow you to display the date formatted 'most any way you'd like.

Example: To display the current time and date:

date

Time Display Options

%H	hour (00...23)
%I	hour (01...12)
%k	hour (0...23)
%l	hour (1...12)
%M	minute (00...59)
%p	locales AM or PM
%r	time, 12-hour (hh:mm:ss [AP]M)
%s	seconds since January 1, 1970 00:00:00 (the Unix epoch)
%S	second (00...61)
%T	time, 24-hour (hh:mm:ss)
%X	locales time representation (%H:%M:%S)
%z	RFC-822 style numeric time (e.g., +200, -900)
%Z	time zone, or nothing is no time zone is determinable

Date Display Options

%a	locales abbreviated weekday name (Sun...Sat)
%A	locales full weekday name, variable length (Sunday...Saturday)
%b	locales abbreviated month name (Jan...Dec)
%B	locales full month name, variable length (January...December)
%c	locales date and time (Sat Nov 04 12:02:33 EST 1989)
%d	day of month (01...31)

%D	date (mm/dd/yy)
%h	same as %b
%j	day of year (001...366)
%m	month (01...12)
%U	week number of the year with Sunday as first day of the week (i.e., if January 1 is on a Thursday, that week is week 0)
%V	week number of year with Monday as first day of week as a decimal
%w	day of week (0...6) with 0 corresponding to Sunday
%W	week number of year with Monday as first day of week (00...53).
%x	locales date representation (mm/dd/yy)
%y	last two digits of year (00...99)
%Y	year (1970....)

Literal Display Options

%%	literal %
%n	newline
%t	horizontal tab
-(hyphen)	do not pad the display field with zeroes
_(underscore)	pad the field with spaces instead of zeroes

Setting the Time and Date

A new time and date are specified by an all-digit string of the form:

MMDDHHMM[[CC]YY][.SS]]

where the variables stand for the following:

MM month

DD day of the month

HH hour

MM minute

CC first two digits of year (optional)

YY last two digits of year (optional)

SS second (optional)

***-d** DATESTR, **--date=**DATESTR*	Display the time and date as specified in DATESTR instead of the current time and date.
***-f** DATEFILE, **--file=**DATEFILE*	Parse each line in the specified datefile and display the resulting time and date.
--rfc-822	Display the time and date using the RFC-822-specified format, %a, %_d %b %Y %H:%M:%S %z. If --utc is also specified, use GMT in place of %z.
***-r** FILE, **--reference=**FILE*	Rather than current date, display the time and date reference according to the last modification time of FILE.
***-s** DATESTR, **--set=**DATESTR*	Set the time and date to DATESTR, See -d above.
-u, --utc, --universal	Print or set the time and date in Universal Coordinated Time instead of in local (wall clock) time.

Miscellaneous

fortune [-aefilosw] [-n *length*] [-m *pattern*] [[n%] file/dir/all]

Display a random quote/joke/adage. Typically included in .profiles to spit out some cheerful time-wasting quote at login time.

Example: To display a semi-amusing random quote:

fortune

```
Bolt your doors, up your car insurance and don't
leave any booze in plain sight. It's St. Patrick's
day in Boston again. Legend has it that St. Patrick
drove the snakes out of Ireland. Actually, he was
```

```
arrested for drunk driving. The snakes left because
people kept throwing up on them.
```

-a	Choose from all lists, regardless of offensiveness.
-e	Consider all fortune files to be of equal size.
-f	Display list of files that would be searched without printing out a fortune.
-l	Long fortunes only.
***-m** pattern*	Print out all the fortunes matching the specified pattern.
***-n** length*	Specify the longest length of a "short" fortune (usually 160).
-o	Offensive fortunes only.
-s	Short fortunes only. (See -n option for more information on "short".)
i	Ignore case for -m patterns.
-w	Wait before termination for an amount of time calculated from the number of characters in the message. Useful when fortune is included as part of a logout script.

ispell [common-flags] [-M|-N] [-*Lcontext*] [-V] *files*

ispell [*common-flags*] -l

ispell [*common-flags*] [-f file] [-s] {-a|-A}

ispell [-d *file*] [-w *chars*] -c

ispell [-d *file*] [-w *chars*] -e[e]

ispell [-d *file*] -D

ispell -v[v]

Ispell is a spell checker. It will check words in a file against a dictionary and suggest alternate spellings.

Example: To check the spelling of the words in the file "thesis.txt":

ispell thesis.txt

ispell is somewhat interactive; the following keys are active:

R	Replace the misspelled word completely.
Space	Accept the word this time only.
A	Accept the word for the rest of this ispell session.
I	Accept the word, capitalized as it is in the file, and update private dictionary.
U	Accept the word, and add an all lowercase version to the private dictionary.
0-n	Replace with one of the suggested words.
L	Look up words in system dictionary (controlled by the WORDS compilation option).

X	Write the rest of this file, ignoring misspellings, and start next file.
Q	Exit immediately and leave the file unchanged.
!	Shell escape.
^L	Redraw screen.
^Z	Suspend ispell.
?	Give help screen.

Command Line Options

-M	Display a mini-menu at bottom of screen.
-L	Include the specified number of lines of context in the display.
-V	Display in the style of "cat -v".
-t	Specify that the input file is in TeX or LaTeX format.
-n	Specify that the input file is in nroff/troff format.
-b	Tell ispell to create a backup file by appending ".bak" to the name of the input file.
-x	Don't create a backup file.
-B	Report run-together words with missing blanks as spelling errors.
-C	Consider run-together words as legal compounds.
-P	Don't generate extra root/affix combinations.
-m	Make possible root/affix combinations which aren't in the dictionary.
-S	Order the list of guesses by probable correctness.
***-d** file*	Specify an alternate dictionary file.

***-p** file*	Specify an alternate personal dictionary.
***-w** chars*	Specify additional characters that can be part of a word.
***-W** n*	Specify length of words that are always legal.
***-T** type*	Assume a given formatter type for all files.
-n	Specify nroff/troff input mode.
-t	Specify TeX/LaTeX input mode.
-b	Generate backup file for each input file.
-x	Do not generate backup file unless errors occur.
-B	Treat run-together words (e.g., runtogether) as errors.
-C	Treat run-together words (e.g., runtogether) as legal compound words.
-m	Always display suggested root/affix combinations for inclusion in dictionary.
-P	Display only suggested root/affix combinations for inclusion in dictionary when there are no reasonable possibilities in the current dictionary.
-S	Do not sort the list of possible replacement words.
***-d** file*	Use specified dictionary file rather than the default.
-p	Use the specified personal dictionary file rather than the default.
-w	Allow specified non-alphabetic characters.
-W	Specify an "always-legal" word length.
-T	Specify a default formatter type for use in generating string characters.
-l	Generate a list of misspelled words.

printf *FORMAT* [ARGUMENT]...

Similar to the C printf function. FORMAT includes:

%d, %i	Decimal number
%o	Unsigned octal
%x, %X	Unsigned hexadecimal
%u	Unsigned decimal number
%c	Single character
%s	String of characters
%f	Double; default precision of 6 [-]m.dddddd
%e, %E	Double, default precision of 6 [-]m.dddddd e+/-xx [-]m.dddddd E+/-xx
%g, %G	Double; use %e if exponent less than -4 or >= the precision
p	void *; pointer
%	Literal %

rpm -i [install-options] <*package_file*>+

rpm -q [*query-options*]

rpm -V|-y|--verify [*verify-options*]

rpm --checksig <*package_file*>+

rpm -e <*package_name*>+

rpm -[b|t]O [build-options] <*package_spec*>+

rpm --rebuilddb

rpm --setperms [*query-package-specifiers*]

rpm --setugids [*query-package-specifiers*]

rpm --showrc

Red Hat package Manager. RPM has ten modes of operation: Install, Query, Verify, Signature Check, Uninstall, Build, Rebuild Database, and Show RC.

Example: To install the WordPerfect package from CD-Rom:

rpm -i /mnt/cdrom xwp-7.0-242.i386.rpm

General Options

-vv	Very verbose. Print a great deal of debugging information.
--keep-temps	Do not remove temporary files.
--quiet	Don't print anything except (possibly) error messages.

--help	Display a long usage message.
--version	Display version number.
--rcfile file	Use the specified file instead of /etc/rpmrc and $HOME/.rpmrc.
--root dir	Use the system rooted at <dir> for all operations.
--dbpath path	Use RPM database in path.
--ftpproxy host	Use the specified host as an FTP proxy.
--ftpport port	Use the specified port as the FTP port.

Install and Upgrade Options

-i	Install new package.
-U	Upgrade an Installed Package.

TIP Note that in the above two cases, the package file may be specified as a ftp style URL. If so, rpm will first complete the download before installing it.

--force	Same as using both --replacepkgs, --replacefiles, and --oldpackage.
-h, --hash	Display 50 hash marks as the package archive is unpacked. Use with -v for a nice display.
--oldpackage	Allow an upgrade to replace a newer package with an older one.
--percent	Display percentages as files are unpacked from the package archive.
--replacefiles	Force rpm to install the packages even if they replace files from other, already installed, packages.
--replacepkgs	Force rpm to install the packages even if some of them are already installed on this system.

--allfiles	Install or upgrade all the missingok files in the package, regardless if they exist.
--nodeps	Don't do a dependency check before installing to upgrading a package.
--noscripts	Suppress execution of the preinstall and postinstall scripts.
--notriggers	Suppress execution of scripts which are triggered by the installation of this package.
--excludedocs	Do not install documentation files.
--includedocs	Install documentation files. Since installation of documentation is automatic, this option is necessary only if excludedocs: 1 is set in an rpmrc file.
--test	Do not actually install the package, just report any potential problems with the installation.
--prefix *path*	Use the specified path as the installation prefix for relocatable packages.
--ignorearch	Force the installation or upgrade even if the architectures of the binary RPM and host don't match.
--ignoreos	Force the installation or upgrade even if the operating system versions of the binary RPM and host don't match.

Query Options

-q *package_name*	Tell rpm to query the specified package.
-a	Query all installed packages
--whatrequires *<capability>*	Query all packages that require the specified <capability> for proper functioning.
--whatprovides *<virtual>*	Query all packages that provide the <virtual> capability.
-f *<file>*	Query package owning <file>.

--requiredby *<package>*	Query all of the packages which contain triggers scripts that are triggered by <package>.
-p *<package_file>*	Query an (uninstalled) package <package_file>.

Information Selection Options

-i	Display package information (name, version, and description).
-R	List the packages which this one depends on.
--provides	List the capabilities this package provides.
--changelog	Display change information for the package.
-l	List files in the package.
-s	Display the states of files in the package (normal, not installed, replaced).
-d	List only the documentation files.
-c	List only configuration files.
--scripts	List any package specific shell scripts used as part of the installation/uninstallation process.
--triggers	Display any trigger scripts contained in the package.

--dump	Dump file information as follows: path size mtime md5sum mode owner group isconfig isdoc rdev symlink. This must be used with at least one of -l, -c, -d.
-V, -y, --verify	The verify options compare the installed package with information stored in the rpm database. Output from the verify option is a string of 8 characters, either a period denoting that the test passed or one of the following characters indicating that a test failed: 5 MD5 Sum S File size L Symlink T Mtime D Device U User G Group M Mode (includes permissions and file type)

Signature Checking

--checksig	Check the PGP signature built into a package to ensure the integrity and origin of the package.

Uninstall Options

***-e** package_name+*	Uninstall the specified package.
--allmatches	Remove all versions of the package which match package_name.
--noscripts	Suppress execution of the preuninstall or postuninstall scripts.
--notriggers	Don't execute scripts which are triggered by the removal of this package.
--nodeps	Tell rpm to suppress dependency check usually performed before uninstalling the packages.
--test	Don't actually uninstall stuff, just test to see if it will go smoothly.
--nodeps	Suppress the check for broken dependencies normally performed before removing the package.

Build Options

-b	Used to specify that the build source is a spec file.
-t	Used to specify that the spec file is contained in a gzipped tar file.
-bp	Execute the "%prep" stage from the spec file. Normally this involves unpacking the sources and applying any patches.
-bl	Tell rpm to perform a check to make sure the files all exist.
-bc	Tell rpm to execute the "%build" stage from the spec file.
-bi	Tell rpm to perform the "%install" stage from the spec file.
-bb	Tell rpm to build a binary package.
-ba	Tell rpm to build binary and source packages.

Other Options

--short-circuit	Skip straight to the specified stage.
--timecheck	Specify a maximum age, in seconds, for a file being packaged.
--clean	Delete the build tree after the packages have been made.
--rmsource	Tell rpm to remove the source and spec files after the build.
--test	Suppress execution of the build stages.
--sign	Tell rpm to embed a PGP signature in the package.
--rebuild *<source_package_file>+*	Build a new binary package.

Signing an Existing RPM

--resign *<binary_package_file>+*	Insert new PGP signatures for the existing packages.

PGP Signatures

Obviously, in order to use PGP signatures, RPM must be able to find the PGP software package and there must be a public key ring with RPM public keys in it. If the PGP package is located anywhere other than the default, you should set the following variables in your /etc/rpmrc file:

pgp_path	Replacement path for /usr/lib/rpm. Must contain your key rings.
signature	The signature type. Right now only pgp is supported.
pgp_name	The name of the "user" whose key you wish to use to sign your packages.
--sign	This option will result in your being prompted for a "pass phrase" when building packages.

Rebuild Database Options

--rebuilddb	Rebuild database information
rpm --showrc	Show the values RPM will use for all options that may be set in rpmrc files.

FTP Options

Rpm sources may be FTP sites. Use the following URL syntax:

ftp://<user>:<password>@hostname/path/to/package.rpm

--ftpproxy *<hostname>*	Use specified hostname as proxy server for all transfers.
--ftpport *<port>*	Use specified TCP port number for ftp connection.

strfile [-iorsx] [-c *char*] *sourcefile* [*outputfile*]

unstr [-c *char*] *datafile*[.ext] [*outputfile*]

strfile takes as input a file containing groups of lines delimited (by default) by a % sign. It creates a data file containing a header structure and a table of file offsets (sourcefile.dat, unless otherwise specified).

unstr prints out the strings contained in the sourcefile in the order that they are listed in the header file datafile.

Example: This command really isn't good for much except maintaining the fortune program database. To display the contents of the fortune file pithy.dat:

unstr pithy

-c char	Change the delimiter to the specified character.
-i	Ignore case when ordering the strings.
-o	Order the strings in alphabetical order.
-r	Randomize access to the strings.
-s	Silent option (no summary message upon completion.)
-x	Set the STR_ROTATED bit in the header.

PART

4

NETWORKING

CHAPTER

29

TCP/IP

Introduction

TCP/IP stands for Transmission Control Protocol/Internet Protocol and refers to a collection of data transmission protocols used for transmitting messages among a distributed network of computers.

The examples in this section will be based on the following network (see Figure 29-1):

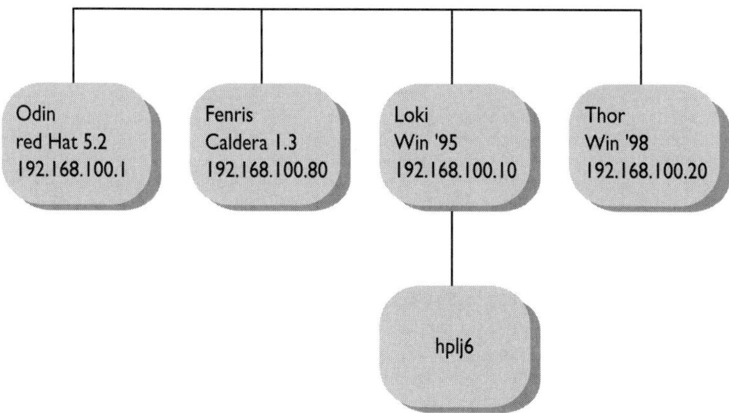

Figure 29-1 Sample Network

OSI Reference Model

Most discussions of TCP/IP open with a few words about the OSI (Open Systems Interconnect) reference model. The OSI model was created in 1978 to specify a standard used for the development of network systems. Real world protocol designers have been cheerfully ignoring it ever since, but it comes up whenever people start to talk about TCP/IP. Rather than break tradition, I hereby include the 7-layer OSI reference model:

Application	The application which you are invoking at the command line to do stuff (e.g., **telnet**)
Presentation	This layer concerns itself with the format in which data will be handed to the adjoining layers. For example, EBCDIC to ASCII translation or encryption might be handled here.
Session	As the name implies, this layer is concerned with setup and shutdown of a communication session between two machines.
Transport	Concerned with reliable delivery and data integrity.
Network	This layer concerns itself with the routing of packets from one point in the network to another.
Data Link	In this layer, the bits received from the adjoining layers are grouped into logical units called **frames**.
Physical	This layer includes cabling and whatnot, and is responsible for the actual transmission of data over an actual physical link.

TCP/IP Protocol

Like most network protocols, TCP/IP bears only a peripheral resemblance to the OSI model. The TCP/IP designers had their own layers in mind:

Application	Implementation of a protocol for a specific task (e.g., Simple Mail Transport Protocol—SMTP—for mail, telnet for remote logins).
Transport	The procedure two machines use to communicate with one another. For example, the TCP protocol which exists at this layer is a reliable, connection-oriented protocol (see definitions, below).
Internet	This layer is concerned with shuffling information (arranged into packets called datagrams) between two hosts. The hosts need not know anything about how the network is organized or how the data will get there.
Host-to-Network	Concerned with the physical connection to a network and the transmission of data across subnetworks.

IP Addresses

An **IP address** is a sequence of 4 bytes used to uniquely identify a host on a network. The bytes are usually presented in dotted octet form. For example:

127.0.0.1

is the **loopback address** which is included in the ***/etc/hosts*** file to enable a machine to refer to itself.

Recall that a **byte** is a set of eight binary digits (zeros or ones) called **bits**. Because each byte contains eight bits, the maximum value a single byte can take is 255:

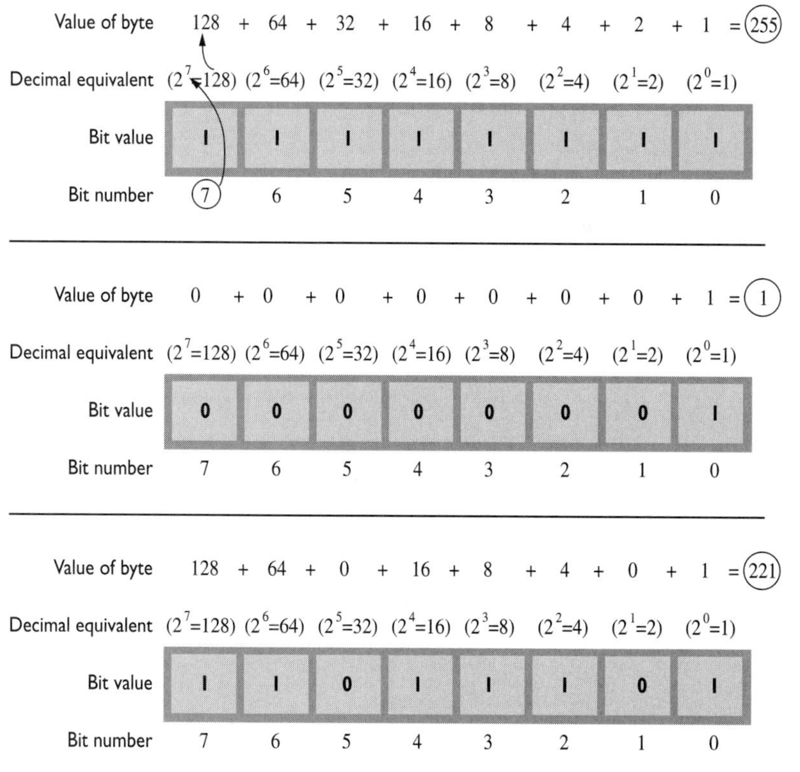

Figure 29-2 **Byte Values**

Address Classes

IP addresses are divided into **classes**. Depending on the class, either the first byte, the first two bytes, or first three bytes of the IP address refer to the Network address of the node. The remaining bytes refer to the host address. The way to tell what class an IP address is in is to look at the value of the first byte:

1st Byte	Address Class	Bit Division	Example
< 128	A	**net**.host.host.host	32.103.26.2
128-191	B	**net.net**.host.host	129.32.101.7
192-223	C	**net.net.net**.host	196.78.33.101

Subnet Masks

A **subnet mask** is another dotted octet sequence used to specify which bits in the IP address will refer to the network address and which will refer to the host address. In the simplest case, the bits used in the subnet mask are determined by the address class:

Address Class	Default Subnet Mask
A	255.0.0.0
B	255.255.0.0
C	255.255.255.0

Note that the above subnet mask is only the default—masking doesn't *have* to be done at the byte boundaries. However, a full description of subnetting is beyond the scope of this book. If you're connecting to a network that uses some funky subnet mask, talk to your network administrator. Otherwise, just accept the default for now.

Jargon

Any non-trivial endeavor will generate buzzwords, and networking is no exception. Here is a sampling of the jargon you're likely to run across in this chapter:

TIP Name resolution adds a layer of complexity to the networking process. If a command doesn't work with a hostname (e.g., ping fenris), you ought to try pinging the actual IP address (e.g., ping 192...). If the latter works but the

Reliable	When used in the network context, this word refers to a protocol that guarantees delivery of all packets transmitted.
Unreliable	Protocols described as unreliable are not necessarily unreliable in the common English sense of the word; they just don't guarantee delivery of any particular packet.
Connection-Oriented	A protocol is connection-oriented if it establishes a connection between the two communicating hosts. A **connectionless** protocol transmits data without any direct communication ("**handshaking**") between the two hosts.
Name Resolution	The process of turning a dotted octed IP address into an English word (e.g., 192.168.100.1 = odin).

former doesn't, you have a name resolution problem. Cheer up, things could be worse.

TIP

Most network problems are physical. For example, I spent almost an hour last Saturday trying to figure out why me & the little woman couldn't get X-Wing vs. TIE fighter to work before realizing that Puppy Dog had chewed up the cable. Similar things happen in industry, particularly when your wiring runs through the sales department.

The following commands are covered in this chapter:

arp	Maintain the Address Resolution Protocol table
bootpd	Network boot daemon
bootptab	Dump bootp table
bootpgw	bootp gateway
bootptest	Test bootp
dip	Handle dialup IP links
hostname	Set or display host name
gated	Implementation of the gated routing protocol
gdc	Gated controller

ifconfig	Configure network interface
in.identd	User identification protocol
netstat	Network status information
nslookup	Query Internet domain server
rmail	Handle mail received via uucp
route	Display or manipulate IP routing
routed	Network routing daemon
rusers	Similar to who, but works across the network
tcpdchk	Check TCP wrapper
tcpdmatch	Predict response to TCP request
traceroute	Trace route of IP packet from specified host

Related Files

/etc/networks	Specify network masks
/etc/hosts	IP address to hostname translation table
/etc/ethers	Ethernet addresses for diskless workstations
/etc/passwd	Defines users on the system
/etc/diphosts	Dialup IP hosts
/etc/bootptab	Database file read by bootpd.
/etc/bootpd.dump	Debugging dump file created by bootpd.
/etc/services	Internet services by port number.

/tftpboot	Current directory typically used by the TFTP server and bootpd.
/etc/resolv.conf	Initial domain name and name server addresses.
$HOME/.nslookuprc	User's initial options.

Commands

arp [-vn] [-H type] [-i if] -a [*hostname*]

arp [-v] [-i if] -d *hostname* [pub]

arp [-v] [-H *type*] [-i if] -s *hostname hw_addr* [temp]

arp [-v] [-H *type*] [-i if] -s hostname hw_addr [netmask nm] pub

arp [-v] [-H *type*] [-i if] -Ds *hostname* ifa [*netmask nm*] pub

arp [-vnD] [-H *type*] [-i if] -f *filename*

This command is used to maintain the kernel's Address Resolution Protocol (ARP) cache. You can add, delete, or display an entry in the ARP cache. For this command, hostname may either be a symbolic hostname or an IP address.

Example: To obtain network address information (hardware type, ethernet address, address class, interface device) for the host fenris:

TCP/IP

arp fenris

-v, --verbose	Verbose operation.
-n, --numeric	Use numeric rather than symbolic IP addresses.
-H *type,* ***--hw-type*** *type*	Specify a type of entries (ether, arcnet, pronet, ax25, netrom) to be checked.
-a *[hostname],* ***--display*** *[hostname]*	Display entries of the specified host only.
-d *hostname,* ***--delete*** *hostname*	Remove all entries for the specified host.
-D, --use-device	Use the interface ifa's hardware address.
-i If, --device If	Specify an interface for dumping.
-s *hostname hw_addr,* ***--set*** *hostname*	Specify a new ARP address hostname-to-hardware-address-class mapping entry.
-f *filename,* ***--file*** *filename*	Specify a filename (frequently /etc/ethers) containing address mappings. The file format is a hostname, the associated hardware address, and optional pub, temp, and netmask flags delimited by whitespace.

bootpd [-i -s -t *timeout* -d *level* -c *chdir-path*] [

bootptab [*dumpfile*]]

bootpgw [-i -s -t *timeout* -d level] *server*

The **bootpd** daemon is the Internet bootstrap protocol (BOOTP) server which allows computers to get network and boot information via a network interface. Bootpgw is a gateway used to forward requests between clients on one subnet and a BOOTP server.

Normally, one host on the network runs bootp in "inetd mode."

Example: To invoke bootp via inetd, include the following lines in ***inetd.conf***:

```
bootps  dgram  udp  wait  root  /etc/bootpd  bootpd bootptab

bootps dgram udp  wait  root  /etc/bootpgw  bootpgw server
```

When invoking **bootp** in inetd mode, set a timeout using the **-t** option on the command line. (10 minutes is a good timeout value.) TIP

You can also invoke **bootpd** and **bootpgw** from the command line or a shell script.

Invoke bootp from a shell script at startup time when it has a large configuration database (and thus loads slowly). TIP

-t timeout	Specify a timeout value in minutes.
-d debug-level	Specify a debug level (higher == more information).
-c chdir-path	Specify the current directory used by bootpd when checking the existence and size of client boot files.
-i	Force bootpd and bootpgw to run in inetd mode.
-s	Force bootpd and bootpgw to run in standalone mode.
bootptab	Specify a configuration database of known clients.
dumpfile	Specify a file into which bootpd will dump its internal database up receiving a SIGUSR1 flag.
server	Specify a server to forward all BOOTREQUEST packets to.

TCP/IP

bootptest [-f bootfile] [-h] [-m magic_number] server-name [template-file]

This command is used to test the **bootp** daemon. It sends **bootp** requests to the specified host at one-second intervals until a response is received or ten requests have gone unanswered.

Example: Assuming that the **bootp** server is running on the server fenris, test **bootp** with the following command:

testbootp fenris

-f bootfile	Specify a bootfile for use in the request.
-h	Tells bootp to use the ethernet (hardware) address to identify the client.
-m	Specify a magic number to initialize the first word of the vendor options field.
template-file	File used in initializing the options of the request packet.

dip [-v] [-m *mtu*] [-p *proto*] *scriptfile*

dip -t [-v]

dip -i [-a] [-v]

diplogin [*username*]

diplogini

dip [-v] -k [-l *tty_line*]

This program handles the connections needed for dialup IP links (e.g., SLIP, PPP).

Example: To allow the user testdip to login using dialup IP protocol, set **diplogin** as the default shell in their ***/etc/passwd*** file entry:

```
testdip:x:501:Dialup IP User:/home/testdip:/usr/sbin/diplogin
```

-v	This mode interprets the specified scriptfile to dial out and open an IP connection.
-t	Run dip interactively.
-i	Dial in mode. Handle incoming connections.

-a	Prompt for user name and password.
-k	Kill the dip process that has locked the specified tty device.
***-l** tty_line*	Use with -k option. Specify the line to be killed.
-m	Specify the maximum transfer unit (MTU).

TIP

In general, smaller MTU blocks work better.

***-p** proto*	Specify the line protocol (options are SLIP, CLSIP, PPP, TERM).
-t	Run in test mode.
-v	Verbose operation.

Modes of Operation

Dip has three modes of operation:

Mode	How to invoke
Interactive	(-t option) Set up an outgoing IP connection interactively.
Dialout	(-t with scriptfile specified) Setup a connection automatically.
Dialin	Specify **dip** as the login shell in ***/etc/passwd***.

In interactive mode, the following commands apply:

label:	Define a label.
***beep** [times]*	Beep on user's terminal the specified number of times.
***bootp** [howmany [howlong]]*	Use BOOTP protocol to retrieve local and remote IP addresses.
break	Send a BREAK.

TCP/IP

chatkey *keyword [code]*	Add to dip's collection of modem response words.
config [interface|routing] [pre|up|down|post] {arguments...}	Store interface configuration parameters.
databits 7|8	Set the number of data bits.
dec *$variable [decrement-value\|$variable]*	Decrement a variable. The default decrement-value is 1.
default	Tell DIP to set up the default route to the remote host to which it made a connection.
dial *phonenumber [timeout]*	Dials the specified phone number.
echo on|off	Enable or disable the display of modem commands.
exit [exit-status]	Exit script leaving established [C]SLIP connection intact and dip running.
flush	Flush input on the terminal.
get $variable [value | ask | remote [timeout_value | $variable]]	Get or ask for the value of a variable.
goto *label*	Transfer control to the indicated label in the chat script.
help	Print list of commands.
if expr goto label	Conditional branch. expr is of the form: **$variable op constant** where op is one of: == != < > <= >=.
inc $variable [increment-value\|$variable]	Increment a variable. The default increment-value is 1.
init *init-string*	Set the initialization string (sent to the modem before dialing) to the indicated string (default ATE0 Q0 V1 X1).

mode SLIP|CSLIP|PPP|TERM	Set the line protocol (default SLIP).
***modem** modem-name*	Set the type of modem. Currently, only HAYES is valid.
netmask xxx.xxx.xxx.xxx	Specify a netmask to be used.
parity E|O|N	Set the type of parity.
password	Prompt for a password and send it.
proxyarp	Request Proxy ARP to be set.
print $variable	Display the contents of some variable.
psend** command **[arguments]	Send the output of command to the serial driver, optionally passing arguments to command.
***port** tty_name*	Set the name of the terminal port to use. (The path /dev/ is assumed.)
quit	Exit with nonzero exit status.
reset	Reset the modem. (Sends "+++" then "ATZ".)
***securidf** fixedpart*	Store the fixed part of the SecureID password.
securid	Prompt for the variable part of the password generated by the ACE System SecureID card.
***send** text-string*	Send a string to the serial driver.
***shell** command [parameters]*	Execute command through the default shell with parameters as the command-line arguments.
skey** [timeout / **$variable]	Tell dip to look for an S/Key challenge from the remote terminal server. dip then prompts the user for the secret password, generates the response, and sends it to the remote host. Timeout sets how long dip waits to see the challenge.

sleep *time-in-secs*	Wait for the specified length of time.
speed *bits-per-sec*	Set port speed (default 38400).
stopbits 1/2	Set the number of stop bits.
term	Enter a terminal mode.
timeout *time-in-sec*	Set timeout.
wait *text* *[timeout_**value / $variable]***	Wait for some string to arrive.

Special Variables

$errlvl	Holds the result of the previous command.
$locip	IP number of local host in dotted quad notation.
$local	Fully qualified local host name.
$rmtip	IP number of remote host in dotted quad notation.
$remote	Fully qualified remote host name.
$mtu	Maximum Transfer Unit (maximum number of bytes transferred at once).
$modem	Modem type (at present the only valid value is HAYES).
$port	The name of the terminal port to use.
$speed	Transfer rate between the local host and the modem, in bits/sec.

hostname [NAME]

Display or set the hostname of the local machine.

Example: To display the host name of the local machine:

hostname

--help	Display help information.
--version	Display version information.

gated [-c] [-C] [-n] [-N] [-t *trace_options*] [-f *config_*file] [*trace_*file]

Gated is a routing service which handles a variety of routing protocols. It may be configured to some or all of the protocols which it is capable of handling.

Example: It's a good idea to invoke this command via **gdc**. But to invoke from the command line as a background process (&), type:

gated &

-c	Tell gated to parse the configuration file, report any syntax errors, and exit.
-C	Tell gated to parse the configuration file for syntax errors.
-n	Prohibit gated from modifying the kernel forwarding table.
-N	Tell gated not to run as a daemon.
***-t** trace_options*	Allow the user to specify a comma-separated list of trace options on the command line.
***-f** config_file*	Specify a non-default configuration file.

TCP/IP

gdc [-q] [-n] [-c *coresize*] [-f *filesize*] [-m *datasize*] [-s *stacksize*] [-t *seconds*] *command*

This command is the **gated** controller, a user interface for controlling the **gated** routing daemon. You can use it to stop, start, signal, maintain configuration files, and generate or maintain core dumps.

Example: To invoke **gated** and send all output to the system log:

gdc -q start

TIP In order for these controls to take effect, you must start **gated** with **gdc**.

-n	Do not check the kernel forwarding table.
-q	Quiet operation. Log any output to the system log.
***-t** seconds*	Allow the user to specify how long gdc will wait for gated to complete startup, shutdown, and other operations.
***-c** coresize*	Specify an upper limit on the size of core dumps which may be generated by gated. Typically used to up the system default when it is too small to be useful.
***-f** filesize*	Specify a maximum file size which a gated started with gdc can produce.
***-m** datasize*	Specify an upper limit on the size of the data segment of a gated started with gdc.
***-s** stacksize*	Specify the maximum size of a stack of a gated started by gdc.

The following actions may be specified at the command line:

checkconf	Check **/etc/gated.conf** for syntax errors.
checknew	Check **/etc/gated.conf+** for syntax errors.
newconf	Replace **/etc/gated.conf** with /etc/gated.conf+.
backout	Move the old configuration file (/etc/gated.conf-) back into place as the current active gated.conf. Also rotates the current /etc/gated.conf to **/etc/gated.conf+**
BACKOUT	Same as backout (above), but will overwrite any existing /etc/gated.conf+
modeconf	Set all configuration files to mode 664, owner=root, group=gdmaint.
createconf	If /etc/gated.conf+ does not exist, create a zero length file with the file mode set to 664, owner=root, group=gdmaint.
running	Test to see if **gated** is currently running.

start	Start **gated**.
stop	Stop **gated**.
restart	Stop and restart **gated**.
rmcore	Delete any **gated** core dump file.
rmdump	Delete any **gated** state dump file.
rmparse	Delete any parse error file generated by checkconf or checknew.

ifconfig [interface]

ifconfig interface [aftype] options | address ...

This command is used to configure network interfaces resident in the kernel. With no arguments, it displays the status of the currently resident interfaces. When only a single interface is specified (with no other options), it displays the status of that interface only.

Example: To display the status of the network interfaces:

ifconfig

TIP

This command can provide information handy in debugging network problems.

interface	The driver name of the interface.
up	Activate the specified interface.
down	Deactivate the specified interface.
[-]arp	Enable or disable the use of the ARP protocol on this interface.
[-]promisc	Activate or deactivate the promiscuous mode of this interface. When activated, all packets on the network will be received.
[-]allmulti	Activate or deactivate all-multicast mode. When active, all multicast packets on the network will be received.

metric *N*	Specify an interface metric of N.
mtu *N*	Specify a Maximum Transfer Unit (MTU) for an interface.
netmask *addr*	Set the IP network mask for an interface.
add addr/prefixlen	Add an IPv6 address to an interface.
del addr/prefixlen	Remove an IPv6 address from an interface.
tunnel aa.bb.cc.dd	Create a new SIT (IPv6-in-IPv4) device, tunnelling to the given destination.
irq *addr*	Specify the interrupt request used by this device.
io_addr *addr*	Specify a start address in I/O space for this device.
mem_start *addr*	Specify a start address for shared memory used by this device.
media *type*	Set the physical port or medium type to be used by the device (10base2, 10baseT, AUI).
[-]broadcast *[addr]*	If the address argument is given, set the protocol broadcast address for this interface. Otherwise, set or clear the IFF_BROADCAST flag for the interface.
[-]pointopoint *[addr]*	Enable the point-to-point mode of an interface.
hw *class address*	Specify the hardware address of the interface, assuming the device driver supports this operation.
multicast	Set the multicast flag on the interface. Normally this is done without help from the user.
address	Specify the IP address to be assigned to this interface.
txqueuelen length	Specify the length of the transmit queue of the device.

/usr/sbin/in.identd [-i|-w|-b] [-t<*seconds*>] [-u<*uid*>] [-g<*gid*>] [-p<*port*>] [-a<*address*>] [-c<*charset*>] [-C[<*key-*

file>]] [-o] [-e] [-l] [-V] [-m] [-N] [-d] [-F<*format*>] [*kernelfile* [*kmem*file]]

This program is an implementation of the TCP/IP IDENT user identification protocol. It looks up TCP/IP connections and returns the user name of the process which owns the connection.

Example: Typically, this command is started automatically by inetd. To start **identd** with **inetd**, add the following entry to your ***/etc/inetd.conf*** file:

```
auth stream tcp nowait nobody /usr/sbin/in.identd in.identd -l -e
```

Modes of Operation

-i	Use when starting with nowait option in /etc/inetd.conf. Starts one identd daemon for each connection request.
-w	Use when starting from inetd with the wait option in the */etc/inetd.conf* file.
-b	Use when running the daemon from the command line.

Options

-t<seconds>	Specify the timeout (the length of time a server started with the -w option will wait before dying) in seconds.
-u<uid>	Specify the user id which ident will switch to after binding itself to the TCP/IP port (-b mode only).
-u<uid>	Specify the group id which ident will switch to after binding itself to the TCP/IP port (-b mode only).
-p<port>	Specify an alternative port to bind to when using -b mode. Default is 113.
-a<address>	Specify the local address to bind the socket to when using -b mode.
-V	Display version information.
-l	Tell identd to use the system logging daemon.
-o	When used, identd will not reveal the type of its operating system.

-d	Return UNKNOWN-ERROR rather than NO-USER or INVALID-PORT errors.
-c<charset>	Add the optional character set designator to the reply generated.
-C[<keyfile>]	Tell identd to return DES-encrypted tokens rather than user names.
-n	Tell identd to return numbers rather than user names.
-N	Tell identd to check for a .noident file in each home directory which it is about to return a user name for.
-m	Allow multiple requests to be processed each session.
-d	Debug mode. Not normally used as it creates some security problems.
-F	Format output according to the following: **%u** print user name **%U** print user number **%g** print (primary) group name **%G** print (primary) group number **%l** print list of all groups by name **%L** print list of all groups by number **%p** print process ID of running process **%c** print command name **%C** print command and arguments **%e** print the environment

netstat [-venaoc] [--tcp|-t] [--udp|-u] [--raw|-w] [--unix|-u] [--inet|--ip] [--ax25] [--ipx] [--netrom]

netstat [-veenc] [--inet] [--ipx] [--netrom] [--ddp] [--

ax25] {--route|-r}

netstat [-veenac] {--interfaces|-i} [iface]

netstat [-enc] {--masquerade|-M}

netstat [-cn] {--netlink|-N}

netstat {-V|--version} {-h|--help}

This command displays information (network connections, routing tables, interface statistics, masquerade connections and netlink messages) about the local network.

Example: To display information about the network status:

netstat

```
Active Internet connections (w/o servers)
Proto Recv-Q Send-Q Local Address          Foreign Address         State
tcp        0      0 odin:1051               fenris:telnet
    ESTABLISHED
udp        0      0 odin:netbios-dgm       *:*
udp        0      0 odin:netbios-ns        *:*
udp        0      0 odin:domain            *:*
udp        0      0 localhost:domain       *:*
Active UNIX domain sockets (w/o servers)
Proto RefCnt Flags       Type       State         I-Node Path
unix  2      [ ]         STREAM                   115034 /tmp/.X11-unix/X0
unix  2      [ ]         STREAM     CONNECTED     115033
unix  2      [ ]         STREAM                   114985 /tmp/.X11-unix/X0
unix  2      [ ]         STREAM     CONNECTED     114983
unix  2      [ ]         STREAM                   114448 /dev/log
unix  2      [ ]         STREAM     CONNECTED     114447
unix  2      [ ]         STREAM                   113290 /tmp/.X11-unix/X0
unix  2      [ ]         STREAM     CONNECTED     113288
unix  2      [ ]         STREAM                   59282  /tmp/.X11-unix/X0
unix  2      [ ]         STREAM     CONNECTED     59281
unix  2      [ ]         STREAM                   59277  /tmp/.X11-unix/X0
unix  2      [ ]         STREAM     CONNECTED     59276
unix  2      [ ]         STREAM                   59235  /tmp/.X11-unix/X0
unix  2      [ ]         STREAM     CONNECTED     59234
unix  2      [ ]         STREAM                   59196  /tmp/.X11-unix/X0
unix  2      [ ]         STREAM     CONNECTED     59142
unix  2      [ ]         STREAM                   1886   /dev/log
unix  2      [ ]         STREAM     CONNECTED     1885
unix  1      [ ]         STREAM                   1646
unix  2      [ ]         STREAM                   1566   /dev/log
unix  2      [ ]         STREAM     CONNECTED     1565
unix  2      [ ]         STREAM                   1521   /dev/log
unix  2      [ ]         STREAM     CONNECTED     1520
unix  2      [ ]         STREAM                   1465   /dev/log
unix  2      [ ]         STREAM     CONNECTED     1464
unix  2      [ ]         STREAM                   1252   /dev/log
unix  2      [ ]         STREAM     CONNECTED     1251
```

Example: To see whether your routing table contains a route to the network 192.249.100 (**r** prints routing table information, **n** is the numeric option):

netstat -nr | grep '192.168.100'

Modes

-r, --route	Display kernel routing tables.
-i, --interface iface	Display all (or only the specified) network interfaces.
-M, --masquerade	Display a list of all masqueraded sessions.

TIP Use -M in conjunction with -e option for sequence numbering and deltas caused by data rewrites on FTP sessions.

-N, --netlink	Get information about creation or deletion of interfaces or routes.

Options

-v, --verbose	Verbose operation.
-n, --numeric	Display numeric addresses rather than attempting to resolve them into symbolic host, port or user names.
-A, --af family	Set the address families as a comma separated list of keywords (inet, unix, ipx, ax25, netrom, ddp).
-c, --continous	Update the display every second until interrupted.

Output Description

* Active Internet connections (TCP, UDP, RAW)

Proto	The protocol (tcp, udp, raw) used by the socket.
Recv-Q	The count of bytes not copied by the user program connected to this socket.
Send-Q	The count of bytes not acknowledged by the remote host.

Local Address	Local address (hostname) and port number of the socket.
Foreign Address	Remote address (hostname) and port number of the socket.
State	State of the socket.
ESTABLISHED	The socket has an established connection.
SYN_SENT	The socket is actively attempting to establish a connection.
SYN_RECV	The connection is being initialized.
FIN_WAIT1	The socket is closed, and the connection is shutting down.
FIN_WAIT2	Connection is closed, and the socket is waiting for a shutdown from the remote end.
TIME_WAIT	The socket is waiting after close for remote shutdown retransmission.
CLOSED	The socket is not being used.
CLOSE_WAIT	The remote end has shut down, waiting for the socket to close.
LAST_ACK	The remote end has shut down, and the socket is closed. Waiting for acknowledgment.
LISTEN	The socket is listening for incoming connections.
CLOSING	Both sockets are shut down but we still haven't sent our data.
UNKNOWN	The state of the socket is unknown.
User	The name or the UID of the owner of the socket.
Proto	The protocol (usually Unix) used by the socket.
RefCnt	The reference count (i.e., attached processes via this socket).
Flags	The flags displayed are SO_ACCEPTON (displayed as ACC), SO_WAITDATA (W) or SO_NOSPACE (N).
Type	There are several types of socket access:

SOCK_DGRAM	The socket is used in Datagram (connectionless) mode.
SOCK_STREAM	This is a stream (connection) socket.
SOCK_RAW	Raw socket.
SOCK_RDM	Reliably-delivered messages.
SOCK_SEQPACKET	This is a sequential packet socket.
SOCK_PACKET	RAW interface access socket.

State **One of the following:**

FREE	Unallocated.
LISTENING	Socket is listening for a connection request.
CONNECTING	Socket is about to establish a connection.
CONNECTED	The socket is connected.
DISCONNECTING	The socket is disconnecting.
(empty)	The socket is not connected to another one.
UNKNOWN	This state should never happen.

Path Path name as which corresponding processes are attached to the socket.

nslookup [-option ...] [host-to-find | -[server]]

The **nslookup** command is used to query Internet domain name servers. When invoked from the command line it can be passed a host name and return the associated IP address (or vice-versa) or to return information about a domain. It can also be used interactively, to return various combinations of information about hosts and domains.

Example: To use nslookup to find information about the server www.yahoo.com:

nslookup www.yahoo.com

nslookup invokes interactively in two ways:

a) when invoked with no arguments

b) when the first argument is a hyphen and the second argument is the IP address or host name of a name server.

To invoke **nslookup** non-interactively, just pass in the name or IP address of the host to be looked up. Optionally, you may specify a name server as the second argument.

TIP

If you use **nslookup** a good bit, set your favorite options in a ***.nslookuprc*** file in your home directory.

Interactive Commands

host [server]	Look up information for the specified host using the optionally specified server.
server domain, lserver domain	Change the default server to domain; lserver uses the initial server to look up information about domain, while server uses the current default server.
root	Change the default server to the server for the root of the domain name space.
finger [name] [> filename], finger [name] [>> filename]	Connect with the finger server on the current host.
ls [option] domain [> filename]	
ls [option] domain [>> filename]	List the information available for the specified domain, optionally creating or appending to filename.
-t querytype	List all records of the specified type (see querytype below).
	-a List aliases of hosts in the domain.
	-d List all records for the domain.
	-h List CPU and operating system information for the domain.
	-s List well-known services of hosts in the domain.

view filename	Sort and list the output of previous ls commands with more.
help, ?	Prints a brief summary of commands.
exit	Exit the program.
***set** keyword [=value]*	This command is used to change state information that affects the lookups. Valid keywords are:

all	Print current values.
class=value	Change the query class to one of:

IN	the Internet class
CHAOS	the Chaos class
HESIOD	the MIT Athena Hesiod class
ANY	wildcard (any of the above)

[no] debug	Turn debugging mode on and off.
[no] d2	Turn exhaustive debugging mode on and off.
domain=name	Specify a new default domain.
srchlist=name1/ name2/...	Specify an ordered list of domains to be searched (maximum 6 domains). name1 becomes default domain.
[no] defname	Append default domain name to a single component lookup request.
[no] search	Append domain names in domain search list to the request until an answer is received.

port=value	Change the default TCP/UDP name server port to value.
querytype=value **type=value**	Change the type of information query to one of:

A	the host's Internet address.
CNAME	the canonical name for an alias.
HINFO	the host CPU and operating system type.
MINFO	the mailbox or mail list information.
MX	the mail exchanger.
NS	the name server for the named zone.
PTR	the host name if the query is an Internet address; otherwise, the pointer to other information.
SOA	the domain's "start-of-authority" information.
TXT	the text information.
UINFO	the user information.
WKS	the supported well-known services.

[no] recurse	Tell the name server to query other servers if it does not have the information.
retry=number	Specify the number of times to retry a request.
root=host	Change the name of the root server to host.
timeout= **number**	Specify the initial timeout interval in seconds.

[no] vc	Always use a virtual circuit when sending requests to the server.
[no] ignoretc	Ignore packet truncation errors.

rmail user ...

This command interprets incoming mail received via uucp.

Example: To handle mail for user somebody:

rmail somebody

route [-CFvnee]

route [-v] [-A family] add [-net|-host] *target* [netmask Nm] [gw Gw] [metric N] [mss M] [window W] [irtt I] [reject] [mod] [dyn] [reinstate] [[dev] If]

route [-v] [-A *family*] del [-net|-host] target [gw Gw] [netmask Nm] [metric N] [[dev] If]

route [-V] [--version] [-h] [--help]

This command is used to display or manipulate the kernel's IP routing table. Typically it is used to set up static routes to specific hosts after it has been configured with the **ifconfig** program.

Example: To display the current routing table:

route

Example: To add a route to the local network to odin's routing table:

route add -net 192.168.100.0 eth0

Output

The output of the kernel routing table is organized in the following columns:

Destination	Destination network or destination host.
Gateway	The gateway address or "*" if none set.
Genmask	Netmask for the destination network.
Flags	Possible flags are: **U** (route is up) **H** (target is a host) **G** (use gateway) **R** (reinstate route for dynamic routing) **D** (dynamically installed by daemon or redirect) **M** (modified from routing daemon or rederict) **!** (reject route)
Metric	Distance to the target (usually presented in hops).
Use	Count of lookups for the route.
Iface	Interface to which packets for this route will be sent.
MSS	Maximum Segment Size for TCP connections over this route.
Window	Default window size for TCP connections over this route.
irtt	Initial RTT (Round Trip Time).
HH	Number of ARP entries and cached routes that refer to the hardware header cache for the cached route.
Arp	Whether or not the hardware address for the cached route is up to date.

-v	verbose operation.
-A family	Tell route to use the specified address family.

-n	Use numeric addresses rather than attempting to resolve into host names.
-e	Display the routing table in netstat format.
-net	The target is a network.
-host	The target is a host.
-F	Display the kernel FIB routing table.
-C	Display the kernel's route cache.
del	Delete a route.
add	Add a route.
target	IP address or hostname of the network destination or host.
netmask *Nm*	Net mask of the route to be added.
gw *Gw*	Route any IP packets for the target network/host through the specified gateway.
metric *M*	Set the metric field in the routing table (used by routing daemons) to M.
mss *M*	Specify the TCP Maximum Segment Size (MSS) for connections over this route to M bytes.
window *W*	Set the TCP window size for connections over this route to W bytes.
irtt *I*	Set the initial round trip time (irtt) for TCP connections over this route to I milliseconds (1-12000).
reject	Install a blocking route, which will force a route lookup to fail.
mod, dyn, reinstate	Install a dynamic or modified route.

***dev** If*	Force the route to be associated with the specified device, as the kernel will otherwise try to determine the device on its own.
***If** dev*	If is the last option on the command line, so the word dev may be omitted, as it's the default.

routed [-d] [-g] [-q] [-s] [-t] [logfile]

Routed is the daemon used to manage the network routing tables. **Routed** listens on the udp socket for the route service for routing information packets and updates the internal routing tables.

Example: Routed is usually invoked at startup time via the script ***/etc/rc.d/init.d/routed***, but the call is pretty simple:

routed

-d	Log additional debug information.
-g	On internetwork routers, this flag is used to specify a possible route to the default destination.
-s	This option forces routed to supply routing information regardless of whether or not it is acting as an internetwork router.
-q	Inverse of the -s option.
-t	Display all packets sent or received to standard output.

/etc/gateways

Routed relies on the ***/etc/gateways*** file, each line of which is formatted as follows:

```
<net | host> name1 gateway name2 metric value <passive | active | external>
```

The **net** or **host** keyword indicates if the route is to a network or specific host.

net	Indicates that the route is to a network.
host	Indicates the route is a specific host.
name1	Name of destination network or host.

name2	Address of the gateway to which messages should be forwarded.
value	A metric indicating the hop count to the destination.
< passive | active | external >	Indicates nature of the gateway.

rusers [-al] [*host* ...]

Produces output similar to who for all machines on the local network.

Example: To get **rusers** information for all hosts on the network:

rusers -a

-a	Display all machines responding even if no one is logged in.
-l	Output long listing. Includes user name, host name, tty, date & time logged in, idle time, and remote host (if applicable).

tcpdchk [-a] [-d] [-i *inet_conf*] [-v]

This command examines the tcp wrapper configuration and points out any potential problems it identifies. In some cases, it suggests fixes as well.

Example: To check the tcp wrapper configuration on the current host:

tcpdchk

-a	Report access control rules that permit access without an explicit ALLOW keyword.
-d	Examine hosts.allow and hosts.deny files in the current directory instead of the default ones.
-i inet_conf	Use this option when tcpdchk is unable to find your inetd.conf or tlid.conf network configuration file.
-v	Display the contents of each access control rule.

tcpdmatch [-d] [-i *inet_conf*] *daemon client*

tcpdmatch [-d] [-i *inet_conf*] *daemon*[*@server*] [user@]client

This programs offers predictions about how the tcp wrapper would offer a specific request for service.

Example: To predict how odin would react to a telnet request:

tcpdmatch in.telnetd fenris

If you're having network service problems, it's not a bad diagnostic aid.

TIP

-d	Examine hosts.allow and hosts.deny files in the current directory instead of the default ones.
-i inet_conf	Specify this option when tcpdmatch is unable to find your inetd.conf or tlid.conf network configuration file, or when you suspect that the program uses the wrong one.

traceroute [-dFInrvx] [-f *first_ttl*] [-g *gateway*] [-i *iface*] [-m *max_ttl*] [-p *port*] [-q *nqueries*] [-s *src_addr*] [-t *tos*] [-w *waittime*] *host* [*packetlen*]

This command is used to print the route that packets take to the network host.

Example: To print the route a packet would take to the host www.themes.org:

traceroute www.themes.org

-f	Set the initial time-to-live used in the first outgoing probe packet.
-F	Set the "don't fragment" bit.
-d	Enable socket level debugging.
-g	Specify a loose source route gateway (8 maximum).
-i	Specify a network interface to obtain the source IP address for outgoing probe packets.

TCP/IP

-l	Use ICMP ECHO instead of UDP datagrams.
-m	Set the max time-to-live (max number of hops) used in outgoing probe packets.
-n	Print hop addresses numerically rather than symbolically and numerically.
-p	Set the base UDP port number used in probes.
-r	Bypass the normal routing tables and send directly to a host on an attached network.
-s	Use the following IP address as the source address in outgoing probe packets.
-t	Set the type-of-service in probe packets to the following value (default zero).
-v	Verbose output.
-w	Set the time (in seconds) to wait for a response to a probe (default 5 sec.).
-x	Toggle checksums.

CHAPTER

30

NETWORKING APPLICATIONS

Introduction

Purists among you will note that the commands covered in this section are usually associated with TCP/IP and thus might organizationally have been included in that chapter. My justification for organizing them into two chapters is that these commands are concerned with accomplishing actual work in a network environment, whereas the commands in the TCP/IP chapter are more concerned with the infrastructure used to facilitate that work. Also the TCP/IP chapter was getting awfully long.

The commands covered in this chapter include:

ftp	Transfer files between networked machines
hostname	Display or set name of host
netstat	Display network usage information
ping	Request confirmation packed from remote host
rarp	Reverse Address Resolution Protocol
rcp	Remote copying service
rdate	Get date information across network

rdist	Distribute files across network
rlogin	Login to a remote computer
rsh	Execute a remote shell
rusers	Network user information
rwall	Write to all users on network
rwho	Network user information
telnet	Remote access to network host
tftp	Trivial File Transfer Protocol

Related Files

/etc/services	Associates services with port numbers
/proc/net/dev	Devices information
/proc/net/raw	RAW socket information
/proc/net/tcp	TCP socket information
/proc/net/udp	UDP socket information
/proc/net/unix	Unix domain socket information
/proc/net/ipx	IPX socket information
/proc/net/ax25	AX25 socket information
/proc/net/appeltalk	DDP (appeltalk) socket information
/proc/net/nr	NET/ROM socket information
/proc/net/route	Kernel IP routing information

/proc/net/ax25_route	Kernel AX25 routing information
/proc/net/ipx_route	Kernel IPX routing information
/proc/net/nr_nodes	Kernel NET/ROM nodelist
/etc/services	Maps service name to socket number
/etc/hosts	Maps host name to Internet address
/etc/exports	Filesystems which are to be exported

Commands

ftp [-v] [-d] [-i] [-n] [-g] [*host*]

The **ftp** command is used to transfer files between two network sites. It is an implementation of the Arpanet File Transfer Protocol. The command is interactive; the options listed below may be specified either on the command line or at the **ftp** prompt.

Example: To transfer the file test.txt from the local host (odin) to the remote host (fenris):

ftp fenris

ftp> put test.txt

To abort a file transfer, use the terminal interrupt key (Typically <Ctrl>-C) TIP

-v	Verbose operation. Show all responses from the remote server.
-n	Do not attempt to log in automatically upon making initial connection. Without this option, ftp will check the user's *~/.netrc* file for information about the account on the remote machine and use that information to log in. If there is no entry in the ~/.netrc file for the current machine, ftp will prompt the user for login information as appropriate.
-i	Disable interactive prompting when performing multiple file transfers.

-d	Debug mode.
-g	Disable file name globbing.
host	The client machine with which ftp is to connect.

The ftp program is interactive. The following commands are valid at the "ftp>" prompt.

! [command [args]]	Execute an interactive shell on the local machine. The first argument to ! is taken as a command to be executed; any successive arguments are taken as arguments to the first command.
$** macro-name **[args]	Execute the specified macro. Macros are defined with the macdef command. Any arguments are passed unglobbed.
*account **[passwd]***	Supply login information (account & password) for access to a remote system.
append** local-file **[remote-file]	Append the local-file to the remote-file.
ascii	Set file transfer type to network ASCII (default mode).
bell	Sound a bell after each transfer completed.
binary	Set file transfer type to binary.
bye	Close any connections and exit ftp.
case	Convert filenames to lowercase letters when transferring to the local machine.
***cd** remote-directory*	Change to the specified directory on the remote machine.
cdup	Change to the parent directory of whatever the current directory is on the remote machine.
***chmod** mode file-name*	Change the file permissions on the remote system as specified.

close	Close the FTP session with the remote host, but do not exit FTP.
cr	Toggle carriage return stripping during ASCII type file retrieval. The default is to strip carriage returns to conform with Unix standards.
delete *remote-file*	Delete the specified file on the remote machine.
debug [debug-value]	Specify a debug level.
dir [remote-directory] [local-file]	Display a list of the contents of the specified remote directory or information about the specified file. If a local-file argument is specified, the listed files will be sent there.
disconnect	Same as close.
form format	Set the file transfer form to format.
get *remote-file [local-file]*	Transfer the specified file from the remote machine to the local machine.
glob	Toggle filename expansion for mdelete, mget and mput.
hash	Toggle hash-sign ("#") printing for each 1024-byte data block transferred. The size of a data block is 1024 bytes.
help [command]	Display help information for the specified command.
idle [seconds]	Set the idle timer on the remote machine to the specified number of seconds.
lcd [directory]	Change directory on the local machine.
ls [remote-directory] [local-file]	Display a list of the contents of the specified remote directory or information about the specified file.
macdef *macro-name*	Define a macro. The subsequent lines make up the content of the macro; end the macro definition by entering a null line.

***mdelete** [remote-files]*	Delete the specified files on the remote machine.
***mdir** remote-files local-file*	Like dir, except multiple remote files may be specified.
***mget** remote-files*	Get the specified files from the remote machine.
***mkdir** directory-name*	Create a directory on the remote machine.
***mls** remote-files local-file*	Display a list of files on the remote machine. There may be more than one remote file specified, and the local file argument (to which the listing is sent) is mandatory.
***mode** [mode-name]*	Specify the file transfer mode. The default is "stream".
***modtime** file-name*	Display the most recent modification time of the specified remote file.
***mput** local-files*	Transfer each file specified to the remote machine.
***newer** file-name [local-file]*	Retrieve the specified file if the modification time is more recent than the copy on the local machine.
***nlist** [remote-directory] [local-file]*	Display the files in the specified remote directory. If a local-file is specified, output from this command will be sent to it rather than the screen.
***nmap** [inpattern outpattern]*	Toggle the file mapping mechanism. If inpattern and outpattern are specified, files are automatically renamed during transfer according to the specified mapping pattern.
***ntrans** [inchars [outchars]]*	Toggle filename character translation. If a character mapping is specified, file name characters will be automatically translated as specified during file transfers.
***open** host [port]*	Connect to the specified host FTP server.
prompt	Toggle interactive prompting during multiple file transfers.

proxy *ftp-command*	Execute an ftp command on a secondary control connection. This command allows simultaneous connection to two remote ftp servers for transferring files between the two servers.
put *local-file [remote-file]*	Transfer a local file to the remote machine.
pwd	Display the current working directory on the remote machine.
quit	Equivalent to bye.
quote *arg1 arg2 ...*	Sends the specified arguments, verbatim, to the remote FTP server.
recv *remote-file [local-file]*	Equivalent to get.
reget remote-file [local-file]	Similar to get, but if local file exists and is smaller than the remote file, it is presumed to be an incomplete transfer. Transfer is continued from the apparent point of failure.
remotehelp *[command-name]*	Get help from the remote FTP server on the specified command.
remotestatus *[file-name]*	Display status of the remote machine or the specified file on the remote machine.
rename [from] [to]	Rename a file on the remote machine as specified.
reset	Clear the reply queue.
restart *marker*	Restart the immediately following get or put at the indicated marker.
rmdir *directory-name*	Delete the specified directory on the remote machine.

runique	Toggle storing of files on the local system with unique filenames. If the target file of a transfer already exists and unique mode is set, the file will not be overwritten. Instead, a new file with the same base name but a ".1" extension is appended to the filename (or ".2", or ".3", ... , ".99").
send *local-file [remote-file]*	Equivalent to put.
sendport	Toggle the use of PORT commands.
site *arg1 arg2 ...*	The specified arguments are sent (verbatim) to the remote FTP server as a SITE command.
size *file-name*	Display the size of the specified file on remote machine.
status	Show the current status of ftp.
struct *[struct-name]*	Set the file transfer structure to struct-name. By default "stream" structure is used.
sunique	Toggle storing of files on remote machine under unique file names (see runique, above).
system	Display operating system information for the remote host.
tenex	Set file transfer type such that TENEX machines can be communicated with.
trace	Toggle packet tracing.
type *[type-name]*	Set file transfer type as specified. The default is network ASCII.
umask *[newmask]*	Set the default umask on the remote server as specified.
user *user-name [password] [account]*	Send your user information to the remote FTP server.

verbose	Toggle verbose mode.
? [command]	Equivalent to help.

hostname [NAME]

Display or set the hostname of the local machine.

Example: To display the host name of the local machine:

hostname

--help	Display help information.
--version	Display version information.

netstat [-venaoc] [--tcp|-t] [--udp|-u] [--raw|-w] [--unix|-u] [--inet|--ip] [--ax25] [--ipx] [--netrom]

netstat [-veenc] [--inet] [--ipx] [--netrom] [--ddp] [--ax25] {--route|-r}

netstat [-veenac] {--interfaces|-i} [iface]

netstat [-enc] {--masquerade|-M}

netstat [-cn] {--netlink|-N}

netstat {-V|--version} {-h|--help}

This command displays information (network connections, routing tables, interface statistics, masquerade connections and netlink messages) about the local network.

Example: To display information about the network status:

netstat

Example: To see whether your routing table contains a route to the network 192.249.100 (**r** prints routing table information, **n** is the numeric option):

netstat -nr | grep '192.249.100'

Modes

-r, --route	Display kernel routing tables.
-i, --interface iface	Display all (or only the specified) network interfaces.
-M, --masquerade	Display a list of all masqueraded sessions.

TIP Use -M in conjunction with -e option for sequence numbering and deltas caused by data rewrites on FTP sessions.

-N, --netlink	Get information about creation or deletion of interfaces or routes.

Options

-v, --verbose	Verbose operation.
-n, --numeric	Display numeric addresses rather than attempting to resolve them into symbolic host, port or user names.
-A, --af family	Set the address families as a comma separated list of keywords (inet, unix, ipx, ax25, netrom, ddp)
-c, --continous	Update the display every second until interrupted.

Output Description

* Active Internet connections (TCP, UDP, RAW)

Proto	The protocol (tcp, udp, raw) used by the socket.
Recv-Q	The count of bytes not copied by the user program connected to this socket.

Send-Q	The count of bytes not acknowledged by the remote host.
Local Address	Local address (hostname) and port number of the socket.
Foreign Address	Remote address (hostname) and port number of the socket.
State	State of the socket.
ESTABLISHED	The socket has an established connection.
SYN_SENT	The socket is actively attempting to establish a connection.
SYN_RECV	The connection is being initialized.
FIN_WAIT1	The socket is closed, and the connection is shutting down.
FIN_WAIT2	Connection is closed, and the socket is waiting for a shutdown from the remote end.
TIME_WAIT	The socket is waiting after close for remote shutdown retransmission.
CLOSED	The socket is not being used.
CLOSE_WAIT	The remote end has shut down, waiting for the socket to close.
LAST_ACK	The remote end shut down, and the socket is closed. Waiting for acknowledgment.
LISTEN	The socket is listening for incoming connections.
CLOSING	Both sockets are shut down, but we still haven't sent all our data.
UNKNOWN	The state of the socket is unknown.
User	The name or the UID of the owner of the socket.

Proto	The protocol (usually UNIX) used by the socket.
RefCnt	The reference count (i.e., attached processes via this socket).
Flags	The flags displayed are SO_ACCEPTON (displayed as ACC), SO_WAITDATA (W) or SO_NOSPACE (N).
Type	There are several types of socket access:
SOCK_DGRAM	The socket is used in Datagram (connectionless) mode.
SOCK_STREAM	This is a stream (connection) socket.
SOCK_RAW	Raw socket.
SOCK_RDM	Reliably-delivered messages.
SOCK_SEQPACKET	This is a sequential packet socket.
SOCK_PACKET	RAW interface access socket.
State	One of the following:
FREE	Unallocated.
LISTENING	Socket is listening for a connection request.
CONNECTING	Socket is about to establish a connection.
CONNECTED	The socket is connected.
DISCONNECTING	The socket is disconnecting.
(empty)	The socket is not connected to another one.
UNKNOWN	This state should never happen.
Path	Path name as which corresponding processes are attached to the socket.

ping [-dfnqrvR] [-c *count*] [-i *wait*] [-l *preload*] [-p *pattern*]

[-s ***packetsize*****]**

Request acknowledgment from a remote host. Terminate ping with <Ctrl>C.

Example: To check the network connection between your computer and the remote host fenris:

ping fenris

TIP

Use this command to see if there is a valid network connection between your computer and another on the network.

-c count	Stop after the specified number of packets have been received.
-d	Set the SO_DEBUG option on the socket being used.
-f	Flood ping. Outputs packets as fast as they come back or one hundred times per second, whichever is more.
-i wait	Wait the specified number of seconds between packets.
-l preload	Send the specified number of packets as fast as possible, then return to normal operation.
-n	Numeric output. Do not resolve addresses into host names.
-p pattern	Pattern is a sequence of up to 16 bytes used to fill out the packet sent.

TIP

Use the **-p** option for diagnosing data-dependent network problems.

-q	Quiet operation. Output summary information only.
-R	Record route.
-r	Bypass normal routing and send directly to a host on an attached network.
-s packetsize	Specify the size of the data packets to be transmitted.
-v	Verbose output.

When setting up a network or debugging network problems, it's a good idea to **ping** yourself first to make sure everything is working correctly on your  end.

rarp [-V] [--version] [-h] [--help]

rarp -a

rarp [-v] -d *hostname* ...

rarp [-v] [-t type] -s *hostname hw_addr*

This command is used to access and manipulate the system's RARP table. RARP stands for Reverse Address Resolution Protocol. The RARP is a system for converting a physical network address into an IP address.

Example: To list the RARP table entries:

ROOT **rarp -a**

-V	Display version information.
-v	Verbose operation.
-t type	Tell rarp which class of entries (ether, ax25, netrom) to look for when setting or reading the rarp table.
-a, --list	List the RARP table entries.
-d *hostname*, ***--delete*** *hostname*	Delete the specified host from the table.
-s *hostname hw_addr*, ***--set*** *hostname hw_addr*	Create an entry in the RARP table for the specified host.

rcp [-px] [-k *realm*] *file1 file2*

rcp [-px] [-r] [-k *realm*] *file ... directory*

Copy a file between two machines on the same network.

Example: To copy the file test.txt from the local host to the directory ***/tmp*** on the remote machine fenris:

rcp test.txt fenris:/tmp

-r	Recursively copy any subdirectories found under the source to the destination.
-p	Attempt to preserve modification times when transferring source files.
***-k** realm*	Attempt to obtain tickets for the remote host in the specified realm rather than the remote host's realm as determined by krb_realmofhost.
-x	Do DES encryption for all data passed by rcp.

rdate [-p] [-s] [*host...*]

Get date and time from the specified host via the network.

Example: To get date information from the remote host fenris:

rdate fenris

-p	Print the date and time (default).
-s	Set local date and time based on the data obtained.

rdist [-DFn] [-A *num*] [-a *num*] [-d *var=value*] [-l <*local logopts*>] [-L <*remote logopts*>] [-f *distfile*] [-M *maxproc*] [-m *host*] [-o *distopts*] [-t *timeout*] [-p <*rdistd-path*>] [-P <*rsh-path*>] [*name ...*]

Networking Applications

rdist -DFn -c name ... [*login@*]*host*[*:dest*]

rdist -Server

rdist -V

This program is used to maintain identical copies of files over multiple hosts. It preserves file data (owner, group, mode, mtime). It reads commands from distfile to direct the updating of files and/or directories. The distfile may be specified on the command line (standard output = "-"), or may be one of "distfile" or "Distfile".

-c	Interpret any remaining arguments as a distfile.
-Server	Attempt to function in server mode.
-A *num*	Specify the minimum number of free files that must exist on a filesystem in order for **rdist** to update or install a file.
-a *bytes*	Specify the minimum amount of free space (bytes) in a filesystem which must exist for **rdist** to update or install a file.
-D	Debug mode.
-d *var=value*	Override the value of *var* specified in the distfile.
-F	Do not fork any child **rdist** processes (effectively, update all clients in sequence).
-f *distfile*	Specify the *distfile* to be used. When distfile is specified as "-", read from standard input.
-l *logopts*	Specify local logging options.
-L *logopts*	Specify remote logging options.
-M *num*	Specify an upper limit on the number of child processes to be run simultaneously.

***-m** machine*	Specify an upper limit on the number of machines to be updated.
-n	Display commands but do not execute them.

TIP

Use rdist with -n option to debug your distfile.

-odistopts Specify which dist options to enable. distopts is a comma separated list of options from the following set:

verify	Verify that the files are all up to date on all the hosts.
whole	Append the whole filename to the destination directory name.
noexec	Do not include executable files.
younger	Update files if their mtime and size disagree.
compare	Perform a binary comparison, updating files where they differ (as opposed to a time & date comparison).
follow	Follow symbolic links to copy files.
ignlnks	Ignore unresolved links.
chknfs	Do not check or update files which reside on NFS filesystems.
chkreadonly	If file resides on a readonly filesystem, do not attempt to update.
chksym	If target on remote host is a symbolic link but is not on master host, allow the remote host to remain a symbolic link. This may lead to Bad Things, but has been retained for compatibility with earlier versions.
quiet	Quiet mode.
remove	Remove extraneous files (files which exist on remote host but not on master).

nochkowner	Do not check ownership of existing files.
nochkgroup	Do not check group ownership of existing files.
nochkmode	Do not check file & directory permission modes.
nodescend	Do not recursively descend into directories.
numchkgroup	Check group ownership via numeric group id rather than name.
numchkowner	Check group ownership via numeric uid rather than name.
savetargets	Save updated files rather than removing them.

-p <rdistd-path>	Specify the path where the rdistd server is searched for on the target host.
-P <rsh-path>	Specify the path where the rsh command may be found.
***-t** timeout*	Specify an upper limit (in seconds) for how long to wait on responses from the rdist server.
-V	Display version information and exit.

Distfiles

Distfiles are of the following format:

```
<variable name> `=' <name list>
[ label: ] <source list> `->' <destination list> <command list>
[ label: ] <source list> `::' <time_stamp file> <command list>
```

rlogin [-8EKLdx] [-e *char*] [-k *realm*] [-l *username*] *host*

Start a terminal session on the specified remote host.

Example: To remotely log in to the host fenris:

rlogin fenris

-8	Permit an eight-bit input data path at all times.
-E	Do not allow the specified character to be recognized as an escape character.
-K	Disable Kerberos authentication.
-L	Permit the rlogin session to be run in litout mode.
-d	Enable socket debugging.
-e	Permit user specification of the escape character.
-k	Request rlogin to obtain tickets for the remote host in the specified realm rather than the remote host's realm.
-x	Turn on DES encryption for all data passed via the rlogin session.

rsh [-Kdnx] [-k *realm*] [-l *username*] *host* [*command*]

Execute a command on the specified host. Standard input, standard output, and standard error are swapped around, as you might expect.

Example: To invoke a shell on the remote host fenris:

rsh fenris

-K	Disable kerberos authentication.
-d	Enable socket debugging.
***-k** realm*	Get rsh to attempt to obtain tickets for the remote host in the specified realm rather than the remote host's realm.
-l	Allow specification of a remote username. (Default is same as local username.)
-n	Redirect input from /dev/null. No, really.
-x	Enable DES encryption on all data transferred.

rusers [-al] [host ...]

Display a list of users logged in on the network.

Example: To display a list of all users currently logged in on the network, and include information on all the hosts on the network regardless of whether anyone is currently logged in (**-a** option):

rusers -a

-a	Display all machines responding even if no one is currently logged on.
-l	Long format listing (user name, host, tty, date & time of login, idle time, and any remote host information)

rwall *host* [*file*]

Display a message to the terminal of all users currently logged in to the specified host. Message may be typed in interactively or may be specified in file.

Example: To display the message contained in the file urgent.txt to all the users currently logged in to the network host fenris:

rwall fenris urgent.txt

rwho [-a]

Display user and machine information for all users on the local network.

Example: To display user information for all users on the network:

rwho

-a	Include all logged in users in output regardless of idle time.

telnet [-8ELadr] [-S *tos*] [-e *escapechar*] [-l *user*] [-n *tracefile*] [*host* [*port*]]

Interact with another machine over the network via the **telnet** protocol. Once you're logged in, network access is pretty much transparent. That is, you'd never know you were logged in across a network rather than directly wired to the machine.

Example: To set up a telnet (interactive network login) session with the remote host fenris:

telnet fenris

-8	Specify 8-bit operation.
-E	Disable escape character.
-L	Use an 8-bit path on output.
-a	Attempt automatic login.
-d	Debug mode. May be interactively toggled back to non-debug mode.
-r	Emulate rlogin(1).
-S *tos*	Use the specified type-of-service.
-e *escapechar*	Specify the escape character.
-l *user*	Attempt to log in to the remote system as the specified user.
-n *tracefile*	Record trace information in the specified tracefile.
host	Specify the network host you wish to log in to.
port	Specify a port number or service name to contact (default = 23).

The **telnet** command is interactive. The following subcommands apply:

auth *argument ...* — This command controls the TELNET AUTHENTICATE protocol option. The following arguments are valid:

disable type	Disable the specified type of authentication.
enable type	Enable the specified type of authentication.
status	List the current status of the various types of authentication.

close Close connection to remote host and return to command mode.

***display** argument ...* Display the set and toggle value specified, or all, if none is specified.

***encrypt** argument ...* Control telnet encryption. Valid arguments are:

disable type [input|output]	Disable specified type of encryption.
enable type [input|output]	Enable the specified type of encryption.
input	Same as "encrypt start input"
-input	Same as "encrypt stop input"
output	Same as "encrypt start output"
-output	Same as "encrypt stop output"
start [input|output]	Attempt to begin encryption.
status	Display current status of encryption module.
stop [input|output]	Stop encrypting.
type type	Specify type of encryption to be used.

***environ** arguments...* Specify environment variables to be propagated across the telnet link. Valid arguments are:

define variable value	Define variable as value.
undefine variable	Remove definition of variable.
export variable	Propagate specified variable to the remote host.

unexport variable	Do not propagate variable to remote host.
list	List the current set of environment variables. * indicates that variable is marked for propagation.

logout	Log out of remote host.
mode *type*	Specify connection mode (character, line, isig, edit, softtabs, litecho).
open *host* ***[[-l]*** *user****][-port]***	Open a connection to the specified host. Optionally, your user id on that host and the port number to be connected to may be specified.
quit	Close connections and exit telnet.
send arguments	Send one of the following telnet protocol character sequences to the remote host:

abort	Abort process.
ao	Abort output (flush all output to the user's terminal).
ayt	Send the Are You There sequence.
brk	Break.
ec	Erase last character entered.
el	Erase current line.
eof	End-of-file.
eor	End of record.
escape	Send telnet escape character.
ga	Go ahead.
getstatus	Send current status (if supported).
ip	Interrupt current running process.

nop	Send the telnet "no operation" sequence.
susp	Suspend process.
synch	Synchronize. Remote system will disregard all typed but unread input.
do cmd, dont cmd, will cmd, wont cmd	Send one of the TELNET DO cmd sequences as specified.
?	Display help information for the send command.

***set** argument value,*
***unset** argument value*

Set or unset the specified argument to value.

ayt	Send an "are you there" sequence to the specified host.
echo	Toggle between doing local echoing of entered characters and suppressing echoing of entered characters.
eof	Send eof to the remote system.
erase	Send a telnet erase character.
escape	Send telnet escape character "^[".
flushoutput	If telnet is in localchars mode and the flushoutput character is typed, a TELNET AO sequence (see send ao above) is sent to the remote host.
forw1, forw2	When in LINEMODE, send partial lines to the remote system.
interrupt	If in localchars mode, send the TELNET IP sequence.
kill	Send a TELNET EL sequence if in LINEMODE.
lnext	If in LINEMODE, this is taken to be the lnext character.
quit	If in localchars mode, send the TELNET BRK sequence.

reprint If in LINEMODE, this is taken to be the reprint character.

rlogin Set the escape character.

start If TELNET TOGGLE-FLOW-CONTROL option has been enabled, this will be taken to be the terminal's start character.

stop If the TELNET TOGGLE-FLOW-CONTROL option has been enabled, this character is taken to be the terminal's stop character.

susp If in localchars mode or LINEMODE is enabled, send a TELNET SUSP sequence.

tracefile Specify file to which output caused by netdata or option tracing being TRUE will be written.

worderase If operating in LINEMODE or line-by-line-mode, this character is taken as the terminal's worderase character.

? Displays the legal set (unset) commands.

slc *state* Set Local Characters to the specified state when TELNET LINEMODE option has been enabled.

check Verify the current settings for the current special characters.

export Switch to the local defaults for the special characters.

import Switch to the remote defaults for the special characters.

? Prints out help information for the slc command.

status Display current status of telnet.

toggle *arguments ...* Toggle the specified argument(s) between true and false.

authdebug Turns on debugging for the authentication code.

autodecrypt When TRUE, automatically enable encryption/decryption.

autologin	Attempt to use TELNET AUTHENTICATION to perform automatic authentication.
autosynch	If autosynch and localchars are both TRUE, then when either the intr or quit characters is typed, the resulting telnet sequence sent is followed by the TELNET SYNCH sequence.
binary	Enable or disable the TELNET BINARY option on both input and output.
inbinary	Enable or disable the TELNET BINARY option on input.
outbinary	Enable or disable the TELNET BINARY option on output.
crlf	If this is TRUE, then carriage returns will be sent as <CR><LF>. If this is FALSE, then carriage returns will be send as <CR><NUL>.
crmod	Toggle carriage return mode.
debug	Toggles socket level debugging.
encdebug	Turns on debugging information for the encryption code.
localchars	If this is TRUE, then the flush, interrupt, quit, erase, and kill characters set (hopefully) appropriate TELNET control sequences.
options	Toggle the display of some internal telnet protocol processing.
prettydump	When the netdata toggle is enabled, if prettydump is enabled the output from the netdata command will be formatted in a more user-readable format.
skiprc	If true, do not read the .telnetrc file.
termdata	Toggles the display of all terminal data.

verbose_encrypt	When TRUE, display a message each time encryption is enabled or disabled.
?	Displays the legal toggle commands.

z	Suspend telnet.
! [command]	Execute a single command in a subshell on the local system.
? [command]	Display help information on the specified command.

tftp [*host*]

This program is an implementation of the Trivial File Transfer Protocol. Tftp is used to transfer files to and from a remote machine. This command is interactive, the following commands apply:

Example: To transfer the binary file "interest" across the network using the tftp protocol and place it in the current directory:

tftp

tftp> **binary**

tftp> **connect fenris**

tftp> **get /usr/bin/interest .**

? command-name ...	Display help information.
ascii	Transfer files in ASCII mode.
binary	Transfer files in binary mode.
***connect** host-name [port]*	Connect to the specified host (and, optionally, port) for file transfer.
***get** filename,* ***get** remotename localname,* ***get** file1 file2 ... fileN*	Retrieve a copy of the specified files and place it on the local host.
***mode** transfer-mode*	Set transfer mode. Allowable values are ASCII and binary.

***put** file, **put** localfile remotefile, **put** file1 file2 ... fileN remote-directory*	Transfer a copy of the specified file(s) from the local host to the remote host.
quit	Exit tftp.
***rexmt** retransmission-timeout*	Specify the per-packet re-transmission timeout (seconds).
status	Show current status.
***timeout** total-transmission-timeout*	Specify the total transmission timeout, in seconds.
trace	Toggle packet tracing.
verbose	Toggle verbose mode.

CHAPTER

31

NIS AND NFS

Introduction

NIS is a suite of programs that allow network configuration databases to be shared across a network. **NFS**, which to a certain extent relies on **NIS** for configuration information, allows filesystems which exist on a machine to be mounted on different machines across a network connection.

NIS

NIS stands for **N**etwork **I**nformation **S**ystem. **NIS** is handy in situations where you have several machines networked together to serve a common group of users. By default, there would be multiple copies of the access control files (e.g. ***/etc/passwd***, ***/etc/hosts***...)—one per machine. This is OK if you have only one or two machines, or only one or two users. But in real world situations where there are dozens of machines and hundreds of users, the man-hours required to keep all those files synchronized can quickly become prohibitively expensive. **NIS** provides a mechanism for replacing the multiple sets of files spread across the network with a single set stored on a central server (or servers). When one of the client machines needs to find out user Timmy's password, it asks the server. When Timmy leaves the company, the system administrator needs to remove him from only one set of files.

NIS data files are referred to as **maps**. A host which requests information from a map is called a **client.** A host which handles client requests for map data is called a **server**. A server which can serve client requests but not modify data in maps is called a **slave server**; a server which can both handle client requests and modify data in maps is called a **master server**. Note that being a server for one map does not necessarily exclude a host from being a client for another map.

Obviously, you want to use NIS to manage files that are more or less the same across all systems on your network. Typically, these might include:

/etc/aliases	Aliases and mail lists
/etc/group	System group definitions
/etc/hosts	IP address to hostname translation table
/etc/passwd	System user definitions
/etc/services	Port number to network service translation table

Setting Up an NIS Server

1. Set the local host's domain name with **domainname.**
2. Initialize a master server with **ypinit**.
3. Initialize any slave servers with **ypinit** (optional).
4. Invoke the **ypserv** daemon on the servers. If your system is a commercial distribution, there is probably already a script for this somewhere under your **/etc** directory. (If not, you can start it by hand—"**ypserv**" will do it.)

Setting Up an NIS Client

1. Put NIS marker entries in all the files you want to refer to the NIS server for information (e.g., in ***/etc/passwd***, include the entry "**+::::::**").
2. Set the domain name with **domainname**.
3. Invoke the **ypbind** daemon.

NFS

NFS is the **N**etwork **F**ile**S**ystem. **NFS** is a way of making the filesystem(s) on one machine accessible to other machines. The beauty of NFS is that an

NFS filesystem mounted across the network appears to the local user almost exactly like a local filesystem mounted from the local hard disk. (See the chapter on filesystems for more information on what it means to "mount" a filesystem.) Again, this is useful in real-world network situations where it would be impractical to maintain multiple copies of files accessed by users across a network.

TIP

Running NFS will open up some security holes on your network. Before setting up NFS, take a little time and read up on the security risks associated with network filesystems. You can't plug all the holes, but you can minimize your risks if you have a better idea of what you're getting yourself into.

Setting Up NFS

1. Invoke the **mountd** and **nfsd** daemons (later you will want to configure your system so this happens automatically at boot time).
2. Edit the **/etc/exports** file on the exporting computer to include the directories you want exported and the domains/users you want them exported to.
3. Edit the **/etc/fstab** file on the mounting computer to include the network filesystem.
4. Mount the filesystem as usual with the **mount** command.

Globbing is the process of referring to multiple files with a single string. For example, the string "a*" would refer to all the files which started with the letter "a".

The commands covered in this section include:

domainname	Show or set the system's NIS/YP domain name.
nisdomainname	Show or set system's NIS/YP domain name.
ypdomainname	Show or set the system's NIS/YP domain name.
makedbm	Convert text file to ypserv database.
ypbind	NIS client daemon.
ypcat	Display keys from the NIS database.

yppasswd	Change user-related info.
ypinit	Initialize a yp server.
yppoll	Return version & master server of NIS maps.
yppush	Copy information from master server to slave servers.
ypserv	NIS network services daemon.
ypset	Get NIS information for a domain.
ypwhich	Return the name of the NIS server or map master.
ypxfer	Copy map databases between servers.

Related Files

/etc/yp.conf	NIS configuration file.
/var/yp/binding/domainname.version	Binding file containing information about domain.
/var/run/ypbind.pid	Contains the process id of the currently running ypbind master process. ypbind sets a write lock to this file to prevent multiple copies of itself from running.
/var/yp/nicknames	Map nickname translation table.
/var/yp/nicknames	Map nickname translation table.
/etc/ypserv.conf	NIS server configuration.
/var/yp/nicknames	Map nickname translation table.
/var/yp/[domainname]/[maps]	Maps for named domain.

Commands

hostname [-v] [-a] [--alias] [-d] [--domain] [-f] [--fqdn] [-i] [--ip-address] [--long] [-s] [--short] [-y] [--yp] [--nis]

hostname [-v] [-F *filename*] [--file *filename*] [*hostname*]

domainname [-v] [-F *filename*] [--file *filename*] [*name*]

hostname [-v] [-h] [--help] [-V] [--version]

dnsdomainname [-v]

nisdomainname [-v]

ypdomainname [-v]

This program will either set or display the specified network name. Note that you cannot change the FQDN with this command.

Example: To set the domain name of the current domain to be asgard:

domainname asgard ROOT

-a, --alias	Display alias name of host.
-d, --domain	Display DNS domain name.
-F, --file *filename*	Specified file contains host name information.
-f, --fqdn, --long	Display FQDN (Fully Qualified Domain Name).
-h, --help	Display help information and exit.
-i, --ip-address	Display IP address(es) of the host.

-s, --short	Display short host name (up to the first dot).
-V, --version	Display version information and exit.
-v, --verbose	Verbose option.
-y, --yp, --nis	Display NIS domain name.

/usr/lib/yp/makedbm [-a | -r] [-b] [-c] [-s] [-l] [-i *YP_INPUT_NAME*] [-o *YP_OUTPUT_NAME*] [-m *YP_MASTER_NAME*] *inputfile dbname*

/usr/lib/yp/makedbm -u *dbname*

/usr/lib/yp/makedbm -c

/usr/lib/yp/makedbm --version

Convert the specified input file and convert it to a **ypserv** database.

Example: To read in the file sample.txt and convert it to the yp database sample:

ROOT **makedbm sample.txt sample**

-a	Support mail aliases.
-b	Insert the YP_INTERDOMAIN into the output.
-c	Clear. Send a YPPROC_CLEAR to the local ypserv.
-l	Convert to lowercase.
***-i** YP_INPUT_NAME*	Create a database entry with the key YP_INPUT_NAME.
***-m** YP_MASTER_NAME*	Create a database entry with the key YP_MASTER_NAME.

***-o** YP_OUTPUT_NAME*	Create a special database entry with the key YP_OUTPUT_NAME.
-r	Treat # as a comment sign and remove the comment.
-s	Secure map. Accept connections from secure NIS networks only.
***-u** dbname*	Dump a ypserv database file.

/usr/sbin/ypbind [-v|-version|--version] [-d|-debug|--debug] [-ipc|--ipc] [-mmap|--mmap] [-broken_server|--broken_server] [-ypset] [-ypsetme] [-no-ping|--no-ping]

This is the NIS client daemon. It locates the server for an NIS domain and stores information about it in a binding file. The binding file is found in ***/var/nis/binding***, and typically has a name formatted as **domain-name.version** (e.g., ***/var/nis/binding/asgard.2***).

Example: To invoke the ypbind daemon on an NIS client machine:

ypbind

ROOT

domain nisdomain server hostname	Use server hostname for the domain nisdomain.
domain nisdomain broadcast	Use broadcast on the local net for domain nisdomain.
***ypserver** hostname*	Use server for the local domain. The IP address of server must be listed in /etc/hosts.
-ypset	Ypset may be used to change the binding for a domain.
-ypsetme	Ypset may be used only from the local host to change the binding for a domain.
-debug	Debug mode. Runs in foreground with debug output written to standard out.
-ipc	Permit use of IPC for master-slave communication. If your root filesystem is on NFS, you must use this option.

-mmap	Permit use of mmap for master-slave communication.
-broken_server	Accept answers from servers running on an illegal port number.
-no-ping	Do not allow ypbind to continually check if the binding is alive.

ypcat [-kt] [-d *domain*] *mapname*

ypcat -x

Display the values of all keys from NIS database specified by mapname.

Example: To display the password map:

ypcat passwd

-d *domain*	Specify a domain other than the default.
-k	Display map keys.
-t	Inhibit map nickname translation.
-x	Display map nickname translation table.

yppasswd [-f] [-l] [-p] [*user*]

ypchfn [*user*]

ypchsh [*user*]

Change password, shell, or GECOS information for NIS. These commands are all links to the same program. This program is very similar to **passwd** in its operation.

Example: To change the password for the user testnfs:

yppasswd testnfs

-f	Update GECOS field.
yppasswd or -l	Change the user's NIS password.
ypchsh or -l	Change the user's login shell.
ypchfn or -f	Change user's full name and related information.

/usr/lib/yp/ypinit [-m] [-s *master_name*]

Build the domain subdirectory of **/var/yp** for the current default domain, then create a set of administrative maps and place them in this directory.

Example: To initialize the current machine as a master server:

ypinit -m ROOT

Example: To initialize the current machine as a slave server to the master server odin:

ypinit -s odin ROOT

-m	If the local host is the NIS master.OK as written?
-s	Set up a slave server with the database from master_name.

ypmatch [-kt] [-d *domain*] *key ... mapname*

ypmatch -x

Display the values of one or more keys from the NIS database specified by mapname.

Example: To display the password file entry for the user testnfs:

ypmatch testnfs passwd

***-d** domain*	Allow user to specify a domain.
-k	Display map keys.

-t	This option inhibits map nickname translation.
-x	Display the map nickname translation table.

yppoll [-h *host*] [-d *domain*] *mapname*

Return version and master server of an NIS map.

Example: To get the version and master server of the hosts map:

ROOT **yppoll hosts**

-h host	Request information on mapname from the specified host.
-d domain	Specify a domain other than the default.

/usr/sbin/**yppush** [-d *domain*] [-t *timeout*] [-p *# parallel jobs*] [-h *host*] [-v] *mapname* ...

Copy updated NIS databases or maps from the master NIS server to the slave servers within an NIS domain. This program is used by master servers to maintain map databases on slave servers when changes are made.

Typically, this is handled automatically by the NIS make utility.

Example: To overwrite the passwd map on slave servers:

ROOT **yppush passwd**

-d *domain*	Specify a domain.
-t *timeout*	Specify a timeout value in seconds.
-p *# parallel jobs*	Perform transfers serially (complete the transaction with the current slave before talking to the next one).
-h *host*	Transfer a map to a user-specified machine or group of machines rather than the list of servers contained in the ypservers map.

/usr/sbin/ypserv [-b] [-d [*path*]] [-p *port*]

ypserv is the NIS network lookup service daemon.

Example: To invoke the NIS network daemon on a server:

ypserv &

-d --debug [path]	Run the server in debugging mode.
-b --dns	If a particular host is not found in the host map, query DNS for more host information.
***-p --port** port*	Bind to the specified port.
-v --version	Display version information.

ypset [-d *domain*] [-h *hostname*] *server*

This command tells **ypbind** to get NIS services for the specified domain from the **ypserv** process running on the server. In order to use **ypset**, ypbind must be initiated with the **ypset** or ypsetme **options**.

Example: To invoke **ypbind**, telling it to get NIS services for the domain midgard from the server helga:

ypset -d midgard helga

ROOT

***-d** domain*	Specify a domain other than the default.
***-h** hostname*	Set NIS binding on host rather than the local machine.

ypwhich [-d *domain*] [-Vn] [*hostname*]

ypwhich [-d *domain*] [-t] -m [*mname*]

ypwhich -x

This command returns the name of the NIS server or map master.

Example: To find out who your NIS server is:

ypwhich

***-d** domain*	Specify a domain other than the default domain.
-t	Inhibit map nickname translation.
***-m** mname*	Find the master NIS server for a map.
-x	Display the map nickname translation table.
-Vn	Version of ypbind(8), V2 is default.

/usr/lib/yp/ypxfr [-f] [-c] [-d *target domain*][-h *source host*] [-s *source domain*][-C *taskid program-number ipaddr port*][-p *yp_path*] *mapname* ...

Copy an NIS database from the NIS master server to a slave server, using the NIS service.

Example: To transfer the aliases map from a master server to a slave (the command is run on the slave):

ROOT **ypxfr aliases.byname**

-f	Force a map transfer.
-c	Do not send a "clear current map" request to the ypserv process running on the local host.
***-d** domain*	Specify a domain other than the default NIS domain.
***-h** source host*	Force **ypxfr** to get the map from the specified host.
***-s** source domain*	Specify a source domain from which to transfer a map that should be the same across domains.
***-C** taskid program-number ipaddr port*	Specify that **ypxfr** should call back a **yppush** process at the host with IP address ipaddr, registered as program, listening on the specified port and waiting for a response to transaction taskid.

***-p** yp_path*	Change directory for the maps to yp_path/[domainname].
mapname	One or more names of the map to transfer.

CHAPTER

32

DOS & WINDOWS

Introduction

The world being what it is, the odds are that even the most fervent Linux partisan will, from time to time, be forced to interact with the various Microsoft products. The commands in this section enable Linux to work directly with Microsoft file systems and networking protocols. In the discussion below, the term "Windows" is used as shorthand for the DOS, Windows, and OS/2 operating systems.

The differences between the Linux environment and the Windows environment are as innumerable as the differences between good and evil. For that reason, the introduction to this chapter is likely to be a little topheavy. I want to give you enough information to get the job done, but at the same time this book needs to be light enough for an average human to lift it without mechanical assistance. Let me know if you need more details.

Windows Filesystems

Historically, Windows used the FAT (File Allocation Table) filesystem. The FAT system stores information on file size, type (e.g., archive, system, hidden, read-only), and modification time. As the FAT system was designed to be run on a single-user PC, there is no provision for access control. The m* suite of commands (**mcopy, mdir**...) are designed to access FAT filesystems directly from Linux. More recently, we've seen the introduction of NTFS, the NT filesystem which provides for access control information.

In the Windows environment, path delimiters are backwards: "\" instead of "/". Also, drives are specified by letters. By convention **A:** is the floppy disk drive, **C:** is the primary hard disk (which may have further logical subdivisions—**D:, E**:...). For example, the file **test** in the subdirectory **examples** of the floppy disk drive would be specified as:

A:\examples\test

Windows Networking Concepts

Windows networking uses the **S**erver **M**essage **B**lock (**SMB**) protocol for communication between networked machines. Broadly speaking, the SMB protocol provides the following functionality:

- Opening & closing files
- Reading and writing data blocks
- Retrieving directory information
- Maintaining the list of Universal Naming Convention (UNC) names for shared resources (e.g., printers, files)
- Associated operating system overhead

The SMB protocol is roughly analogous to a combination of the Unix **NFS** networking protocol and **lpd** line printer daemon.

Note: In comparison to Unix, SMB has a *lot* of commands. This means that SMB is more complicated and more likely to have bugs, but at the same time quicker in that a single SMB command can suffice for two or three NFS commands.

The **SMB** protocol runs on top of the **NetBIOS** network interface. **NetBIOS** stands for **Net**work **B**asic **I**nput **O**utput **S**ystem. It is a session-level (of theOSI model) network interface typically used on Windows networks. NetBIOS provides the following three basic services:

Name Service	Maintain name database for applications
Session	Handle connection/disconnection and communication between two applications
Datagram	Transmit datagrams (fundamental packets of data) to network, receive those addressed to you

NetBEUI is a non-routable networking protocol designed for Lan-Manager networks. It is a prominent implementation of NetBIOS.

The **Uniform Naming Convention** (UNC) is the syntax used to specify shared network resources ("shares") on a Windows machine. UNC names are of the form:

\\server\sharename\subdirectory\subdirectory\...\filename

The server and sharename are mandatory; subdirectory and filename specifications are optional. For example, in the sample network described in the start of this section, my printer share is called:

\\Loki\HPLJ6

and this chapter is shared as

\\Loki\e\My Documents\Linux Book\26-dos

Windows networks come in two flavors: **workgroups** and **domains**. **Workgroups**, which may be run without an NT machine, are peer-to-peer networks, usually of Windows 95/98 machines. Workgroups allow shared access to resources (printers, directories) across a network. Workgroups have very limited security features, but it is possible to set a password for a printer or other share.

Domains, which require an NT machine, implement centralized access control and are chock full of user level security mechanisms. The NT-server machine which stores account information for a domain is called the **primary domain controller.**

Note: NT domains and Internet domains are two totally different concepts.

The process of viewing the resources available on a Windows network is known as **browsing**. In order to facilitate browsing, Windows networks require that one of the machines on the network maintains a centralized list of browsable resources. The list is known as the **browse list**, the computer that maintains it is known as the **master browser**.

The **Windows Internet Name Service (WINS)** is a client-server mechanism for resolving Internet domain names into IP addresses. The ***LMHOSTS*** file is a text file used by Windows systems to associate NETBIOS network names with IP addresses (not unlike the /etc/hosts file on Linux). It is found either in the ***\WINNT\system32\drivers\etc*** directory (Windows NT) or the ***\WINDOWS*** directory (Windows 95/98).

Samba is a suite of programs which run on Linux (or other Unix) machines but use the SMB networking protocol. Linux machines running Samba can act as file and print servers for Windows machines. Samba can be obtained from:

http://samba.anu.edu.au/pub/samba

The samba configuration file, **smb.conf** contains the configuration information for both smb and nmbd.

The commands covered in this section include:

mattrib	Set attributes on an MS-DOS file
mbadblocks	Test MS-DOS disk for bad blocks
mcd	Change directories on DOS filesystem
mdel	Delete file from DOS directory
mdeltree	Delete directory tree on DOS filesystem
mdir	Display DOS directory contents
mdu	Display usage of DOS disk
mformat	Format DOS disk
mlabel	Label DOS disk
mmd	Make DOS directory
mrd	Remove DOS directory
mmove	Move file on DOS filesystem
mtype	Display contents of DOS file
xcopy	Recursively copy contents of DOS directory
nmbd	Provide NetBIOS nameserver support
smbclient	Access Windows machines on the network
smbd	Provide LanManager services to network clients
smbmount	Mount LanManager filesystem
smbstatus	Status information about SMB connection

smbumount	Unmount LanManager filesystem.
testparm	Test SMB configuration file parameters

Related Files

/usr/local/samba/lib	Default samba directory
/etc/lmhosts	IP to hostname mapping for SMB

Commands

The following options apply to all of the mtools commands:

-o	Overwrite primary names by default.
-O	Overwrite secondary names by default.
-r	Rename primary name by default.
-R	Rename secondary name by default.
-a	Autorename primary name by default.
-A	Autorename secondary name by default.
-s	Skip primary name by default.
-S	Skip secondary name by default.
-m	Ask user what to do with primary name.
-M	Ask user what to do with secondary name.

mattrib [-a|+a] [-h|+h] [-r|+r] [-s|+s] [-/] [-X] *MSDOSFILE* [*MSDOSFILES* ...]

This command is used to add or remove attribute flags on an MS-DOS file.

Example: To make the MS-DOS file "secret.txt" on the floppy disk invisible to the dos **dir** command:

mattrib +h secret.txt

a	Archive bit.
r	Indicates a read-only file.
s	Indicates an operating system file.
h	If set, this bit makes file hidden from the DIR command.
/	Recursive listing of attributes in subdirectories.
X	Display attributes without padding with whitespace.

mbadblocks DRIVE:

Scan an MS-DOS disk for bad blocks.

Example: To scan the floppy disk in the drive for bad blocks:

mbadblocks

mcd [*MSDOSDIRECTORY*]

If invoked with no arguments, this command displays the current working directory. If invoked with arguments, it changes the current working directory as specified.

Example: To change to the subdirectory "examples" on the floppy disk:

mcd examples

mcopy [-b/ptnvmoQOsSrRA] *SOURCEFILE TARGETFILE*

mcopy [-b/ptnvmoQOsSrRA] *SOURCEFILE* [

SOURCEFILES...] *TARGETDIRECTORY*

mcopy [-tnvm] *MSDOSSOURCEFILE*

This command copies files as specified from source to destination. The source and target may be either MS-DOS or Linux files.

Example: To copy the Linux file **/etc/hosts** to the MS-DOS formatted floppy disk in */dev/fd0* (a.k.a. the A: drive):

mcopy /etc/hosts A:

b	Optimize operation for large recursive copies.
/	Recursive copy.
p	Preserve attributes of copied files.
Q	When mcopying multiple files, tells mcopy to quit as soon as a copy fails.
t	Text file transfer.
n	Tell mcopy to overwrite Unix files without prompting.
m	Retain file modification time.

mdel [-v] *MSDOSFILE* [*MSDOSFILES* ...]

Delete a file from an MS-DOS filesystem. This command will prompt before deleting a read-only file.

Example: To delete the file "test" from the floppy disk in the A: drive:

mdel A:\test

mdeltree [-v] *MSDOSDIRECTORY* [*MSDOSDIRECTORIES...*]

This command is used to remove a directory and all the files and subdirectories contained therein.

Example: To remove the entire subdirectory tree rooted at examples:

mdeltree examples

DOS & Windows

mdir [-/] [-f] [-w] [-a] [-X] *MSDOSFILE* [*MSDOSFILES*...]

This command is used to display the contents of an MS-DOS directory.

Examples: To display the contents of the directory examples on the floppy disk:

mdir

/	Recursive output.
w	Wide output—lists filenames across the display with no other information.
a	Include hidden files in the list.
f	Specify fastest possible operation.
X	Concise listing.

mdu [-a] [*MSDOSFILES* ...]

List the space used by a directory, including its subdirectories and files.

Example: To display the space used by the subdirectory examples on the floppy disk in the A: drive:

mdu

a	Include all files.
s	Summary information only.

mformat [-t *CYLINDERS*] [-h *HEADS*] [-s *SECTORS*] [-l *VOLUME_LABEL*] [-F] [-I *FSVERSION*] [-S *SIZECODE*] [-2 *SECTORS_ON_TRACK_0*] [-M *SOFTWARE_SECTOR_SIZE*] [-a] [-X] [-C] [-H *HIDDEN_SECTORS*] [-r *ROOT_SECTORS*] [-B *BOOT_SECTOR*] [-0 *RATE_ON_TRACK_0*] [-A *RATE_ON_OTHER_TRACKS*] [-1] [-k] *DRIVE*:

Format a diskette with a minimal filesystem (boot sector, FAT, root directory).

Examples: To format the floppy disk in the A: drive for use by MS-DOS:

mformat

I've got no particular reason to be suspicious of the mformat command, but I think that, in general, it's best to let each operating system format it's own disk space. You might want to consider this command a backup, to be used only when there are no DOS/Windows machines around.

TIP

t	Specify the number of cylinders.
h	Specify the number of heads (sides).
s	Specify the number of sectors per track.
l	Specify volume label.
S	Specify sizecode.
2	Force 2m format.
1	Do not use 2m format.
M	Specify software sector size.
a	Force generation of an Atari-style serial number.
X	Format disk as an XDF disk.
C	Create the disk image file to install the MS-DOS filesystem on it. Obviously, this is useless on physical devices such as floppies and hard disk partitions.
H	Specify number of hidden sectors.
n	Serial number.
F	Format the partition as FAT32 (experimental).
I	Sets the fsVersion id when formatting a FAT32 drive.
c	Specify size of a cluster (in sectors).
r	Set the size of the root directory (in sectors).
B	Use bootsector stored in the file or device.

k	As much as possible, keep the existing boot sector.
0	Data transfer rate on track 0.
A	Data transfer rate on tracks other than 0.

mlabel [-vcs] *DRIVE*:[*NEW_LABEL*]

Add a volume label to a disk. If no label is specified, it will prompt the user to enter one. (Volume labels show up in **mdir** listings.)

Example: To label the disk in the current drive "Linux_Ports":

mlabel A:Linux_Ports

c	Clear the existing label.
s	Show the existing label.

mmd [-voOsSrRA] *MSDOSDIRECTORY* [*MSDOSDIRECTORIES...*]

Create the specified directory on an MS-DOS filesystem.

Example: To create the subdirectory "examples" on the disk in the floppy drive:

mmd examples

mrd [-v] *MSDOSDIRECTORY* [*DOSDIRECTORIES...*]

Delete a subdirectory from an MS-DOS filesystem.

Example: To remove the subdirectory "examples" from the disk in the floppy drive:

mrd examples

mmove [-voOsSrRA] *SOURCEFILE TARGETFILE*

mmove [-voOsSrRA] *SOURCEFILE* [*SOURCEFILES...*]

TARGETDIRECTORY

Rename an existing MS-DOS file or subdirectory.

Example: To move the file "smbstuff" into the directory examples from the root directory of the floppy drive:

mmove smbstuff examples

mtype [-ts] *MSDOSFILE* [*MSDOSFILES...*]

Display contents of an MS-DOS file to the screen.

Example: To display the contents of the file "smbstuff.txt" to the screen:

mtype smbstuff.txt

t	Optimize for text file viewing.
s	Strip high bit from the data.

xcopy *source_dir target_dir*

Recursively copy one directory to another.

Example: To recursively copy the contents of the subdirectory "examples" to the subdirectory "text":

xcopy examples text

nmbd [-D] [-H *netbios hosts file*] [-d *debuglevel*] [-l *log basename*] [-n *netbios name*] [-p *port number*] [-s *configuration file*]

The **nmbd** daemon is the part of the samba suite which handles **netbios** name server requests. It also has the capability of working as a WINS (Windows Internet Name Server).

Example: Inetd (see the chapter on daemons) can be used to start **nmbd** and **smbd** as appropriate. To do so, include the following entries in the ***/etc/services*** file:

```
netbios-ssn 139/tcp
netbios-ns 137/udp
```

which associates the netbios-ssn service with port 139 and the netbios-ns service with port 137. Once the association has been made, inetd can monitor ports 137 and 139 for requests. Upon receiving a request, inetd will look in the ***inetd.conf*** file for instructions on how to handle it. You will need to add the following lines to the ***inetd.conf*** file to tell it how:

```
netbios-ssn stream tcp nowait root /usr/sbin/smbd smbd
netbios-ns dgram upd wait root /usr/sbin/nmbd nmbd
```

TIP When configuring **samba** on NFS machines, remember that you must modify the ***/etc/services*** file on the NIS master.

-B	Obsolete. Included for backward compliance.
-I	Obsolete—replaced by the interfaces option in smb.conf.
-D	Tell the server to operate as a daemon.
***-C** comment string*	This option has been replaced by the "server string" option in smb.conf.
-G	This option has been replaced by the "workgroup" option in smb.conf.
***-H** netbios hosts file*	Allow command-line specification of a file containing a list of netbios names which the server is allowed to reply to. file is formatted like: [IP address | hostname][netbios name]
-N	This option has been replaced by the "interfaces" option in smb.conf.
***-d** debuglevel*	Specify debug level.
***-l** logfile*	Specify a path and base filename for storing login information.
***-n** netbios_name*	Specify a netbios name other than the default.
-a	Append to log files rather than overwrite.

***-p** port number*	Specify port number.
***-s** configuration file*	Specify a default configuration file other than /etc/samba.conf.

smbclient servicename [password] [-E] [-L *host*] [-M *host*] [-I IP *number*] [-R *name resolve order*] [-N] [-P] [-U *username*] [-d *debuglevel*] [-l *log basename*] [-n *netbios name*] [-W *workgroup*] [-O *socket options*] [-p *port number*] [-c *command string*] [-T *tar options*] [-D *initial directory*]

smbclient is a client program designed to communicate with a Lan Manager server. Its functionality is not unlike **ftp** in that it is mostly used for the getting and putting of files and directory information. It can also be used as an interface to other server resources (e.g., printers).

Example: To use smbclient to print the file test.txt to the printer HPLJ6 on the server Loki:

cat test.txt | smbclient '\\Loki\HPLJ6'

Example: The following example shows me using **smbclient** to retrieve the file "test" from the "e" drive on the machine "Loki." Commands which I actually typed are in boldface, the machine responses are in regular text:

```
[shawkins@odin shawkins]$ smbclient '\\Loki\e'

Server time is Sun Aug  1 14:16:50 1999

Timezone is UTC-4.0

Password:

security=share

smb: \> get test.txt localtest.txt

getting file \test.txt of size 30 bytes as
localtest.txt (3.66206 kb/s) (average 3.66211 kb/s)

smb: \> quit
```

TIP

You will need to quote your backslashes when typing UNC names within a Linux shell (e.g., "\\Loki\HPLJ6" rather than \\Loki\HPLJ6). Forward slashes will also work on Samba versions greater than 1.9.17. (e.g., //Loki/HPLJ6).

servicename	Name of the server service which you wish to access. Service names are in the UNC format: \\server\service, where server is the netbios name of the server and service is any service which is offered (e.g., a particular printer, <some other shared resource>). Note that the netbios name of the server may be distinct from the host name of the same server.
password	Allow the user to specify a password for the service which it is attempting to access.
-R *name_resolve_order*	Specify a method for name resolution. If used, this overrides the default value specified as the "name resolve order" of smb.conf.
-L	List the services available on the specified server.
-M	Send messages via the WinPopup protocol. After a connection is established, type your message, terminating with ^D (Control + D). Note that if the target computer is not running WinPopup, your message will disappear without any error messages.
-E	Tell smbclient to send any error messages to standard error rather than standard output.
-I *IP number*	Specify an IP number of the server to which you wish to connect.
-N	Suppress the normal password prompt.
-O *socket options*	See the socket options section of smb.conf for details.
-P	Specify that the service smbclient is connecting to is a printer service.
-U *username*	Specify a username for use in accessing services.
-d *debuglevel*	Specify a debug level from 0 (less detail) to 5 (more detail).

***-l** basename*	Specify a non-default base file name to which logging messages are send.
***-n** netbios name*	Specify a name other than the (all-uppercase) hostname of the current machine as the netbios name.
***-W** workgroup*	Specify a workgroup to be used for the connection.
***-p** port number*	Specify a port number used for making connections to the server. Overrides the default of 139.
-T <c|x>[IXbgNa]	Tar operation. The above options correspond to the following actions:

c	Create a tar file.
x	Restore a local tar file back to a share.
I	Include the specified files and directories (default behavior).
X	Exclude the specified files and directories.
b	Blocksize.
g	Incremental. Tells tar to back up only those files with the archive bit set.
N	Newer than <specified file>.
a	Reset the archive bit once the file is backed up.

***-D** initial directory*	Tell smbclient to switch to the specified directory before starting.
***-c** commandstring*	Execute the specified list of commands rather than prompting. Commandstring is delimited by colons.

Smbclient is interactive. The following commands are valid at the **smb** command prompt ("smb: <current directory>>").

? [command], help [command]	Help. Either prints information on the specified command or, if none specified, on all available commands.
! [shell command]	Run the specified shell command on the local machine.
***cd** [directory]*	Change to the specified directory.
***del** <mask>*	Delete all files matching the specified mask.
***dir** <mask>, **ls** <mask>*	List all files in the current directory matching the specified mask.
exit, quit	Close connection and exit.
***get** <remote file name> [local file name]*	Copy file from the server to the local machine.
***lcd** [directory name]*	Change directories on the local machine.
lowercase	Toggle the conversion of filenames to lowercase letters.
mask	Specify a mask for use during recurive use of the mget and mput commands. Masks consist of a label and the pattern to be used in place of that label, e.g., source *.c
***mget** <mask>*	Copy all files matching the specified mask from the server to the client.
***mkdir** <directory name>, **md** <directory name>*	Create a new directory on the server.
***mput** <mask>*	Copy all files matching the specified mask from the client to the server.
***print** <file name>*	Print the specified file from the local machine through a printable service on the server.

printmode *<graphics or text>*	Toggle the print mode between graphics and text.
prompt	Toggle prompting for filenames when executing mget and mput commands.
put *<local file name> [remote file name]*	Copy the local file from the client to the server.
queue	Display print queue information
recurse	Toggle recursion on|off of the mget and mput commands.
rm	Delete all files matching the specified mask from the server.
rmdir *<directory name>,* ***rd*** *<directory name>*	Attempt to remove the specified directory from the server.
tar *<c|x>[IXbgNa]*	Perform one of the following tar operations: **c** Create a tar file. **x** Restore a local tar file back to a share. **I** Include the specified files and directories (default behavior). **X** Exclude the specified files and directories. **b** Blocksize. **g** Incremental. Tells tar to back up only those files with the archive bit set. **N** Newer than <specified file>. **a** Reset the archive bit once the file is backed up.
blocksize	Specify a blocksize in multiples of 512 bytes.

smbmount *servicename mount-point* **[-h] [-C] [-n] [-P** *password* **] [-s** *server name* **] [-c** *client name* **] [-I** *hostname/IP* **] [-U** *user name* **] [-D** *domain name* **] [-u** *uid* **] [-g** *gid* **] [-f** *file mode* **] [-d** *dir mode* **] [-m** *max xmit* **] [-p** *port* **]**

This program enables you to mount an SMB filesystem on a Linux machine.

Example: To mount the e directory of the Win-95 machine "Loki" at the ***/mnt/loki*** directory of the Linux machine odin:

ROOT **smbmount //Loki/e /mnt/loki**

In order to do this, you first have to set up the directory as a share on the Win-95 machine. Create a directory, right-click on it, choose the Properties menu item, then choose the Sharing tab and specify what kind of access you want.

servicename	The service you want to use on the server. Format is //server/service/rootdir.
mount-point	The directory over which you wish to mount the filesystem.
-h	Display help information.
-C	Do not convert passwords to uppercase.
-n	Use this argument when mounting shares which do not require a password.
-P *password*	Allow user to specify the password on the command line.
-s *netbios_server_name*	Enable specification of netbios server name when it is distinct from the servername.
-c *netbios_client_name*	Enable specification of netbios client name when it is distinct from the servername.
-I *hostname/IP of the server*	Specify hostname or IP address of the server when distinct from netbios name.

-U *user name*	Used to specify Lan Manager side user name, if distinct from Linux user name.
-D *domain name*	Used to specify domain name at login time.
-u *uid,* ***-g*** *gid*	Enables command line specification of user and group ids (default = current user).
-f *file mode,* ***-d*** *dir mode*	Specify file and directory modes for mounted filesystems.
-p *port*	Specify TCP port to connect to on the server (default = 139).
-m *max xmit*	Specify maximum packet size transmitted.

DOS & Windows

smbd [-D] [-a] [-d *debuglevel*] [-l *log file*] [-p *port number*] [-O *socket* options] [-s *configuration file*]

This program is a server which provides SMB (a.k.a. LanManager) services to clients. Clients include MSCLIENT 3.0, Windows for Workgroups, Windows 95, Windows NT, OS2, DAVE for Macintosh, and smbfs for Linux.

The configuration file (***smb.conf***) is automatically reloaded every minute.

Example: Inetd (see the chapter on daemons) can be used to start **nmbd** and **smbd** as appropriate. To do so, include the following entries in the ***/etc/services*** file:

```
netbios-ssn 139/tcp
netbios-ns 137/udp
```

which associates the netbios-ssn service with port 139 and the netbios-ns service with port 137. Once the association has been made, inetd can monitor ports 137 and 139 for requests. Upon receiving a request, inetd will look in the ***inetd.conf*** file for instructions on how to handle it. You will need to add the following lines to the ***inetd.conf*** file to tell it how:

```
netbios-ssn stream tcp nowait root /usr/local/samba/bin/smbd smbd
```

```
netbios-ns dgram upd wait root /usr/local/samba/bin/nmbd nmbd
```

-D	Tell the server to run as a daemon.
-a	Tell smbd to overwrite log files with each new connection rather than append.
***-d** debuglevel*	Specify level of detail (0-10) for debugging output. Detail of output increases with debuglevel.
***-l** log file*	Specify a base filename into which operational data will be logged.
***-p** port number*	Specify a port number other than the default of 139.
***-s** configuration file*	Specify a file containing configuration information other than the default.

smbumount *mount-point*

Unmount an smb filesystem.

Example: To unmount the smb directory mounted in the smbmount example:

ROOT **smbumount /mnt/loki**

mount-point	mount-point is the directory you want to unmount.

smbstatus [-b] [-d] [-p] [-s *configuration file*]

This program is used to display status information on current samba connections.

Example: To display status information on current samba connections:

smbstatus

-b	Brief output.
-d	Verbose output.

-p	Display a list of smbd processes and exit.
-s configuration file	Specify a configuration file other than the default.

testparm [*configfilename* [*hostname hostIP*]]

This command is used to test the **smbd** configuration file for internal correctness.

Example: There really aren't that many options on this command. To use:

testparm

configfilename	Specify the configuration file to be checked.
hostname	Check host access of the specified machine. Use in conjunction with the hostIP address.
hostIP	Specify the IP address of a previously specified hostname.

CHAPTER

33

MAIL & OTHER COMMUNICATION

Introduction

Modern email systems are a suite of programs working together. **User agents** (e.g., **elm, mail**) are the programs which interface with the end user for creation and display of email. **Transport agents** (**sendmail, smail, fetchmail**) are responsible for forwarding mail to the system for which it is intended. *Delivery agents* (**rmail**) put mail in the system in the proper mailbox.

The topic of configuring an Internet-connected email service would fill a large book by itself (in fact, it does: *Sendmail*, 2nd edition, the definitive reference). The **sendmail** and **fetchmail** commands are included in this section primarily to give a feel for how they fit into the overall Linux world.

In addition, Linux provides several utilities (**wall, write, talk, rwall**) for communicating directly with another user's terminal. These are fairly invasive programs and should be used sparingly. If having messages show up on your screen uninvited irritates you, use the **mesg** utility to deny other users permission to display to your terminal.

biff	Toggle message notification.
elm	Email user interface.
fetchmail	Retrieve mail from remote servers.

formail	Mail filter.
mail	Email user interface.
makemap	Create sendmail's database maps.
mesg	Toggle your terminal's writability.
mimencode	Encode binary files.
rmail	Interpret incoming mail.
rwall	Write to all users on remote systems.
sendmail	Mail transport agent.
talk	Talk interactively to another user.
uuencode	Encode binary file for mail transmission.
wall	Write to all users on local system.
write	Write to a particular user.

Related Files

/usr/local/lib/elm-help.*	help files
/usr/local/lib/aliases.text	system alias source
/usr/local/lib/aliases.dir	system alias dbz directory table
/usr/local/lib/aliases.pag	system alias hash table
/usr/local/lib/aliases	system alias data table
/usr/local/lib/aliases.hash	system alias hash table
/usr/local/lib/aliases.data	system alias data table
$HOME/.elm/aliases.text	user alias source

$HOME/.elm/aliases.dir	user alias dbz directory table
$HOME/.elm/aliases.pag	user alias dbz hash table
$HOME/.elm/aliases	user alias data table
$HOME/.elm/elmrc	customized mailer parameters
$HOME/.elm/elmheaders	customized message headers
/tmp/snd.$$	outgoing mail edit buffer
/tmp/mbox.logname	temporary mailbox
$HOME/ELM:debug.info	debug output if turned on
/etc/sendmail.cf	sendmail configuration file

Commands

biff [ny]

Biff toggles the system's message notification system. Biff alerts you when mail arrives and tells you who it is from. Biff n turns off notification.

Example: To set your system to notify you when mail arrives:

biff y

n	Turn notification off.
y	Turn notification on.

elm [-achkKmrtwz] [-f *alternate-folder*] [-d *debug level*]

elm [-s *subject*] *list of aliases or addresses*

elm is a screen oriented program for sending and receiving mail. It is usually used interactively, but may be used to send mail from the command line.

Example: To mail the file message.txt to jones@abc.com with a subject line of "Important":

elm -s "Important" < message.txt

-a	Specify use of the arrow cursor (as opposed to the default, reverse video cursor).
-c	Expand listed aliases and return.
***-d** level*	Specify the debug level. Output from debug goes to $HOME/ELM:debug info.
***-f** alternative-folder*	Tell elm to read from the specified folder instead of the inbox.
-h, -?	Print help information.
***-i** file*	Tell elm to open with the specified file in the edit buffer.
-k	Force knowledge of the HP terminal keyboard.
-K	Enable use of softkeys (HP terminals only).
-m	Turn the menu off to make more room for mail headers.
***-s** subj Subject*	Allow user to specify mail subject on the command line.
-t	Turn usage of termcap/terminfo ti/te sequences.
-v	Display version information.
-z	Tell elm not to bother opening up if there is no new mail.

fetchmail [options] [*mailserver...*]

fetchmailconf

Fetchmail gets mail from remote mail servers and forwards it to your local client machine's delivery system. Typically, this is run as a daemon to check remote mail servers over a PPP/SLIP link. However, it can also be used to gather mail by machines which do not permit their mail servers to initiate an SMTP connection.

Note that fetchmail is not a mail reader. To actually read your mail once retrieved, you must use **elm**, **mail**, **mailx** or some other mail reader.

Example: To retrieve the mail from the server pop3.isp.com using the pop3 protocol:

fetchmail -p pop3 pop3.isp.com

General Options

-V, --version	Display version information.
-c, --check	Check to see if there is mail waiting, but do not retrieve it.
-s, --silent	Do not display the normal complement of progress messages.
-v, --verbose	Pass any control messages sent between fetchmail and the mail server on to the display.

Disposal Options

-a, --all	Tell fetchmail to get both new messages and messages which have already been displayed.
-k, --keep	Tell fetchmail to keep any retrieved messages on the mail server, rather than delete them (which is the default).
-K, --nokeep	Tell fetchmail to delete any retrieved messages from the mail server.
-F, --flush	Tell fetchmail to delete old messages before retrieving any new messages.

Protocol and Query Options

-p, --protocol *proto* Specify the protocol to use in communications with the remote server.

POP2	Post Office Protocol 2
POP3	Post Office Protocol 3

APOP	POP3 with MD5 authentication.
RPOP	POP3 with RPOP authentication.
KPOP	POP3 with Kerberos V4 authentication on port 1109.
SDPS	Use POP3 with Demon Internet's SDPS extensions.
IMAP	IMAP2bis, IMAP4, or IMAP4rev1 (fetchmail autodetects their capabilities).
IMAP-K4	IMAP4 or IMAP4rev1

-U, --uidl	Force UIDL (Unique ID Listing) use when using POP3.
-P, --port	Use the specified port rather than the default.
-r folder, --folder *folder*	Use the specified mail folder rather than the default.
-S host, --smtphost *host*	Specify a hunt list of hosts to forward mail to (one or more hostnames, commaseparated).
-D domain, --smtpaddress *domain*	Specify the domain to be put in RCPT TO lines shipped to SMTP rather than the default localhost.
-Z nnn, --antispam *nnn[,nnn[,nnn...]]*	Specify the list of numeric SMTP errors that are to be interpreted as a spamblock response from the listener.
-m, --mda	Specify that mail will be passed to an MDA directly rather than port 25.

Resource Limit Control Options

-l, --limit	Specify a maximum octet size argument. Messages exceeding this size limit will not be fetched or marked as seen.
-b, --batchlimit	Specify a limit to the number of messages shipped out to an SMTP listener in a single session. The default is unlimited.
-B, --fetchlimit	Specify a limit to the number of messages accepted from server in a single poll. The default is unlimited.
-e, --expunge	Specify that fetchmail should issue expunges only after the Nth delete. (Expunges force a deletion to be performed immediately, which is sometimes a performance drag.)

Authentication Options

-u *name,* ***--username*** *name*	Specify the user identification to be used when logging in to the mailserver.
-I *specification,* ***--interface*** *specification*	Tell fetchmail that the specified device must be up and have a specific local IP address before polling.
-M *interface,* ***--monitor*** *interface*	Specify a system TCP/IP interface to be monitored constantly.
-A, --auth	Specify a preauthentication type (password | kerberos_v5 | kerberos).

Miscellaneous Options

-f *pathname,* ***--fetchmailrc*** *pathname*	Use the specified name as the .fetchmailrc file.
-i *pathname,* ***--idfile*** *pathname*	Use the specified name as the .fetchids file.

-n, --norewrite	Disable rewrite of address headers. Of interest only to those truly paranoid about having a machine rewrite their email headers. Prevents addition "@hostname" clauses to the address.
-E, --envelope	Change the header which fetchmail assumes will carry a copy of the mail's envelope address.
-Q, --qvirtual	Remove the specified string prefix from the user name found in the header specified with the envelope option.
--configdump	Tell fetchmail to parse the ~/.fetchmailrc file, interpret any command line options it finds there, and dump a configuration report to standard output.

formail [+skip] [-total] [-bczfrktnedqBY] [-p *prefix*] [-D *maxlen idcache*] [-x *headerfield*] [-X *headerfield*] [-a *headerfield*] [-A *headerfield*] [-i *headerfield*] [-I *headerfield*] [-u *headerfield*] [-U *headerfield*] [-R *oldfield newfield*][-m *minfields*] [-s [*command* [*arg* ...]]]

formail is a mail filter. It puts mail into mailbox format, does "From" escaping, generates autoreplying headers, does simple header munging/extracting or splits up the specified mailbox/digest/articles file.

If **formail** is started without any command line options, it will force any mail coming from stdin into mailbox format and will escape all bogus "From" lines with a ">".

Example: To remove all fields except To:, From:, and Subject: from the header:

formail -k -X To -X From: -X Subject:

-b	Don't escape any misformatted mailbox headers.
***-p** prefix*	Specify a quotation prefix.
-Y	Tell formail to use traditional Berkeley mailbox format.
-c	Concatenate continued fields in the header.
-z	Zap fields containing only a space.

-f	Don't force generation of a "From" line.
-r	Generate an auto-replay header.
-k	Tell formail to retail the message body when generating an auto-reply header or extracting fields.
-t	Trust that the sender has a valid return address in the header.
***-s** program*	Separate input into distinct mail messages and pipe into the specified program.
-n	Do not wait for a program to finish before starting the next.
-e	Do not require empty lines to precede the header of a new message.
-d	Disable recognition of the Content-Length: field.
-B	Tell formail it is splitting up a BABYL rmail file.
***-m** minfields*	Specify the minimum number of consecutive fields which will constitute the start of a new message.
-q	Quiet operation. Do not display error messages on write errors, duplicate messages, and mismatched Content-Length: fields.
***-D** maxlen idcache*	Detect if the Message-ID of the current message has already been seen using an idcache file of approximately maxlen size.
***-x** headerfield*	Extract contents of the specified headerfield from the header and display it as a single line.
***-X** headerfield*	Extract contents of the specified headerfield from the header and display it as a single line and preserve the field name.
***-a** headerfield*	Append the specified headerfield to the header if and only if a similar field does not exist yet.
***-A** headerfield*	Append the specified headerfield to the header.

-i headerfield	Append the specified headerfield to the header, adding the word "Old-" to any similar field.
-I headerfield	Append the specified headerfield to the header, but remove any similar field.
-u headerfield	Make the first occurrence of the specified headerfield unique. (Delete all subsequent occurrences.)
-U headerfield	Make the last occurrence of the specified headerfield unique. (Delete all previous occurrences.)
-R oldfield newfield	Rename all instances of oldfield as newfield.
+skip	Skip the specified number of messages.
-total	Specify a upper limit of messages to output.

mail [-ilnv] [-s *subject*] [-c *cc-addr*] [-b *bcc-addr*] *to-addr...*

mail [-ilnNv] -f [*name*]

mail [-ilnNv] [-u *user*]

Mail is a mail processing (send, receive, view) system. It can be used either interactively or strictly from the command line.

Example: To send the file blah.txt to user Susie from the command line with subject "Homework":

mail -s "Homework" susie < blah.txt

-v	Verbose mode.
-i	Ignore tty interrupt signals (good for use over noisy phone lines).
-I	Force interactive mode.
-n	Do not read /etc/mail.rc on startup.
-N	Do not perform the initial display of message headers.

***-s** subject*	Specify subject on the command line.
***-c** user [user, ...]*	Copy the message to the specified users.
***-b** user [user, ...]*	Send blind copies to the specified users.
***-f** file*	Use the specified file as your mailbox.
-u	Is equivalent to: mail -f /var/spool/mail/user.

To use mail interactively, type "mail" at the command line. It will get any mail you have from your default p.o. box and display headers to the screen. You can then use the following commands:

-	Print preceding messages
?, help	Display help screen.
! command	Execute the specified shell command.
Print, P, Type, T	Display message to screen including ignored header fields.
Reply, R	Reply to sender of current message.
alias	Print out all aliases or (if any specified) the specified alias only.
alternates	Specify alternate email accounts, usually on other machines s.t. mail will not copy those accounts in replies.
chdir	Change user's working directory to specified directory (if any) or to the login directory by default.
copy	Save as specified but do not mark for deletion.
***delete** message, message, ...*	Mark the specified messages as deleted.
dp	Delete current message and print the next.

edit	Edit the specified list of messages.
exit, xit, x	Quit without modification.
file, fi, folder	Use the specified folder as input.
folders	List the names of the folders in your folder directory.
from *message [, message, ...]*	Print the headers from the specified list of messages.
headers [+/-]	List the current range of headers, or the previous (-) or the following (+).
hold, preserve, pre	Mark specified messages to be saved in user's system mailbox.
ignore	Add specified list of headers to the ignored list.
mail username [, username, ...]	Send mail to the specified list of users.
mbox	Send the specified list of messages to mbox in your login directory when you quitmail.
next, n, +, <Enter>	Go to next message in list.
print message [, message, ...]	Display the specified message to the terminal.
quit	End session.
reply, respond	Reply to sender and all other recipients.
retain	Add the specified list of header fields to the retained list.
save, s *[messages] [file]*	Save message to specified file.
set *[variable=value]*	Set the variable to the specified value or (if no arguments) print all variables.

shell, sh	Invoke the shell.
size	Print out the size of the characters in the specified list.
source file	Read commands from the specified file.
***top** message [,message, ...]*	Print the top few lines of each specified message.
***unalias** alias [, alias, ...]*	Discard the previously specified aliases.
***undelete** message, [,message, ...]*	Mark the specified messages as undeleted.
***unread** message, [,message, ...]*	Mark the specified messages as unread.
unset option	Discard the specified option values.
***visual** message [, message, ...]*	Use the display editor on each specified message.
write	Save message but not the associated header.
z [-]	Move forward or backward [-] one windowful.

makemap [-N] [-d] [-f] [-o] [-r] [-v] *maptype mapname*

Sendmail uses keyed maps for lookups. The makemap command creates and maintains the map database. maptype must be one of dbm, btree, or hash. Input is read from standard input and is formatted like:

key value

where key is the database key and value is the corresponding value, separated by white space(s).

Example: To input the contents of the /etc/hosts file to makemap:

awk '/^[^#]/ {print $2, $1}' /etc/hosts | makemap

-N	Do not trim the null byte which terminates the string when creating the map.
-d	Permit duplicate keys.
-f	Do not translate (fold) uppercase letters to lowercase.
-o	Append to an existing file.
-r	Permit replacement of existing keys.
-v	Verbose output.

mesg [y|n]

This command specifies whether you will allow other users to write to your terminal.

Example: To turn off the other user's ability to display messages (via **write**, **talk**, etc.) to your screen:

mesg n

mimencode[-u] [-b] [-q] [-p] [*file name*] [-o *outputfile*]

Used to attach a binary file to a mail message. Reads from standard input (by default) and sends a base64 encoded version to standard output. If a file is specified, mimencode will use that rather than standard input.

Example: To format the file spreadsheet.xls for attachment to a mail message and store it in ss.mme:

mimencode spreadsheet.xls -o ss.mme

TIP **mimencode** is more reliable than **uuencode**.

-q	Use the specified quoted-printable encoding rather than base64.
-u	Decode standard input rather than encoding.

-p	Translate decoded carriage return/line feed sequences into whatever the local newline convention is during decoding.
-o file	Send output to the specified file rather than standard output.

rmail *user ...*

rmail interprets incoming mail received via **uucp**. It collapses From lines into a single line of the form "return-path!finder" and passes the processed mail on to **sendmail**.

rwall *host* [*file*]

The **rwall** command sends a message to all users logged in to the specified host. By default, the message is taken from standard input, but if a file is specified, that will be used instead.

Example: To send the message contained in the file go.away users currently logged in to the host local.net:

rwall local.net go.away

sendmail [*flags*] [*address ...*]

newaliases

mailq [-v]

Sendmail is responsible for delivering messages to the intended recipients. It transports messages across networks as necessary. It is not designed for contact with the end user; other programs (**mail, elm**) handle that phase of the mail process.

Example: To invoke sendmail as a foreground daemon in verbose mode:

sendmail -bD -v

***-B**type*	Specify the body type of the message. Current legal values 7BIT or 8BITMIME.
-ba	Specify ARPANET mode.

-bd	Tell sendmail to run as a daemon.
-bD	Tell sendmail to run in foreground as a daemon.
-bh	Display the persistent host status database.
-bH	Empty the persistent host status database.
-bi	Initialize the alias database.
-bm	Deliver mail in the usual way (default).
-bp	Display a listing of the queue.
-bs	Tell sendmail to use the SMTP protocol as described in RFC821 on standard input and output.
-bt	Run in address test mode.
-bv	Verify names only - do not try to collect or deliver a message.
-C*file*	Tell sendmail to use the specified configuration file.
-d*X*	Set debugging value to X.
-F*fullname*	Set the full name of the sender.
-f*name*	Set the name of the sender of the mail.
-h*N*	Set the hop count to the specified number.
-i	Ignore dots alone on lines by themselves in incoming messages. This should be set if you are reading data from a file.
-N *dsn*	Set delivery status notification conditions to dsn, which can be one of: never, failure, delay, or success.
-n	Specify no aliasing.
-O *option=value*	Set the specified option to the specified value.
-ox *value*	Set option x to the specified value.

-pprotocol	Specify the protocol used to receive the message.
-q[time]	Specify the interval at which to process the saved messages in the queue.
-qIsubstr	Limits the processing to jobs which have substr as a substring of the queue id.
-qRsubstr	Limit the processing to jobs which contain substr as a substring of one of the recipients.
-qSsubstr	Limit the processing to jobs which containing substr as a substring of the sender.
-R *return*	Specify the amount of the message to be returned if message bounces (one of [full|headers]).
-rname	Same as -f (obsolete).
-t	Scan the To:, Cc:, and Bcc: lines for message recipients.
-U	Initial (user) submission. Used with user agents (e.g. Mail, elm) but never with network delivery agents.
-V *envid*	Tell sendmail to set the original envelope id.
-v	Verbose mode.
-X *logfile*	Tell sendmail to log all traffic in the specified file.
AliasFile=file	Tell sendmail to use the specified alias file.

talk user[ttyname]

Set up a **talk** session. When a talk session is open, you and another user can write directly to a section of each other's terminals. Terminate the session with Ctrl-C.

Example: To attempt to initiate a **talk** session with user Darrell: 

talk darrell

user	Specify the user to whom you wish to talk.
ttyname	Specify the tty with which you wish to open a talk session. Useful when the other user is logged in more than once.

uuencode [-m] [*file*] *name*

uudecode [-o *outfile*] [file]...

The **uuencode/uudecode** programs are used to encode binary files for transmission over media which support only transmission of ASCII data.

Example: To encode the binary file program and mail to user someguy@wherever.com:

uuencode program | mail someguy@wherever.com

-m	Use base64 encoding format.
-o	Write output to the specified file.

wall [*message*]

Display the specified message to the terminals of all users currently logged in. **wall** does not write to the terminals of those users whose mesg value is set to no.

Example: To send the message "Go away" to all users currently logged in:

wall "Go away"

write *user* [*ttyname*]

Display the specified message to the terminal of another user.

inode The data structure which is used by Linux to store information about files.

jihad Holy war. e.g. "My operating system can beat up your operating system."

local When used as an adjective, implies that the associated noun (e.g. drive, printer) is attached to the current actual physical machine; and not accessed via the network.

major device number Number used by the kernel to specify which device driver is associated with a particular device.

minor device number Number used by the kernel to distinguish among a group of devices all using the same driver.

parent process The process which initiates a fork() system call which ultimately results in a child process.

process An executing program.

PID, process id Numeric value used by the system to uniquely identify a process.

PPID, process parent id PID of the process which created the current process.

priority Numeric value associated with a process used in computing who will next be allocated CPU time. Default 0, negative values imply higher priority, positive values lower priority.

recursive Something which refers to itself is said to be recursive. In the context of computer science, the term is usually used in reference to a function or algorithm which, as part of its execution, calls itself.

GLOSSARY

child process The process resulting from a fork(exec() sequence of system calls. process which initiated the fork called the parent.

exec() A system call which, when inv transfers the attributes and reso of the currently executing proce another (presumably different) gram specified as a parameter c system call. In this way are new cesses made.

fork() A system call which creates a exact (everything but PID) dup of the currently executing pr Used in conjunction with exe start up new programs.

gid Group id. Numeric value asso with some group identity. Specifi /etc/group.

hard link A second (or third, or fourth...) which points to a file.

sammich Good, pleasant, useful, e.g. "Linux is very sammich." Origins obscure.

soft link A link to another path in the filesystem (a k a symbolic link).

standard input Where a program gets its input. By default, the keyboard, but may be attached to the output of another program.

standard output Where a program sends its output. By default, the monitor, but may be attached to the standard input of another computer.

superuser The user with a UID of zero, implying full access (read/write/execute) to all system resources.

symbolic link A link to another path in the filesystem.

system call An invocation of a function provided by the operating system, e.g., fork(), exec().

transparent Not seen by the user. Typically has positive connotations, e.g. "transparent access via NFS" means the user doesn't need to care that the filesystem is on a machine three thousand miles away.

uid Numeric value used by the system to uniquely identify a user. Defined in the ***/etc/passwd*** file.

zombie processes A process which is no longer executing but has not been removed from the table of executing processes.

Index

Symbols

Numerics

A

B

C

T

U

V

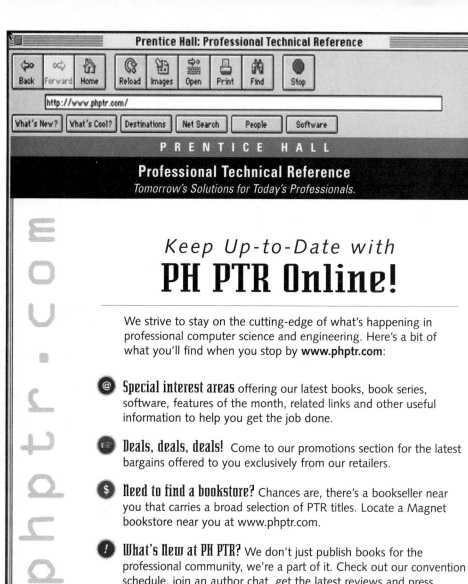